I Dedicated This Book To My Three Children
And to Their Resourcefulness

Mark Hall

Matt Hall

Jessica Hall

DRAGON SLAYING

FROM DRAGONS TO PRINCES

Meta-Stating Dragon States

Revised Second Edition
2000

L. Michael Hall, Ph.D.

© First Edition, 1996 L. Michael Hall, Ph.D.
   Second Edition, 2000
Dragon Slaying: From Dragons to Princes
   Library of Congress — TXu - 749-316   Washington DC.
   ISBN — 1-890001-09-0

First Edition, 1996 Published by **E.T. Publications**
Second Edition, 2000 Published by **Neuro-Semantics®**
First German Edition, 1999, Junferman Press, Germany

Published By
E.T. Publications (*Empowerment Technologies*)
P.O. Box 8
Clifton, CO 81520
(970) 523-7877

Printed By:
Action Printing
Jerry Kucera, Owner
516 Fruitvale Court, Unit C
Grand Jct. Co. 81504
(970) 434-7701

Description: *Dragon Slaying* presents the *Meta-States* model as it describes a way of working with those emotional states that feel like Dragons to us. These painful constructions arise from how we have used (or more correctly *misused*) our higher states of consciousness (the mind-body or neuro-linguistic states). *Dragon Slaying* therefore focuses on how we can effectively work with the higher (or meta) states of our mind by which we create toxic, morbid, and unsane patterns or maps. These *states-about-states* structures (or meta-states) arise when mind or consciousness reflexively loops back onto itself to generate thoughts-and-feelings about previous thoughts-feelings. This creates our higher frames of awareness, layers of thinking and feeling, and can create painful neuro-semantic states that we here call "Dragon States."
   A more theoretical version of this material appears in *"Meta-States: Self-Reflexiveness in Human States of Consciousness"* (1995/ 2000 second edition).

TABLE OF CONTENTS

Preface ... 5

PART I: THE INSIDE STORY ABOUT DRAGONS ... 9

Ch. 1: *Sometimes I Feel Like A Dragon/Sometimes I Don't!* ... 11
    Mind-Body or Neuro-Linguistic States

Ch. 2: *Sometimes I Feel Like a Meta-Dragon!* ... 37
    When Dragons Govern our Higher Mind

Ch. 3: *Dragon Slaying* ... 65
    How to Slay, Tame, Transform & Even Slap Dragons

Ch. 4: *Consciousness & State Management* ... 79
    Tracking the Brain Through all its Contortions

Ch. 5: *Meta-Stating* ... 99
    Setting Mental Frames At Higher Levels

Ch. 6: *Flushing Out Old Dragons for New Meta-Stating* ... 115

Ch 7: *Designing & Installing Empowering Meta-States* ... 127
    That Tame Dragons

Ch.8: *Dragon Slaying #101* ... 147
    The Science & Art of Handling Dragons
    Dragon Meters ... 171

Ch. 9: *Semantic Dragons* & Meta-Dragons ... 173
    Meaning—The Mechanism that Feeds Dragons

PART II: INTO THE FRAY OF DRAGON SLAYING ... 187

Ch. 10: *Slaying the Dragon of Self-Contempt* ... 189
    And Casting a Spell for Self-Esteeming

Ch. 11: *Slaying the Whiny Dragon That Acts Like a Victim* ... 207
    And Casting a Spell for Resilience

Ch. 12: *Slaying the Dragons of Reactivity & Defensiveness*   223
       And Casting a Spell for Proactivity

Ch. 13: *Slaying the Dragons of Criticism & Insult*   237
       And Casting a Spell for Un-Insult-Ability

Ch. 14: *Slaying Nasty Little Resentful & Grudge Holding Dragon*   251
       And Casting Spells for Magnanimity & Forgiveness

Ch. 15: *Slaying the Dragons of Internal Conflict & Disquietude*   271
       And Casting a Spell for Serene Inner Peace

Ch. 16: *Slaying and/or Taming All Dragons!*   289
       All Other Dragons Put on Notice!

Appendix A   E-Prime / E-Choice   296
Glossary   299
Bibliography   302
Trainings   304
About the Author   307

PREFACE

I wrote *Dragon Slaying* because we humans so easily and frequently find ourselves in emotional states and states of mind that we can only call "D*ragon* states." I wrote it also because by using *Meta-States* we can fairly easily get ourselves out of those states. Would you like to have *that* kind of power and elegance in managing your states? You can. With *the Meta-States Model* (which you'll learn about in this book), you will be able to consciously shift from a dragon-like state and put yourself into a princely state.

How does such magic occur?

It emerges from the power of discovering how to effectively manage not only your states but your higher states of mind-and-emotion, your meta-states. By discovering and developing skills for state management, you will be able to tame, transform, or slay dragons the dragons that roar and pillage in your mind.

What do all of us need when we access a dragon state of anger, fear, dread, negativism, fatigue, sadness, discourage, etc.?

We need a **model** whereby we can *understand the experience* itself, how we created it (yes, it's all a matter of our own creations), and what we can do about it.

- What in the world is going on?
- Why do I feel this way?
- When I feel this way, what causes me to think, perceive, and behave as I do?
- How do I sabotage myself and my relationships when I get into these dragon states?
- How did I ever get into this frame of mind and how can I get out of it?

Understanding alone (as we all know far too well) does not, and will not, empower us to actually change things. We also need an ability. We need *the ability to take control of our states*. We need the personal power to take effective action in doing something effective and productive so that we do not let our Dragon States sabotage us. The ability to take effective action, which is what we mean by personal "power," comes with practice, training, and skill development. We also need a *process* that assists us in developing the quality of personal power of "running our own brain" as we learn to take charge of our states.

I have based this work on *the Meta-States model* which grew out of several fields: Neuro-Linguistic Programming (NLP), Cognitive Behavioral psychology (i.e. REBT, Rational-Emotive Behavioral Therapy), Korzybski's General Semantics model of the Levels of Abstraction, Bateson's Levels of Learning, Viktor Frankl's Logotherapy and paradoxical intention, Glasser's Reality Therapy /Control Theory, etc. This has given rise to an extension and expansion of NLP which we call *Neuro-Semantics®.* These fields provide the basic theoretical basis for this meta-level model and how it allows us to work with consciousness in a more systemic way.

The Meta-States model (1995) revolves about an understanding and appreciation of *the levels of thought.* Using the mechanism of self-reflexivity, we simply follow the flow of thought as it *reflects* back onto itself as we think about our previous thinking.

What did you think about that?
What do you now think about your thinking about that?

Meta-States puts this information together in an organized way in order for us to track our jumps to higher levels and the loops we move around in (conceptually) as we generate higher and more complex mental and emotional states.

This allows us to consider our *states* of mind-emotion-and-body and the different kinds of states we get into, as well as the effect that states have on our everyday experiences. And what value does *that* hold for us? It allows us to *observe* these loops without getting caught up in them or dominated by them. When that happens, a "Dragon" state typically emerges.

After I first wrote the first book on *Meta-States* and focused on "reflexivity in human states of consciousness," many said that they found that it too theoretical, academic, and complex. "Can't you boil it down? Can't you make it more simple?"

Dragon Slaying (as both a book and training) represents the first attempt at making *Meta-States* more user friendly and easier to access and use. In this work I have attempted to put into a form that I think you will find readable, immediately useable, insightful, and practical.

What you have in your hands is essentially a transcript of the first *Meta-States* training workshop which was entitled, *Dragon Slaying / Taming.* I have also included Peanuts cartoons in order to keep the reading interesting and illustrative. Originally, I had hoped to have reproduce the cartoons, but upon contacting Charles Schultz and discovery that it would cost over $300 for each cartoon, I decided *not* to go that route. I do trust that you'll get the point and enjoy the humor even from the written form.

Prepare yourself also for encounter some words that may be new to you. If you find it strange or happen to miss the initial definition of some term (and don't want to reread pages to find it), skip to the back to the *glossary of terms.*

Finally, I gratefully thank my associates *Dr. Bob Bodenhamer* and *Debra Lederer* for working through the text proofing and adding valuable comments and to my son *Mark Hall* for his extensive art work as well as to my daughter, *Jessica Hall* for her contributions to this latest edition.

And now, may you thoroughly *enjoy your exploration and learning*
as you *allow yourself* to *become truly curious*
about how you can empower your mind-and-emotions
in new and enhancing ways
as you discover some exciting ways
to simply bring some resourceful thoughts and feelings
upon some of your mental and emotional states
so that you *become fascinated by the playful interaction*
of your consciousness thinking about itself
as you access some of your higher states,
and wonder, really wonder,
just which dragon states you'd like to deal with first,
and whether you need to tame it,
transform its energy, or slay it,
and whether when you do that
some new princely state will automatically emerge,
or whether it just opens up space
so that you can begin to design engineer for yourself
some highly resourceful states
that would put more vitality and zest into everyday life,
but you can ... now ... even as you begin...

PART I:

THE INSIDE STORY ABOUT DRAGONS

Dragons— They're everywhere. Push any human being to his or her limits and, presto, out pops a Dragon. Some will roar. Others will whimper. Some will huff and puff and rage and carry on in dramatic and melodramatic ways. Others will just roll over and act dead.

Dragons— They undermine our sense of personal mastery, empowerment, and happiness. Yet they emerge as simply functions of our mind-body states of consciousness. As such, they simply represent our neuro-linguistic energy fields that govern our lives and determine the quality of our experience.

Dragons— Some are just plain downright toxic and need to be slain. Others are just out-of-control mind-body states that need to be tamed and harassed and used for more energy and vitality in life. Others are states that need to be tempered and balanced by other resources.

Welcome then to the Inside Story about Dragons ... when you emerge on the other side, you'll be a *Dragon Master* and ready to Manage your Mind-Body states for health, happiness, wholeness, and fun.

Chapter 1

"SOMETIMES I FEEL LIKE A DRAGON SOMETIMES I DON'T!"

- What do you think of the title of this chapter?
- Do you identify with that statement?
- Do you sometimes feel like a dragon? And then, do you at other times feel like you have a dragon by the tail?

Dragon states afflict us all. We get into states of mind-and-body wherein we feel like a raging, fire-breathing dragon. When was the last time that you felt that? When was the last time you encountered a Dragon State in someone else? What kind of a Dragon were you up against? A Dragon of Rage, Fear, Disgust, Victimization, Abuse, Criticism?

Actually, almost any state of consciousness involving a "negative" emotion (e.g., fear, anger, sadness, regret, upsetness, stress, disgust, etc.) can become a "Dragon" to us. And when it does, it can turn into a dragon state toward others as well.

Of course, talking about *Dragon States* like this brings up the subject of *"states."* By that term, I simply refer to the "states of mind" and "states of body" that we all experience every day. We more frequently describe these states as the attitudes, moods, predispositions, places, etc. that we get into and operate from. All of these different terms describe the same phenomenon, namely, our mind-body state of consciousness.

[By the way, you will see "mind" and "body" put together throughout the pages of this book as *mind-body* or as *thought-emotion,* etc. because these words designate an interlocking *system* that cannot really be pulled apart and treated as separate except in language and in concept. These elements seem as separate processes due to the way we have languaged them. And yet they always and inevitably operate as a systemic process.]

So what? What's so important about our *mind-body states?* Most of the time we live and operate out of *states* that we find so habitual that we hardly notice them. Noticing them may even take a lot of time and trouble. Why go to such trouble?

We go to all that trouble because our states completely determine the quality of our lives.

Your states completely determines your level of effectiveness, happiness, resourcefulness, and ability to navigate life. It's that important. Does that sufficiently explain the vital importance of your states? No? Then let me add yet another one.

The quality of your life can be no better than the quality of your states.

Everyday you wake up and move through life in various states. You experience positive states of excitement, anticipation, joy, laughter, humor, playfulness, fun, commitment, passion, relaxation, teasing, relating, etc. You also experience negative states of fear, anger, worry, dread, frustration, stress, grief, etc. Such give definition and texture to your life.

With that in mind, we can easily see the importance of developing *awareness* of our states, *understanding* their composition and the *mechanisms* that drive them. That also alerts us to the importance of discovering some state-of-the-art processes for taking charge of our states. When we do that, we begin to **have** our states, rather than our states **having** us. Imagine living your life like that.

Wouldn't that be a nice shift? If we did that, what would result?

First of all, much better state management. Could you use more skill and ability regarding the management of your states? How many times in a week or a day do you think about that? "I don't like this state, but what in the world can I do with it?"

One of the primary purposes for writing this book is to put into your hands some of the cutting-edge technology from NLP and Meta-States for *discovering and developing the knowledge, skills, and power to manage your primary states as well as your higher level states.* Specifically, we will hone in on the subject of managing our unresourceful dragon states so that we can tame some of those dragons, imprison other dragons, transform others, and slay the rest.

Then we can build some royal states out of which to live.

State Awareness
Identify your current state:
> What would you call your current state of mind-body? What state of emotion? Tired state? Upset? Anticipatory? Learning state? An open and receptive state? An emotionally preoccupied state?

Evaluate that state:
> Do you have the right kind of state of mind-body, emotion to read and study this material? Will it enable you to read well, think and ponder the content profoundly, comprehend and retain, and utilize?

Begin nudging your state:
> Since *the best kind of reading and learning occurs when our minds feel calm, relaxed, open, playful, and curious*— what would you need to do right now (mentally and physically) in order to shift to that kind of state?

State Awareness— Scene 1

In a Peanuts cartoon, Charlie Brown asks Lucy, "Are you going to make any new years resolutions, Lucy?"

Immediately accessing a dragon state and turning around and speaking at a volume that causes Charlie Brown to do a backwards somersault, Lucy replies, "*WHAT?* What for? What's wrong with me now? I like myself just the way I am!"

Continuing in the third frame, she raises her voice even more, "Why should I change?! What in the world is the matter with you Charlie Brown?!!"

And in the fourth frame she raises her fist to the sky and rhetorically continues, "I'm all right the way I am! I don't *have* to improve! How *could* I improve? *How*, I ask you?! *How*?"

Charlie Brown grabs his throat as he leaves muttering, "Good grief."

Now I'd call that a dragon state! Lucy seemed okay before Charlie Brown brought up the question that "pushed her buttons" which then sent her into a hot, irritable, and defensive state. This describes one of the most painful dragon experiences that we all know about first hand. When we get into such states, we do not respond *at our best.* We do not think with our highest cognitive skills. We do not emote with our highest emotional skills. We do not communicate or behave with our highest developed skills. Our state has put us in a space of being unresourceful.

What causes such unresourceful states? Sometimes we just don't feel good. Sometimes we failed to get a good night's sleep. Sometimes our biochemistry has gotten out-of-sorts given the way we have eaten or not eaten, exercised or not exercised, etc. Sometimes it arises from the way we have thought.

Consider the way Lucy thought in that scenario. She thought herself as "good enough," even as "un-improvable." That was her frame of reference. So when Charlie Brown suggested the totally unacceptable idea that she make new year's resolutions— she lost it. It violated her frame. Her All-or-Nothing thinking worked as an amplifier. It sent her into a spin and off she took. That happens to be true for most of our states.

State Awareness — Scene 2

Patience obviously represents a state of mind-body. So Linus asks Lucy about it, "Do you think patience is a virtue?"

To this Lucy responds with a calm and cool, "Oh, yes... And I'm proud to say that it is a virtue which I possess."

Linus inquires a second time, "You really would consider patience as a virtue, then?"

Lucy explodes, **"I SAID SO DIDN'T I?"** and Linus does the famous Charles Schultz backward somersault from the blast of her voice.

Lucy actually has two states of consciousness occurring here and one of them references the other one. She felt *proud* of being *patient*. Actually, she felt proud of her *judgment* or *evaluation* that she was patient. Yet this pride in her patience actually moved her to have little patience about Linus questioning her about it. So she must have had yet a another higher frame or state, "Don't question what I say."

So she talked about the patient state *without* demonstrating it. Do you know about that one? And it led to her responding in an incongruent way. Actually this describes a meta-level state because her thoughts-and-feelings of pride referred to her first (assumed) state of patience.

> [We will have more to say about meta-states later. For now, I should note that the term *"meta"* refers to anything that occupies a relationship to something else and so means "above

and beyond" and so "about" or "higher."]

State Awareness — Scene 3
Charlie Brown is standing outside in his neighborhood with a pleasant expression. Nancy approaches and ends her comments by saying, "So there smarty, **Nyah!** Nyah! Nyah!"

Charlie Brown responds with a look of devastation. He seemingly goes into a state of hurt, or rejection, or self-pity. As Nancy walks away, he notes, "Those 'nyahs' get into your stomach, and they just lay there and **burn.**"

What state would you call that one? "Feeling criticized?" "Curious about Nancy?" "Wondering if Nancy needs a nap?"

Information drives states
States of mind-body reflect and correspond to the information that we process. If we don't keep certain pieces of data out from entering consciousness—like those nyahs that hit Charlie Brown, we will typically find ourselves "going into state" without our choice or will. We will feel that our *states just happen to us*. We will feel like a victim of the information around us and in danger of the words and non-verbal communications of those with whom we rub shoulders.

Yet our environment does not drive our states even though, at the feeling level, it may seem to. Typically, we have been trained to think that we go into a state *because* of the environment. Yet we do not. It does not work that way. Just talk to different members of a large household who grew up together. You'll hear different stories, memories, understandings, beliefs, values and states. Roman Emperor Marcus Aurelius said that "men are disturbed not by things, but by *their interpretation* of things." The meanings we give to events and environments as *information* primarily drives and creates our states.

State Awareness — Scene 4
In this next cartoon, we find that Lucy has already accessed a dragon state. It begins with her dressing down her little brother, Linus. "Get out of my way!"

Then raising her fist (one of her common non-verbal gestures), she explains, "When big sisters speak little brothers jump!!"

In the third frame she storms off. To that Linus comments, "Little brothers are the buck privates of life!"

Ah, the buck-private state! Living life in such a way that you feel you must constantly jump at the orders that others bark out. From an information standpoint, Lucy uses many of her communicational channels and processes to induce Linus to buy into the buck-private state. And so he does. This also explains the ultimate induction for any of us. For after all, *what* we say to ourselves, in terms of how we language ourselves, ultimately determines our state. Sadly, the fourth frame ends with Linus making a learning about all of this. He develops a belief that contains a decision which will disempower him, "Little brothers are the buck privates of life."

State Awareness — Scene 5
Linus crosses his arms, tightens his stomach muscles, puts a determined expression on his face and announces, "Boy am I stubborn! I'm the most stubborn person alive!" What state would that kind of self-languaging generate?
Frame two. "I'm like a rock! Permanent! Immovable! Fixed!" Yet this has apparently functioned like a "come-on" (or challenge) to Snoopy, who we see in frame three, comes running like a bowling ball and bowls Linus over.
"Pow!" Then, flat on the floor with fist raised, Linus continues, "Steadfast! Unalterable! Unyielding!"
In this we recognize that a state operates as a mind-body configuration that's made up of thoughts, perceptions, understandings, cognitions—all of the "mental" things by which we develop awareness of the world, ourselves, others, concepts, etc. A state also involves the physical stuff: physiology and neurology. It involves how we breathe, hold ourselves, our posture, facial expressions, movements, etc. In this, I have written about a state of mind **and** a state of body and yet (as noted earlier) this incorrectly describes a state. After all, we never experience a state of mind *without* a state of body. So we need *the hyphen* to remind us of the holistic system of mind-body, neuro-linguistic, neuro-semantic-linguistic-physiological, etc. (This contribution from General Semantics addresses the delusional verbal splits, or elementalism, that we otherwise experience.)
The components of mind-body function as an interactive system contributing to the overall configuration that results in our "state." By definition then, *a mind-body state* refers to the overall configuration which arises from all of our "mental"-"physiological" facets. The two

royal roads to understanding and working with our states consist of our "mind" and our "body."

"Mind" involves *the content* of our internal representations —the *what* that we cognitively present to ourselves. It involves all of the things that we see, hear, smell, taste, feel, etc. on "the theater of our mind" plus the things we say to ourselves about those sights, sounds, and sensations.

Physiology involves the state of our health, body, neurology, and all the factors that make up and that affect our physiological being—our sleeping patterns, eating patterns, exercising, resting, relaxing, recreational patterns, our style of posture, movement, breathing, etc.

These two **royal roads to state** give us two avenues for becoming effectively aware of our states. Via the "mind" we can ask,

> What thoughts flitter across my consciousness? What ideas do I entertain? What visual images play across the theater of my consciousness? What do I represent on that theater in terms of sounds, volumes, pitches, words, etc.?

Our state of "mind" also involves *the meanings* that we give or attribute to things, i.e., the significance, belief, value, etc. of those events.

Via the "body," we can check out the state of our body.

> How do I feel physically? Do I feel tired, fatigued, nervous, sleepy, alert, tense, etc.?

Another window that allows us to become aware of our state involves *the object* of our state. All of our primary states, after all, have some object to which it has reference. If I feel afraid—I feel afraid *of something.* If I feel anger—I experience anger *about something.* If joy fills my heart—then I feel joy *about* something. We always have some *content* in mind that we are referencing when it comes to our states.

> [As an aside: When we lack an object of our state of consciousness and only experience a generalized pervasive state of "fearfulness," "free floating anxiety," "anger-proneness," etc. then we have moved to a meta-state level by creating a higher-level belief about a conceptualization. More about that later.]

Figure 1:1

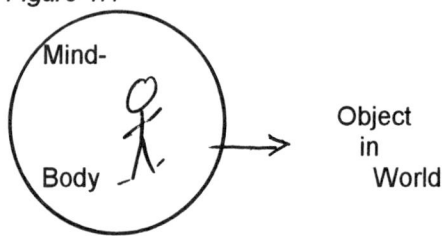

To become aware of our states and manage them, we need to become aware of *the object* that triggers these mind-body experiences.

- What do you think about that object?
- What relationship has your body taken in relationship to that object (the "attitude" you adopt)?
- What history have you had with it?
- What ideas, beliefs, and cognitions has someone trained you to take with respect to it?

Question. What state of mind-body do you typically discover yourself in? Which of these states could you do very well without? Which mind-body states empower you so that you experience more of your personal resources? Use the following list of states to identify those that you primarily and typically live in.

We all live in, and operate out of, various states of mind-body. Out of those states come our emotions, speech, behavior, etc. (the expressions of state). We never leave home without being in some state. I take my states everywhere I go. Yet not all of these *neuro-linguistic states* serve us well. Some states can make life a living hell. Some feel like "dragon" states; some turn us into dragons. All of this reinforces the importance of learning effective state-management skills.

Figure 1:2

Unresourceful States "Dragon" States	Resourceful States "Princely" "Royal"
Stress, Tense, Uptight	Relaxed, calm, reflective
Anger, sarcastic, rageful	Accepting, managing angers well
Fearful, apprehensive	Managing fears well, courageous
Timid, dreadful	Courageous, optimistic
Pessimistic, negative	Optimistic, positive
Worrisome, fretful	Calmly Reflective
Self-contempt, rejection	Self-accepting, esteeming
Sullen, hateful	Connecting, loving
Bitter, resentful	Forgiving, releasing
Overserious	Joyous, Playful

Within the field of NLP, we have numerous and wonderful models, along with technologies, for this very subject of managing states. It specially teaches a person how to "run your own brain." Learning such skills empowers one to feel resourceful, confident, optimistic, and resilient which makes life a whole lot more fun and productive!

STATES OF CONSCIOUSNESS

Our *"primary states"* describe how we think about, give meaning to, and respond to the world at large. States of fear and anger, joy and calmness, sadness and pleasantness, etc. are examples of such everyday *primary* states. The object of these states generally refer to something *outside* of our nervous system. And yet, from these states we live.

They then govern our learning, memory, perception, behavior, communication, etc. (LMPBC). Psychology calls this *state-dependency*. This comprises a critical fact about states and one that provides some major insights and skills for state management.

The state-dependency of knowledge, understanding, emotion, and experience of states means that when we get into an angry state, we can see red anywhere and everywhere. When we access a jealous state, green colors our perceptions and memories. In a depression state, we color everything we hear, feel, and experience dark. In other words, our states control and color (so to speak) the way we perceive things.

When we shift from a ludicrous and silly state in which we laugh at the most ridiculous things to a serious and sober state, we seem to experience an amnesia-like forgetfulness. Suddenly, we seem unable to re-access those silly perceptions or feelings. Out of each and every state also come appropriate and corresponding words and behaviors. When in an angry state, we speak and act angrily. When in a loving and tender state, we behave in loving and tender ways. These *expressions of state* (i.e., speech, behavior, emotions) also arise as *a function of the state*. It describes how we typically express ourselves when in a given state.

With regard to managing states, **if** I remember that all my learning, memory, perception, communication and behavior functions state-dependently, I can take these facets into consideration.

> It makes sense that I should perceive and remember in a depressing way. After all, I have gotten into a down state.
> It makes sense that I will function in a delightful, cheerful, humorous, and joyful way when in a pleasantly cheerful state.

I can even see humor and funniness where it doesn't exist.

> It only makes sense that I should perceive, remember, and feel rejected and insulted when in a put-down and rejection state.

I can even "see" rejection and hurt where another did not intend to offer offense. What does this mean? Frequently our experiences function more as an experience of our state rather than of "reality." This becomes true with a vengeance when it comes to meta-states.

State Induction — Scene 1

Linus responded to something Lucy had said by asking a question, "School President? **Me?**"

Lucy said, "Why not? I'll be your campaign manager."

To this information Linus went into a state of insecurity and lack of self-assurance. "But I could never be school president... think of the work... think of the responsibility." This gives us an idea of where Linus had sent his brain and the ideas (or frames) that he entertained.

Lucy then swished his brain in another direction. "Think of the power."

Frame three shows Linus thinking about the power: his eyes narrow, he takes on a full grin showing his teeth, his hands in fists at his side.

In frame four he raises his arm above his head, *"I'll do it!"*

Not only does information drive states, information also induces and creates states. Via information we send our brains, and the brains of others, to represent new and different things that puts us in various states. Add to that the realization that we all have predispositions toward certain information. We inevitably and inescapably move toward our values, beliefs, and desires. We have a real propensity to move toward some states. If we ask then about the process of *state induction,* we must *go back to the information* (the thoughts) that we entertain. We induce a state of consciousness in ourselves by the mechanism of representation.

Two foci for this state accessing/induction describes two kinds of information: *remembered information and imagined information.*

We can remember a time when we experienced a state and recall what we saw, heard, smelled, tasted, and felt. We can also invent, or create a state out of thin air by using the "what if" frame of reference. What would relaxation look, sound, and feel like? Confidence? Assertiveness? In remembering, we use our mental-kinesthetic memory to *"recall a time when..."* In creating, we use our imagination to wonder about *"what would it look, sound, and feel like if..."*

Now we can code information in our heads in various modalities (modes) of awareness which, in turn, will drive our states. NLP talks about *these modes of awareness* as the sensory-based modes: visual, auditory, kinesthetic, olfactory, gustatory. We also have an evaluative-based mode: language. We also have numerous ways to distinguish and define these modalities. What we erroneously call "sub-modalities" are actually the meta-level qualities and properties of the images, sounds, or sensations. And it lies at this higher or meta-level that we find the semantic mechanisms that truly drive our states (see Figure 1:3).

In talking about *our propensities for accessing various states*, we all have certain states that we can very quickly access, familiar states that we have repetitively induced and which have become so streamlined that we can now *"fly"* into those states. Most people, for example, can really "fly into a state of rage." How about you? Can you do that one? Do you have "flying into a rage" down as a higher developed skill? When you least expect it, can you suddenly "fly into a rage" and get your mind and body and tongue all upset, hot, and bothered?

How about *"flying into a calm?"*

Have you ever experienced being caught up in some dragon state wherein you felt upset, annoyed, angry, fearful, disgusted, etc.? You were going at it with someone and letting them have a piece of your mind. Then all of a sudden, your phone rings. Rrrrinnnnggg.

And you then shift enough to answer it with your pleasant telephone voice. "Hello?"

Can you do that one? If so, then you do have all the necessary neurological equipment you need in order to alter your states, shift your states, and transform your states.

So what actually changes the state? What *mechanism* can we point to that explains the process of such quick, snap-of-the-finger state change?

A new stimulus occurred (i.e., a phone rings) and a new thinking occurs from the enraged thinking.

> I don't want to answer it like a dragon. I don't want to blast the caller, "Who the hell do you want?" I want to present myself as a good, reasonable, thoughtful, and caring human being.

And those instantaneous programmed thoughts (i.e., higher frames about values and beliefs; to wit, meta-states) enable you to immediately "fly into a calm."

So we *already know how* to alter our states and to induce new states, do we not? Our states just never stay the same. In fact, we all experience multiple states every day. Think about all the states you experienced yesterday. How many did you experience? Ten, sixteen, twenty? If you journal or log your states, you will become more conscious of the various states that you access, the triggering stimuli to which you respond, and the internal thoughts that inform those states. You can always count on your states altering, shifting, and transforming. And as you develop greater awareness of this, you can then *take charge* of altering your states at will.

State Induction — Scene 2

Linus said to Charlie Brown while philosophizing on their wall, "I'd like to make a lot of money, but I'd hate to be a snob I've given this a lot of thought." What state would those thoughts induce in you? It sounds like Linus realizes some *incongruity* between these thoughts and has sought to integrate the conflicting desires.

Charlie Brown asks, "So what have you decided?"

Linus responded, "So I've decided to be a very rich and famous person who doesn't really care about money, and who is very humble but who still makes a lot of money and is very famous, but is very humble and rich and famous..."

Charlie Brown concluded by commenting, "Good luck!"

Figure 1:3

Sensory-Based Modalities	Evaluative-Based Modalities
The Representational Systems	The Linguistic Systems
Visual, Auditory, Kinesthetic, etc. (VAK)	Words, language, symbols, etc.
	Submodalities (qualities of sights: i.e. bright/dim, close/far, movie/ snapshot, color/ black & white sounds: i.e., loud/quiet, close/ far sensations: i.e., hot/cold; pressure/ soft)
	Qualities of Symbol Systems
See, hear, feel words	Meaning words
Empirical, "Objective"	Non-empirical, "Subjective"
External References	Internal References
Objects in World	Concepts in "mind"
Words of the world	*Words of the "mind"*
Easy agreement about referent	Difficult agreement about referent
Extensional Orientation--	Intensional Orientation--
Open eyes and point with figure	Close eyes & let words & definitions of words swirl around(!)

Some states *contradict* other states so that if we attempt to access both at the same time, we become internally conflicted with ourselves.

Take a moment to experience this for yourself. Access a state of calmness. Put your body into a place that would correlate to a state of feeling calm and relaxed. For myself, I do that by relaxing my shoulders and letting my arms hang at my side. I shift my breathing so that I breathe deeper and fuller from my stomach.

What do you have to shift? If you need to close your eyes and go back to some relaxing or calming time, then allow yourself to do that completely and honestly as you just allow yourself to access this

resourceful state of calmness.
> [Go ahead and practice this. We'll keep coming back to *relaxation as a resourceful state* that we can use to build some truly royal states later. So the time you begin to spend now will serve you well later!]

We all have different ways of getting there. Some will need pictures— glorious, wonderful, beautiful pictures of comfortable scenes of pleasure. Others will need sounds, i.e., sounds of nature, of an ocean beach, of music, of a calm voice. Others will primarily need to access kinesthetic sensations: feel the sense of the sun's warmth beating down on your body and face, the sense of a soft feather bed as you lay upon it, and sink deep into it. *Now*, at the very same time, *feel really angry*. Try it.

Difficult? Exactly! With regard to contradictory states, we cannot access one state *and simultaneously* the other state. These mixed states, however, sometimes alternate so quickly, first in calm then in anger, then in calm then in anger. First in ambition to become rich, then in humility to not care about making lots of money. And if we keep alternating we can become disoriented, dizzy, conflicted, in a word—internally stressed or dis-eased. Why? Because we have to use the same neuro-pathways to represent and experience both of these states.

State Induction — Scene 3

Charlie Brown said to Lucy, "Look, you don't have to tell me I'm blah!" This indicates one of the identity states that has become habitual for Charlie Brown. He has "mentally" identified himself with a certain quality or trait. And whenever we identify with something (i.e., a person, job, belief, role, experience, etc.), we thereby empower it as we make it our identity. Doing such puts us into, and creates, identity states.

In frame two, Charlie Brown says, "I **know** I'm **Blah!**"

Lucy responded, "Well, then there's still hope for you Charlie Brown." "If you recognize this in yourself then that's the first step up from blahdom!"

Frame four ends with Charlie Brown pondering **"Blahdom?"**

When we use vague, fluffy, and non-referencing words we create miserable, non-productive, and even dragon states for ourselves. Charlie Brown did it around the pseudo-word "blah." Others do it around "loser," "failure," "worthless," "unlovable," "victim," etc. By using such words-of-the-mind (in contrast to words-of-the-world, figure 3, a linguistic distinction we'll explain in more detail later), we induce and create our states and meta-states.

State Induction: Scene 4

Linus sat on the living room floor holding his blanket and sucking his thumb, as Lucy approached him with a series of pseudo-questions. "This is the beginning of a new year, right? **Right!**"

"Now, listen carefully, I have a suggestion. Bad habits are best destroyed at the beginning of a new year, right? **Right!** That stupid blanket you're holding is a bad habit, right? **Right!**"

Linus finally comments in the last frame, "Suddenly I feel very cold..."

Here Linus feels himself physiologically *shifting* from a state of comfort to another kind of state. Listening to his big sister, he senses that she has an agenda to change him! Her languaging led his mind to represent some new and different (and for him) frightening representations. Language, as our meta-sense *above and beyond* (e.g., "meta") our sensory senses of sights, sounds, sensations, smells and tastes, most powerfully induce states.

What we say to ourselves about whatever we hear, see, or experience makes up **the most crucial factor** in terms of the states that result. As we language, so we set higher frames of mind *about* our experience and so everything becomes ordered to fulfill that frame.

If you wanted to access a state of anger, how would you do that? Wouldn't you have to use some words, some angry words, to do that? We have to use words that represent displeasure, violation, and injustice to ourselves. "I can't stand that!" "I hate that!" "She has no right to talk to me that way!" "That's unfair!" "I refuse to take anymore of that from you!"

Angry statements like those inevitably induces angry thoughts-feelings and neurology. Do those statements work for you? Try to feel really, really angry while saying the following in a matter-of-fact tonality, "I would prefer that not to occur." Does that work? The language I use on myself, and others, inevitably corresponds to the states I access and induce. If you want to develop greater state-awareness, listen in on the languaging you do to yourself and others. Our languaging is telling.

If I use insult, degrading, and dignity-denying words on myself or another, guess what state I'll induce? Suppose I use that kind of languaging on another person? What state would I thereby invite them to access? Language provides us with an incredibly powerful state-inducing mechanism.

State Induction: Scene 5

Schultz drew another cartoon. In it Charlie Brown called Snoopy for supper. No response.

Charlie Brown then said, "All right. If you don't want your supper, I'll give it to the cat next door." Immediately we see Snoopy flying through the air as he comes and pounces on his bowl.

Charlie Brown commended, "That usually does it."

What language statements quickly and automatically induce or evoke you to fly into a state? We all invite others to access various states by the statements we make. Every time I open my mouth, I do not just utter mere words, I rather create symbols and referent experiences to which another may powerfully respond.

Knowing this, I will want to speak with more consciousness, care, and awareness with regard as to what effect my words will have, whether I will evoke states that will serve them well or not. For not only will *they* have to live in that state, but *I* will also have to live with them as they experience that state. This sets straight the non-sense of thinking that other people "make" or "cause" me to experience my states. They do not. They cannot. They can only offer the opportunity for others to "go into state." Sometimes they can offer such a strong opportunity, that it seems that they *evoke* or even *provoke* them to step into a state. Yet ultimately, it is still my choice to go.

Physiology represents the second royal road to state. Take a moment and tighten up all your muscles. Make a fist. Clench it hard and as you do allow all of the rest of your muscles in your legs, stomach, chest, neck, face, arms to tighten as much as you can, and now try really hard to think something relaxing as you keep tightening those muscle groups.

Difficult? Yes, indeed. How we use our physiological equipment plays a crucial role in state and state induction. If I wanted to feel depressed, what would I have to do with my physiology to access that kind of a state without thinking depressed? How would you do it *just using your physiological equipment*?

How about loosening your shoulder and arm muscles? Okay. Stoop head, bend back. Look at the ground. Slow down your talk. Use a slow, moaning kind of tonality. Yes. That would work for me! How about you?

One thing we can do in managing our states involves consciously managing our physiology. William Glasser (1967/ 1983), developed *Reality Therapy and Control Theory*, which says that one thing we can always do in controlling ourselves lies in choosing what we **do**. NLP highlights the same principle.

Try this. Access a state of depression by lifting your head, widen your eyes as much as you can, speak in a quick tempo and with an uplifting tonality and when you do, then try to feel as depressed as you can. Can you do it? Such physiology makes the depression much more difficult to access, does it not?

As we develop greater state awareness we discover *the information* or messages that drives our states. We discover the sensory-based information, the linguistic information, and the kinesthetic information that we use to *signal our brain to go into various states*. And as we experience states again and again, they all *habituate*. Any and every state will habituate if we repeat it often enough. The information and signaling in our neuro-pathways will become more and more streamlined and less conscious and eventually become unconscious so that we can "go into state" without even thinking about it. Having looked at the subject of eliciting and accessing states, let's look at how we can interrupt them.

State Interruption: Scene 1

Snoopy sits out in a down pouring rain. He thinks to himself, "So it's raining. Why should I move. I'll just sit here and get wet!"

In frame two, he continues the self-pity. "I'll sit here until I catch pneumonia and die!! Nobody cares anything about me anyway!" Such self-languaging! If you used those language patterns, would that enable you to really get into a state of self-pity and discouragement. Whenever I use that cartoon in workshops on Meta-States or Dragon Slaying, I read that cartoon in a slow, depressing, self-pitying tone. *Tonality* plays a powerful, and usually unconscious role and so profoundly affects us. If you use it and say something positive like, "Everything is going wonderful!" you will not only **not** get an optimistic response, but a strong pessimistic one, especially if you use such tonality in your head, and fail to notice that tonality.

Charlie Brown passed by and seeing Snoopy, yelled at him, "Hey

stupid! Get out of the rain!"
Snoopy responded, "Gee! Somebody cares."
Talk about an interruption! Charlie Brown interrupts Snoopy's state by ordering him to get out of the rain. The information he offered contrasted with his internal thoughts and he "snapped" out of the old state as he re-languaged himself with a new meaning, a new line. "Someone cares!"

Do you have at least five ways to interrupt your state when you get into some unresourceful, unpleasant, unproductive state? I hope so. Actually, the more methods you have for pulling off *a state interruption*, the more control you will experience over your states. It will empower you in the whole process of state management.

Here's one recommendation. The next time you feel depressed, find a corner of a room, go there, and stand on your head. Yes, *stand on your head* with your feet up on the wall. To stand on your head while in that state will undoubtedly severely interrupt your state. I'll bet that you will not have the ability to stay depressed in that position. Try it. After all, your feelings as somatic body sensations have a certain relationship to gravity and when you turn it upside-down, you don't have the neuro-pathways developed to stay depressed on your head. Try it if you don't believe me.

State Interruption: Scene 2

Snoopy says, "Sometimes when I get up in the morning, I feel very peculiar."

Showing his teeth, he continues, "I feel like I've just **got** to bite a cat! I feel like if I don't bite a cat before sundown, I'll go crazy!!"

Do you ever talk that way to yourself? Of course, you probably want to bite someone other than the neighbor's cat. We wake up irritable, annoyed, tense, and feel like we need to let it out in some way.

Sitting up and taking a deep breath, Snoopy says, "But then I just take a deep breath and forget about it." He first changes his physiology. Then he mentally releases it. He comments, "That's what is known as real maturity." Giving it that meaning apparently worked for him.

Snoopy's last line shows us the neuro-semantic and neuro-linguistic frame-of-reference that enabled him to shift. After all, **the meanings** we give to things, and the words we use in labeling things, create our "reality" or frames of states. Snoopy framed, or reframed, taking a deep breath as signifying "maturity," "real maturity." And in so doing, that reframe assisted him in managing his state. What *meanings* help you?

If someone says something to me that I would prefer not to hear, or that I evaluate as information that I would prefer not to receive, I could label that experience as "criticism," "rejection," "insult," "put down," etc. To label it linguistically actually signals the nervous system to create *that kind of phenomenon* within neurology. Yet if I say, "Oh, got up on the wrong side of bed, huh?" "Having a difficult time expressing yourself in a kind and gentle way?" "Feedback." "Valuable information that I can use." Whatever I call it, whatever meaning I attribute to the event—so it becomes to me. By such we can manage or fail to manage our states. This suggests the power of the higher states as frames of meaning that totally reorders perception and meaning.

State Interruption: Scene 3

In one cartoon Lucy really got herself into an unresourceful state. "Everything's wrong! I don't know how I put up with it! And it's getting worse! It's getting worse all the time!" What state would that induce you into? And how could you interrupt someone in such a state?

Linus did an indirect interruption. Commenting to himself by quoting a verse, he said. "Her voice was ever soft, gentle and low, an excellent thing in woman."

Interruption! Lucy said, "What'd he say?"

Here Linus "turned away wrath with a soft answer" (Proverbs 15:1). He offered her something so incongruous to her state that it broke rapport or connection with her. It failed to match or pace her state so much that it jarred her out of her experience. She had to step out of it for a moment, "What'd he say?"

This process of interruption occurs regularly in our everyday lives. Something occurs and we feel interrupted. Later we may even experience a temporary amnesia so that we can't remember our place, activity, or mood before the interruption.

But what do we do about dragon states?

Dragon States: Scene 1

Lucy storms down the sidewalk. Upon meeting Linus she blasts, **"Get out of my way!!"**

Linus and Charlie Brown watch in silence as Lucy stomps on down the road. Charlie Brown finally comments, "I feel sorry for you. How can

you stand it?"
Translation: How do you handle that dragon?
Linus says, "I keep hoping that someday they'll develop a crabbiness vaccine."

Well, while Linus engages in wishful thinking about the development of a crabbiness vaccine, we can learn to more deeply understand people, ourselves, and the states we get into. After all, *the expressions or manifestations of our state* (e.g., behaviors, emotions, words, etc.) *also operate state-dependently.* We can simply expect people in unresourceful states to talk and behave unresourcefully. We can expect people in stressful and irritable states to talk and behave irritably. And if we feel like a victim of their state, how much more them! After all, we can at least leave and go elsewhere. But they can't. They have to carry that state with them everywhere they go until they shift state.

Dragon States: Scene 2
While Charlie Brown pitches the ball from the pitcher's mound, Lucy yells from the outfield. "Hey who told you that you could pitch?" "You pitch like my grandmother! Why don't you give up? You couldn't pitch hay! Why don't you go back where you came from? Booooo!" Finally, exhausted, Lucy heads home. "It's hard work being bitter."

This dragon state operates much more subtly than the dragon states of rage, irritability, stress, etc. This state of ill-will, bitterness, nasty-little thoughts, little mindedness, etc. moves about in sneaky ways.

Dragon States: Scene 3
Lucy says to Charlie Brown. "Charlie Brown, I think you should resolve to be perfect during the coming year."

What thoughts-feelings do those words evoke in you? Charlie Brown says, "Perfect? Good grief, nobody's perfect! What do you expect of me?"

Optimistically Lucy encourages Charlie Brown on, "I think you **can** be if you try. I really do!" Where do those words send your brain?

It hooks Charlie Brown. He takes the bait. "All right, Lucy, if you have that much faith in me, I'll try! I hereby resolve to be perfect during the next year!"

Laughing Lucy says, "You? Perfect? Ha! Ha! Ha! Ha!"

Charlie Brown here faces the dragon of crazymaking because he has received two contradictory messages from Lucy: "You can... You can't!" The first message sets him up, raises his hopes, promises him wonderful things. The second message knocks him down and mocks his naivety. Such double-bind messaging can undermine our grasp of reality so that we don't know where we stand with another or with ourselves. Such communicating drives the Game of "Let Me Drive You Crazy."

State Amplification

We not only use internal representations in all of our sense and language modalities to create a state, we use the same mechanisms to amplify or turn-up the intensity of a state. All states do not have the same level of intensity. Gauging our states and recognizing the "drivers" of our states provides us central mechanisms for state management.

Further, when it comes to state management, we always have a choice about **what** to represent and **how** to code that representation. We can think of this as *representational power*. We have the power to represent whatever information or meaning that we choose, and in whatever manner we choose. This describes the representational coding level of "thoughts." Above that level, that is, *meta* to that level, we have yet another facet of thinking, namely, *the meanings* that we attribute to those representations. These set the frame for how we think about things.

State Manager or Victim

How many of the resourceful states in our initial chart (Figure 1:2) can you access and "fly" into at the snap of a finger? This raises a crucial state management question: Does your state manage you or do you manage it? The two royal roads to state (internal representation of information and physiological cuing) provides you two ways to get yourself into a state, and as you practice doing so, you train your brain-neurology (e.g., neuro-linguistics) to go in a certain direction with greater and greater skill and speed.

You can put yourself into any kind of desired state you choose because states exist as *functions of your mind-body*. Take a moment right now and *access a learning state*. What do you have to do in order to access such?

What does the learning state mean to you? Open, receptive, curious, wondering, playful, etc.? Next check your consciousness: "What do I need to become aware of so that I move into a learning state? What words do I need to say to myself that helps me access that state? What physiological components (e.g., breathing, posture, muscle tension, facial expression, etc.) can I adopt that assists me to feel the feelings of a learning state?" Do you need to sit back, lift your head up, take a deep breath, etc.?

Sometimes we can discover some of these things by engaging in a *contrastive analysis* of our states. So, think about the opposite of a learning state—a closed, rigid, rejecting state. How does that state feel? When you access a non-learning state, notice your muscle tension, eye direction, the words that race through your mind. Doing this contrastive analysis can provide ideas for how to move into a learning state, namely, do the opposite. Go in the other direction! Given the composition of states as we have noted, we can now gain indepth insight about our states and our unique patterns of "stating" (putting ourselves into states) by contrasting resourceful and unresourceful states.

Back to the learning state. What words, statements, and sentences can you say to yourself that facilitates accessing that state?

>"I find this information really fascinating and I really want to learn more."

Language yourself with that one. Does that work for you?

>"This person has information I need." "Focus."

Next, listen to the tone of that voice in your head that expresses those words. How about the volume? Where do you hear these words? Whose voice? You can put anybody's speaking voice in there. Hear Elvis Presley saying/singing, "Be attentive." What if you put in a joyful and playful voice.

Now *gauge the intensity* of your learning state. From "0" for none or "not a chance in hell," and "10" for experiencing it totally and completely, *how much of a learning state* have you accessed? Put a number to it. This helps with state awareness. It assists in understanding whether we have enough *psychic energy* in a state to actually move us so that we can use the state.

To amplify the state, so that you "turn it up" and energize it more, what else you would you need to do? Suppose you wanted to put yourself into **more** of a curious, learning, fascinated, and receptive state? Shift posture, put some desired outcome (goal) in your mind about why you want to access this state. Language yourself with those words in an attractive, compelling tonality.

"I want to learn this in order to develop more skills in self-management."

Frequently, the problem we experience in everyday life involves this issue of neurological intensity. We simply do not have a strong enough state to carry us through. We only have a little weak wimpy state of confidence, anticipation, desire, etc. Suppose you know how to access a caring and loving state, but it lacks enough energy, intensity, and power to move you very much. What then? What do you do if it lacks the strength to get you through the barriers to loving? (Check out a book I wrote many years ago, *Motivation (*1987, Chapter 8.)

Additionally, most of us tend to experience our negative emotional states with much more intensity than our positive emotional states. Does that hold true for you? But why? Undoubtedly because negative emotions function as **warnings** of dangers, problems, and threats to us whereas positive emotions function more like validations and reinforcements for things going well. We feel our negative emotions more intensely because they jerk us around, they slam on the breaks of our processes, and they set off bells and lights of alarm. By contrast, our positive emotions more gently add fuel to keep us moving on down the highway of life.

Next we can do some **state anchoring**. Once we find ourselves, or put ourselves, in a state, we can set up some trigger (i.e., almost any stimuli of sight, sound, sensation, movement, gesture, or word) that will enable us to create a linkage for that state so that by using that stimuli it triggers us back into the state. We call this process "anchoring."

Anchoring takes a Pavlovian conditioning pattern and makes it user-friendly. We take an unconditioned response like experiencing an emotion (e.g. feeling confident, caring, curious, valued, etc.) and then connect a trigger to it so that the new trigger becomes conditioned with the unconditioned response. As a result, this gives us a powerful tool for state management. It enables us to take charge of accessing states instead of just waiting for them to occur. If Pavlov could condition his dogs to access the drooling state via ringing a bell, we can also condition our neurology to access resourceful states via various stimuli.

Working with our states in these ways raises our state consciousness. And the design of this is that we eventually learn our own *state strategies.* The bits and pieces of information, neurology, responses,

etc. that make up or comprise our states occur sequentially.
> "This word leads to that picture which leads to those kinesthetic sensations which leads to this sound, etc."

When we track down such sequences and model the pieces in proper order that generates the "strategy" that creates the state.

Awareness of state strategies puts into our hands *another human technology* for managing our own states so that we can utilize them in ways that enrich our lives. As we discover states which offer resourceful ways to think-feel, perceive, communicate, behave, remember, etc., we can learn to ask and use *the utilization question*. With this focus, we empower ourselves to use states as internal resources that we can take with us wherever we go.

> "Where would I like to use this state?" "What would it look, sound, feel like to have this state in this or that situation?"

Summary

All of this about states and state management underscores the realization that we started with: *our states of mind-body completely determine our level of effectiveness in the world, happiness with ourselves, and resourcefulness.* If we don't learn to develop awareness of our states and management skills over them, we will not develop the ability to control them. That will condemn us to living like a victim of our states. And when we get into unresourceful states we will not function at our best or develop our personal powers.

What key points have I made in this first chapter about how to **"take charge of your states?"**

- We always operate out of some state; we cannot do otherwise. We never leave home without our mental and emotional states.
- Our states arise as "responses" which only we have the "ability" to create, alter, or modify.
- We inevitably and inescapably perceive and experience life from out of our states. We experience perception, learning, memory, communication, and behavior as state dependent.
- We can evaluate our states in terms of whether we find them resourceful or unresourceful, enhancing or unenhancing.
- Our states strongly influence and even determine our

- effectiveness and happiness.
- Our representational powers of thought, information, and meaning drive our states.
- *If we don't manage our states, someone or something else will!*

Effective Actions You Can Take—

1. Journal your states for a week.
Look for the key internal representations (i.e., thoughts, ideas, beliefs, meanings, information) that you use to induce and access your states. Notice also the naturally occurring "anchors" in your life that set off your states. Gauge their intensity. Draw a bubble to represent your state. How long will that bubble last? How many bubbles will you have in a given day?

2. Practice accessing three or four resourceful states this week:
(1) calmness, relaxation, (2) learning, curiosity, (3) playfulness, humor, joy and (4) centeredness.

3. Write out a state induction for yourself for one of these empowering states.

So How Much Did You Learn?
1. How can we develop greater awareness of our states?
2. What does state-dependency mean?
3. How do we induce states in ourselves and/or others?
4. How do we amplify, alter, interrupt states?
5. What does anchoring a state mean? How do we do it?
6. What does an ecology check refer to?
7. What *two royal roads* do we have to "state?"
8. State induction occurs how?
9. What ways do you have to interrupt your dragon states?
10. What resource states do you have plenty of access to?
11. What resourceful states would you like to visit more often?
12. How does *representational power* work powerfully in managing and working with states?
13. What dragon meta-states do you need to slay or tame?

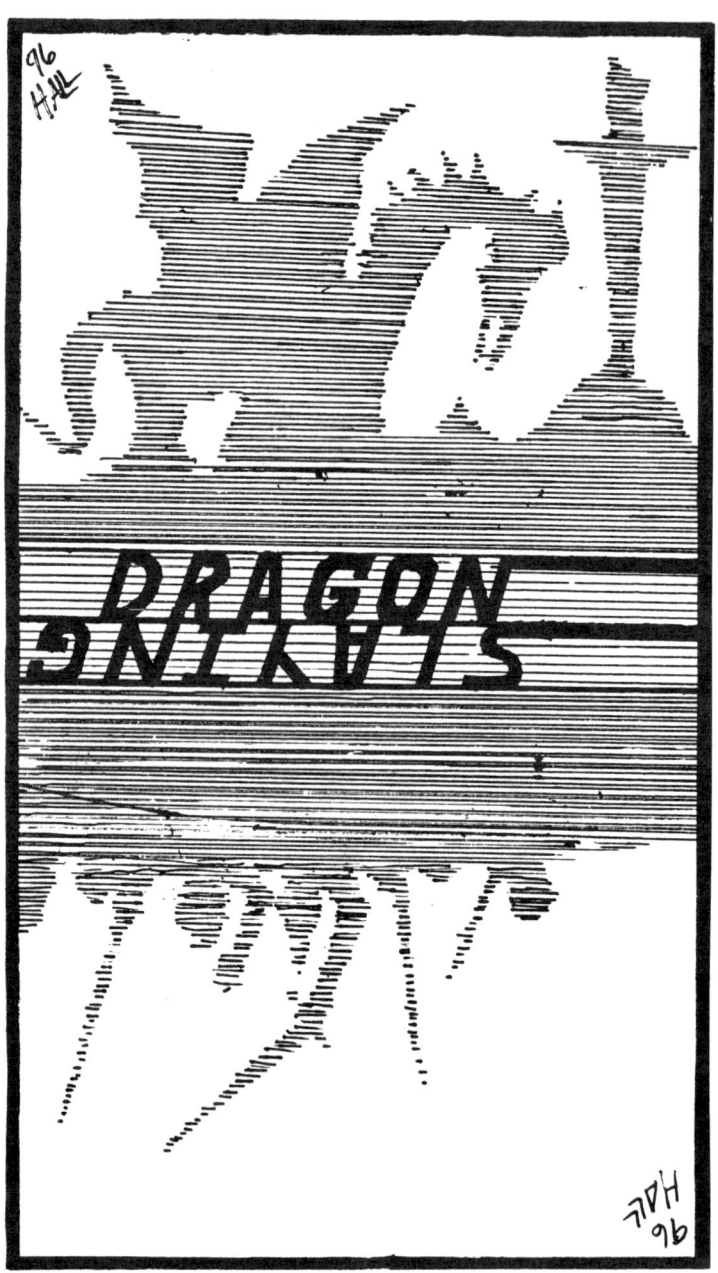

Chapter 2

SOMETIMES I FEEL LIKE A META-DRAGON

When Dragons Govern

I have focused almost exclusively to this point on *primary* states. A primary state refers to those states of thoughts-feelings that generally have reference to some object "out there," some object that we encounter and interact with the external world.

The primary emotions of mad, glad, sad, and fear represent some core primary states. When in these states, we think-feel with anger *about* something external to us that we dislike. We think-feel fear *about* some danger. We think-feel joy and pleasure *about* some source of delight.

Yet all states do not operate on the same logical level. A wild and wonderful thing happens when we access various states and relate them *to other states*. In these more complex "states" which we will hereafter designate as "meta-states," we use our *self-reflexive consciousness* to relate (not so much to the world) but **to** ourselves, or **to** some abstract conceptual mental state.

The word *"meta"* comes from Greek and refers to going *above or beyond* something and having thoughts-and-feelings *about* something. When we *go meta* to a state, we step aside from our primary state of mind-body and we think-feel *about* that state. This wonderful power in human consciousness allows us to become aware of ourselves as "selves" and about many other conceptual abstractions.

For example, in the last chapter I provided a list of states. As you read through that list and thought about the states you frequently experience, and those that you don't, what thoughts-feelings did you experience or access *with regard to* experiencing such states? As one with self-reflexive consciousness, you cannot *not* have additional thoughts-feelings. It comes built in. Your consciousness works in such a way so that you keep reflecting back onto your previous thoughts-and-feelings.

As you look at that list of states, and those that you frequently and habitually get into, now do another jump of levels. Send your thoughts-and-feelings to a higher level as you ask the following questions:

- Does this state serve me well?
- Does it enhance my life or empower me for living?
- Is it the state I want to live in and operate from?

Thinking-and-feeling such things moves us at a meta-level to the primary state. As such, these questions empower us to transcend our primary states. They give us the ability to run a *Quality Control* on our brain. No longer do we have to feel stuck at the primary level of thinking-and-feeling.

Of course, taking charge of your own brain in this way goes against the twentieth century misbelief which the Freudian and other psychotherapies have perpetuated that we must always "be true to our emotions." Numerous problems arise from that limiting belief. After all, many thoughts and emotions contain lots of irrational factors.

We do *not* need to "be true to our emotions." This presupposes that they function as cognitive tools for discerning reality. They do not. Emotions function as somatic signals regarding the relationship between our Map of the World and our Experience of the World. Emotions that provide us valuable information about our beliefs, values, and meanings, and how such higher level thoughts stand up to our ongoing experiences. In this, they function more like warning lights and warning bells to alert us when an experience violates our values and cognitive understandings. They don't tell us anything about "reality." They tell us only about our *thinking* and our *physiological responses* in response to our experience of the outside world.

Think of an *emotion* as the signal that emerges from a set of scales that balances these two facets of our experience. On the one side we have our *Map of the World* and our *Experience of the World.*

E-motions "move" us according to the *evaluations* we make about things. That explains why emotions exist as a mixture of "body" stuff and "mind" stuff—our actual feelings as kinesthetic sensations merge with cognitive awarenesses to generate *a meta-feeling* (a meta-kinesthetic in NLP) which we label "an emotion." Once we have an e-motion (an evaluative-movement), we have somatized a thought or cognition into the body.

Figure 2:1

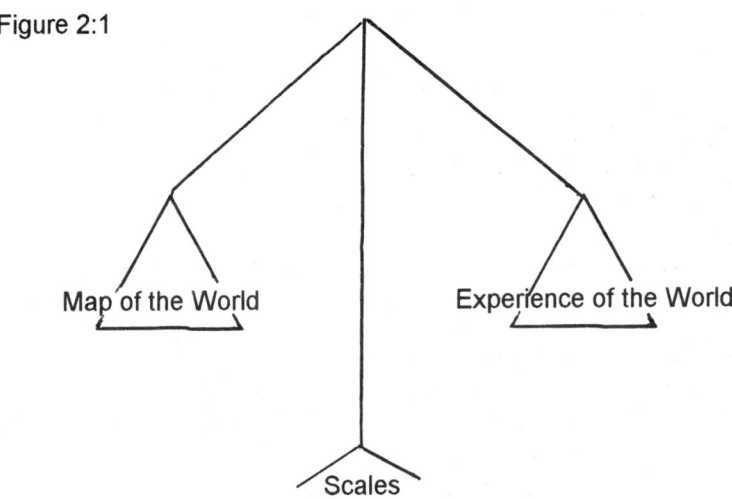

Since emotions operate primarily from our cognitions, we can learn to *track back* from them to the thoughts out of which they arise. After all, when we experience fear in the body we also have fear thoughts plaguing the "mind." When we experience anger, angry thoughts paddle along the stream of consciousness. In joy, joyful thoughts dance around.

By tracking emotions back to the *thinking* from which they arise, we can then *test the thinking*, the cognitions, the meanings, and the beliefs. In a word, we can *check out our mapping.* Accordingly, as we don't have to "be true" to our emotions as if they were some infallible message, we also do not need to "be true to all of our thoughts!" Our thinking suffers from cognitive distortions, erroneous ideas, irrationality, and basic fallibility.

"Being true to our emotions" actually generates a caveman level of authenticity. That would make us less civilized, less moral, less disciplined, less true to the highest values and beliefs that endow us with more humanness.

"Going meta" to our primary states in order to run a reality-test and/or a sanity test on the thoughts-emotions which make up our states gives us the ability to transcend our current states. And in the long run, this enables us to develop a stronger ego-strength so that we can face and adapt to external reality more effectively.

Language — The Meta-Sense

An interesting thing happens with human consciousness after we entertain representations of the world in our "mind," we then say **words** *about* those images, pictures, sights, sounds, sensations, etc. Words about sensory-based representations move us (conceptually) to a higher logical level.

For example, imagine *the sensory qualities* of a strawberry. Allow the sights, sounds, sensations, smells, and tastes of a strawberry or of a plateful of red, juicy strawberries entrance onto the screen of your mind. When you do that, one part of your brain generates an internal experience that re-initiates the experience. And it can come very close to reproducing the experience. But still, there's a difference between all of that internal awareness and actually biting down on a big juice strawberry. It's also very different when we think about *the word* "strawberry" apart from those sensory based details. The word "fruit" takes us even further away, as does "food," "nourishment," "organic substance," etc.

So *above and beyond* what we see and hear on "the theater of our mind," as we use words, we can abstract ideas, concepts, understandings and so create ever higher level awarenesses. Nor does this process stop there. It goes on without end. We can say more words *about* those words, and words *about* those words. Each time we abstract, we can move to a higher logical level of awareness or abstraction. Language, a meta-sense, drives this thinking-experiencing at higher levels. It mediates the conceptual move upward.

As we abstract from the world to make sensory representations in the first place, and then abstract to create word-maps of those sights and sounds, and then more abstract words about those words, etc., we draw conclusions at higher logical levels and invent all kinds of conceptualizations.

We can even over-do all of this. We can engage in this way of operating to such a degree that we can induce ourselves into living in a "world of words" so to speak. It seems to be an occupational hazard of too much college or book learning. Some people can actually do this so much that they lose awareness of their sensory-based representations. Galton found this in the late Nineteenth Century and concluded that "visualization" was for the unsophisticated and intellectually backward. Today we know that keeping alive to seeing, hearing, smelling, tasting, and sensing/feeling keeps us alive to the referents of our words.

Now given this nature of language that moves us to higher and higher logical levels, we can not only access and induce ourselves into *states of thought-and-feeling* about something in the world (the primary states), but we can then develop additional *thoughts-and-feelings about that primary state.* And then we can construct additional thoughts about that meta-state.

Imagine this. I begin with a down state like depressing myself about something that didn't go the way I wanted it to go. Then I think-feel **guilty** about feeling down. Then I feel **embarrassed** about feeling **guilty** about feeling down. Then I feel **angry** for feeling **embarrassed** about my **guilty** feelings about my **depressing.**

Then someone asks, "How do you feel?"

"Well, I feel..."

Our ability to jump logical levels at a single bound causes us to experience complex, layered, and tangled up (even muddled) states-about-states until we don't now what or how we feel. This describes that wild and wonderful experience of accessing states *about* states, or meta-states.

Earlier I used a more formal and technical phrase to describe and explain this—*self-reflexive consciousness.* As our consciousness becomes *reflective* about itself and *reflexes* back onto itself, it develops complexity and layeredness of consciousness.

Suppose you become "angry at your fear." What does that feel like? First you have your experience of fear itself. You feel a dread, apprehension, a moving-away-from energy from some danger. Then you experience an anger *at* your state of fear. In this case, one primary emotion (anger) targets another primary emotional state (fear). Out of the mix comes "self-anger." This really complicates things. It can also create a monster on the inside—a **dragon state.** Sigmund Freud was of the opinion that "anger turned inward" typically shows up as the

depression that self-contempt and self-judgment causes.
   In that case, the state of anger reflexively turning upon itself takes on new complications or gestalts. A *gestalt* refers to a new whole or configuration that we cannot explain in terms of its parts. It exists as an emergent property from the entire system, something "more than the sum of the parts."
   When a state recursively feeds back into another state, it can create a closed-loop system. This can then have the effect of creating the structure of a self-reinforcing, self-validating, and self-fulfilling prophecy. It can create an ever-increasing cycle of thoughts-feelings about thoughts-feelings that no longer relates to the world at all only to other states.
   If I feel frustrated because things just don't seem to open up and move as I feel they should, and then I start feeling disgusted about my self because of this. Now *my consciousness itself has shifted* from the external "aboutness" (my goals and desires of what I wanted to accomplish) to the internal "aboutness." Now I have more *reference* to an abstraction, in this case, my abstraction about my concept of my "self." As I now begin to focus primarily on this concept of "self" (which only exists in my head), I attend more to my feelings of *disgust at "self"* than to the external blocking that stimulated the frustration feelings in the first place.
   What a state!
   What a meta-muddle!
   With all of that, I have just entered into **the semantic zone** (I started to write, Twilight Zone, but it's not that mild or predictable!). I say *"semantic"* to describe this higher level state (and hence, *Neuro-Semantic)* because it operates *exclusively* as a state about my **meanings** (i.e., my concepts, abstractions, and semantics).
   No animal experiences the meta-state of self-disgust in this way. Animals can experience disgust as a primary state. But lacking higher abstraction powers as mediated via symbolic language systems, they do not create the "categories of mind" like we do of "self, time, purpose, causation, gender, significance," etc. And since they cannot get to that level of abstraction, they cannot create higher level thoughts-feelings and direct them toward various conceptualizations. But we do. And we do so with a vengeance!
   And it gets worse.
   My higher level meta-state of self-disgust will operate within me like

primary states in terms of what we call *"state-dependency."* This refers to how a *state* can take on a "life of its own." Once in a state, we tend to think, perceive, feel, remember, talk, and act *according to the nature of the state.* In depressed states, we see, feel, and experience the world as through dark glasses. In an angry state, we can see things to provoke our anger everywhere.

So with the meta-state of self-disgust. Once in that state, it powerfully affects our memories, learning, perceptions, feelings, understandings, communications, behavior, etc. We then tend to engage the external world *through the filter of self-disgust* and constantly nag on ourselves.

"This won't work."
"I hate myself for being this way."
"This is just like me to mess up."

In this way, our meta-states operate as self-fulfilling prophecies, as the higher frame of reference that initiates a self-organizing influence in all of our mind-and-body. As a result, our *expectations about ourselves,* as a meta-state of *self-expectancy* activates our perceptions, neurology, behavior, etc. to bring about that very thing, in this case, self-disgust. [This actually describes the structure of expertise. Set a frame for a mind-set, and we become inwardly organized to manifest it, but that's another story.]

Suppose I *fail* to accomplish something. It could be anything. This describes a primary state. The verb "fail," while not specific, at least describes an action of not fully succeeding to accomplish some outcome. If I then make the verb into a static noun and treat it like a solid, tangible thing, "failure" (a nominalization), I have created an even more abstract map.

If I then define my "self" as *"a failure"* and make that part of my self-definition, I will come to expect *myself* to fail, to "be a failure." What a dragon that creates!

Someone asks, "Well, what other state could we access when we fail to accomplish something we wanted to achieve?"

How about a primary state of "lack of accomplishment?" What else could you expect as your response to that? How about? "Gather more information, then act, continue to produce actions, evaluate, etc." Or, how about "acceptance of failing to accomplish my goal?" Or, how about "curiosity about failing" so we keep learning and using the feedback?

Figure 2:2

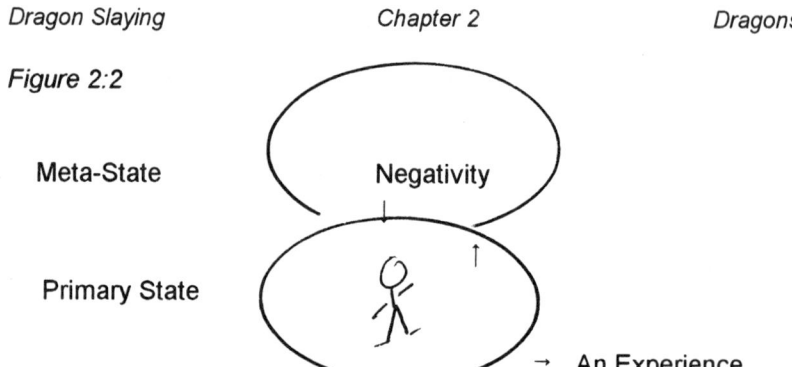

Using the old map of "failure" and then "I am a failure," seems pretty feeble when you consider the range of far more ecological and useful ways to map that experience.

I use that as an example to invite you to consider what happens when we shift to a meta-level *with negative thoughts-feelings*. Suppose we go to a *judgment* state about our self having not accomplished some goal? Then self-contempt, self-judgment, self-rejection, self-discounting, etc., results. We have turned our psychic energy against ourselves. We have generated even more dragon states.

PLAYING WITH THE STATES-ABOUT-STATES INTERFACE

In the spirit of playfulness, imagine all of the wild and weird, helpful and hurtful, and empowering and dis-empowering meta-states that we can generate as we observe how states interact at logical levels (Figure 2:3). Since some have commented that NLP can also stand for *N*ow *L*et's *P*lay, this seems most appropriate here.

Look at "fear of fear." Fear can represent a wonderful, healthy, vigorous, and powerful emotion. It can provide wonderful energy for dealing with appropriate dangers. With inappropriate fear, fear of things that actually represent no danger (i.e., a snake on TV, public speaking, etc.), fear powerfully energizes us also. Yet because we have no true danger to avoid, we then tend to stew in our fear. If we give validity to the "feeling" in and of itself without reference to its context, we can reinforce the inappropriate fear, and become enslaved by it.

Now notice what happens when we become *afraid of our fear?* We become paranoid. We turn our fear against ourselves which can then lead to self-distrust, feeling our selves as dangerous, threatening, out-of-control, etc. The fear frequently becomes displaced on external objects so that we become "fearful" as a quality of our very character. We can then think-and-feel and so respond fearfully in a pervasive way Eventually, we could even end up disordering our personality with agoraphobia and attach fearful thoughts-feelings to nearly everything.

How do we shift out of all of that destructiveness?

We will first want to meta-state ourselves or another person in a new and empowering way. At first, it will seem confusing and paradoxical. Just let it seem that way. "Paradox" occurs whenever we mix levels or fail to take logical levels into consideration. Paradox reveals a category error.

The fearful person will first need to begin to accept and even enjoy the fear. Yes, you read that accurately. *Accept and even enjoy the fear.* I told you it would seem paradoxical. But remember, we have moved to a higher level of mind. We have moved to a level where we no longer fear and reject our emotions as emotions. Here we welcome and accept them, learn from them, and then take counsel of them or refuse to take counsel of them.

When I meet with an agoraphobic, I will ask that person, "I'm just wondering how much can you truly and authentically, I mean honestly, *fully enjoy* your fears?"

Talk about interrupting a state!

"What? I don't understand. What did you say?"

"It's just a curiosity of mine, because we're just talking about an emotion, right? And so I'm wondering how fully you can *just accept and appreciate* that fear fully?"

"Oh, never. I can't do that. That's unthinkable!"

I'm not surprised. It's a place (a semantic zone) that they haven't visited often. So I ask,

> "How skilled would you say you could feel, if you really wanted to, about *appreciating* your fears since they work so wonderfully, powerfully, and pervasively for you? What would it feel like if you did come to the point where you could thank God for your fears and truly celebrate them? Spend a moment

with those thoughts... And as you *enjoy* it when you *breathe* faster, and your heart pounds harder, and you feel butterflies dancing in your stomach, and your head feeling lighter realizing that you have a good healthy and responsive nervous system... And you can now try as hard as you can (intentional state) to really feel even more intense fear."

Agoraphobics do not meta-state themselves in this way. They do not use this kind of meta-stating language on themselves. If they did, they wouldn't be diagnosed as "agoraphobic." Agoraphobics will bring negative thoughts-feelings (states) against their primary state of fear. They will language themselves on on the order of:

"Oh no, this fast breathing and heart pounding **means** I am having a heart attack! It means I'm losing control of myself! It means that I'm going to make a fool of myself."

Then they become afraid of their fear, disgusted with their fear, despise their fear, condemn their fear, etc. Then they will move away from "becoming aware" (a more enhancing state) of their fear. Then they will misdirect and mis-attribute the cause of their fear.

"The mall scares me."
"The streets are dangerous."
"You never know what might happen at the grocery store."

In this way, fear-of-fear becomes *a morbid, sick, and dis-empowering dragon state*. Although in such instances the dragon doesn't devour others (as it does in rage-about-rage), it does devour the persons so ordered by their reflexive thinking.

The same meta-stating process works in a similar way to create dragon states with many of these states-about-states. Pity, for example, feeling pity toward something that calls to our heart when we say, "Her situation is so sad." As such, pity offers us a wonderful emotion. As an emotion, pity allows us to show sympathy and compassion in a human way toward others. But it's a different story when we develop *pity of our pity*. Then we sing a very different song. "I'm such a pitiful thing!" Then we have a morbid state of self-pity.

Even *"belief"* itself represents a wonderful human state of consciousness. Belief speaks about a state of "feeling convinced" about something as valid, useful, or real.

"I believe in exercising regularly." "I believe in God." "I believe in the democratic way, human freedom and the equality of people." "I entrust myself to this person, or idea, or experience."

But what happens when we *believe in our beliefs*? We develop a larger level gestalt called, *fanaticism*. We become fanatics about our beliefs. We feel so sure, so confident, so right, so rigid, that we become arrogant know-it-alls who can't be told anything that differs from the belief. We become intolerant and closed-minded. We have closed the book to learning any more. We have no more questions. Believing in our beliefs puts us on the fast track to closing shop on using our brains. We become unreasonable. We begin to play the "I'm Right" Game, "There's no more to say about the subject" Game. And this too functions as a dragon state, only this time, mostly to those on the receiving end!

Consider sadness. Here we have another great and wonderful emotion. Sadness represents a necessary and valuable emotion that assists us in grieving losses and coming to terms with endings. But it's another thing when we become *sad about our sadness.* What do we have then? Typically, depression. Then we lose the ability to use our sadness in a healthy, vigorous, and productive way in coming to terms with a particular lose. Then we turn our sadness and grief against ourselves and so begin to suffer clinically depression.

In many of these meta-states, we see human nature or experience becoming morbid, hurtful, and dis-empowering. Some states-about-states generate "dragons" that can become highly destructive to us, to our happiness, to our effectiveness, and to our sense of reality.

Figure 2:3
When States Interface with Other States

> curiosity of curiosity → intense curiosity!
> attention of attention → attending attention
> analysis of analysis → study of analysis
> reasoning about reasoning → science
> choice of choice → freedom, lack of blockages
> consideration of consideration → cultured thought
> knowing of knowing→ consciousness of abstracting
> evaluation of evaluation → a theory of sanity
> worry about worry → morbid worrisomeness
> fear of fear → paranoia, agoraphobia
> pity of pity → self-pity, pitifulness
> belief in belief → fanaticism, intolerance, dogmatism

conviction of conviction → dogmatism
ignorance of ignorance → innocence
choice of choice → empowering choice
anger at fear → self-anger
joyful about anger→ celebrative of proper/improper use of anger
sad about anger→ awareness of misusing anger
angry about sadness→ inappropriate sadness
fearful about sadness → self-paranoia, inhibited, unemotional
guilt about angry→ self-judgment for anger, self-condemning
inhibition of an inhibition→ positive excitation
hate of hate → love or nullification of emotion
doubt of doubt → scientific criticism
procrastination of procrastination → taking action
interruption of interruption→ confusion
prohibition of... anger, fear, joy, etc.→ "stuck," inner conflict

Defining "Meta-States"

Our working definition of *a meta-state* focuses on its structure, namely, a meta-state refers to *a state about a state.*

We create this layering effect as we bring *thoughts-feelings and physiology* (the component elements that comprise a "state") to bear upon, and applied it to, another state (i.e., another set of thoughts-feelings and physiology) so that the first state references the second. And that *relationship* determines the critical key of a meta-state. The second state stands in a meta-relationship to the first state. It operates as the Class or Category or Frame for the first state. The first state relates to that higher state as a member of its class.

This relationship of state-*upon*-state can work in a disastrous in human experience as previously noted. And, it can also work in ways that create wonderful and glorious experiences. It can express the very highest and best in human potential.

Consider *curiosity of curiosity.* First I become curious perhaps about what you said. Then, as I become curious about my own curiosity I begin to explore in depth the rich experience it creates for me, and the components that make up my higher level curiosity of my curious state. This amplifies my experience. I begin to experience an even more intense curiosity.

Or, how about *attention about attention?* I first attend something, then I attend my attending. Again, this amplifies my own state. Now suppose you do this to the learning state you accessed earlier; what does the experience then become? Perhaps *learn of learning?* Bateson talked about meta-learning, learning at a higher logical level.

Or how about *joyful about anger?* Try that one on for size. Again, anger represents a wonderful emotion. It provides marvelous information— information that I feel displeased about something, that one of the things that I value feels violated in some way, that something unfair or unjust has occurred. I need this information. If I don't get the warning signal, then major things in my life could become violated or threatened, and I would never know it until it has become too late.

As an emotion, anger simple signals me to *"Stop, Look, and Listen."* It empowers me to check out my current situation (experience of the world) and my thinking (my map of the world). If I can appreciate my anger for this, I can then actually enjoy "anger" as a wonderful emotion.

How about you? Step into appreciating and valuing your ability to get angry as providing you those resources and just notice how that transforms your experience of anger. Appreciation of your anger modifies the anger so that you can use it more appropriately. Yes, I feel glad about my ability to register my anger. Here *content* plays a crucial role. What do you rejoice in regarding your anger? This power of the soul? Or how you can use it to intimidate and cower others? When you set that kind of a semantic frame on anger, it will then typically become a dragon meta-state.

Ah, yes, the *meanings we attribute* to our states, to our thoughts, to our feelings, to what we can do with our states, etc. does create our neuro-semantics.

When you meta-state yourself in the sense of bringing some resourceful positive state to apply to some lower state, you powerfully *modify and modulate* those lower states. It textures them. It layers new qualities upon them. I like starting with appreciation, calmness, acceptance, joy, and optimism and applying these kind of resourceful states to primary states that we experience as unpleasant or "negative."

Yet many people *hate their anger.* They despise their anger and reject it. They even become angry-at-their-anger. Yes, they do it for a positive purpose. They *think* that it will give them more control over their anger. But they are mistaken. Rejecting our primary level emotions, even the unpleasant ones, does not give us more self-management, but less. Doing so misdirects consciousness from objects "out there" that may threaten us in some way. It also targets this energy **against** ourselves and against our nature. And in the end, it only creates internal dragons that roar and rampage around inside. And, simultaneously, it prevents us from using our anger appropriately.

By contrast, we build some wonderful and empowering meta-states when we learn to welcome and to celebrate our anger. I can celebrate that I can use my anger to target true injustices that lie within my power to correct. I can appreciate my anger for the power it gives me to transform hurtful things.

From all of this we now know a great neuro-semantic principle, namely,

Bringing a state to reflect upon another state (meta-stating) gives us a new technology for powerfully managing our states.

Try this. Put yourself into a state of *calm relaxation.* To access your calmness, fully and completely, just allow your thoughts-and-feelings to think back to a time when you felt totally at peace. It might have been on a vacation or perhaps when you rested comfortably in front of a fire on a cold winter day, or on a beach in the summer. Pick a time and place and, just in your mind, go there again...

When you have fully access that state of comfort, snapshot it in your mind. Make a visual snapshot of the pictures, an auditory snapshot of the sounds, and a kinesthetic snapshot of the relaxed feelings in your body. Now, holding all of those feelings constant, begin to recall a time when you became angry, and as you do, take a deep breath and relax your muscles even more.

Then from this state of calmness, calmly notice your anger and wonder, in a relaxed way, about the sources of the anger as both the stimulating event to which you responded and about your processing angry thoughts about that event. *Calmly think* about how you can most effectively address the injustice or violation in a way that will truly make things better, always taking a deep breath and relaxing your arm and leg muscles, and feeling calm about your anger. Because you can. Now.

How resourceful would that make you in handling your anger if you did that every time you got angry? It works for me. It enables me to maintain presence of mind in the presence of my anger. It empowers me to communicate in a kinder/gentler way when I feel displeased and stressed. This gives me a new and un-natural ability to manage my anger states from a much more resourceful meta-state.

Over the years, I've used this as one of many meta-stating processes when working with court-ordered anger control classes. Developing the ability to feel *calmly angry* represents a very different experience for most people. Yet I never stopped there. I always moved on to *respectful* anger, *gentle and thoughtful* anger, *caring and honoring another human being* anger.

What about sadness? How would we deal with a sense of actual loss? With the grief that arises when we have legitimately loss someone close to us?

Use the same meta-stating principle. What higher level thoughts and feelings would you want to bring to bear upon the *sadness* to texture it? Again, we do not want make the sadness go away or evaporate. We only want to make the sadness more acceptable and humane. Imagine feeling calm about your sadness. Imagine feeling appreciative about your sadness, or accepting sadness, even joyful in your sadness about all of the good things that you valued and will forever treasure in that person. And do not "the stages of grief," move us in this direction anyway? Do we not move from denial, rejection, bargaining, depressing, to acceptance, and then to discovering how to think joyfully about that person?

I consciously did this when my dad died suddenly of a massive heart attack. Why did I do so? Because I knew that taking counsel of the natural tendency of my mind to reject the awareness of his death would *not* change things or make things better. Putting myself at odds with the reality of the situation wouldn't do anything positive. It would only delay the grief. So I fully welcomed my grief and sadness, accepting that such feelings were appropriate, that they would help me to register the loss, and to find a way to think about the man who meant the most to me in life in a way that I could treasure him forever.

How different things would been if I had became angry at my sadness and rejected it for being "unmanly," or viewed it as "wrong!" I could have created quite a monster in my soul if I had gone that route. To have done so would have led me to *turn my psychic forces against myself*. Then I would have created a different "mix." I would have textured my sadness with desperation, hatefulness, cruelty, etc. Hate-of-sadness, rejection-of-grief, despising-sadness, etc., these do not help us cope with loss. They only perpetuated the grief state, misdirect our energies, and layer higher level meanings onto our thinking-and-feeling that do not enhance our lives.

META-STATES ALWAYS DRIVE LOWER STATES
Did you notice what happens in all of these examples? *The meta-state inevitably **drives** the lower state.* This gives us yet another neuro-semantic principle. It also offers a description with regard to *how meta-states function.* Because they operate at a higher logical level to the primary state or to the next lower meta-state, they operate in a more extensive, pervasive, and therefore powerful way than the primary state.

Higher states drive, organize, and modulate lower states. They set the frame for the lower states and initiate self-organizing influences.

As a psychotherapist, this explains to me why some people have such a hard time receiving help, making changes, altering their way of thinking-feeling, etc. If I deal with the primary state and offer them ideas, skills, and solutions at that level, those skills and strategies may either not work because some higher level meta-state is negating those skills or distorting them so they not even "make sense" to their understanding.

Agoraphobia
Consider the agoraphobic again. Suppose I tell someone who *fears* his or her fear to just relax. I often did this before I knew better.
"Hey, just take a deep breath and relax."
If I had enough rapport with the person, he would inevitably begin to relax. Yet in doing so, as he would begin to become aware of his body, the feel of his heart beating, the tension in his muscles, he would meta-state his body with fear. He would access thoughts and feelings of fear *about* his physiological responses. Noticing his heart and lungs, in fact, would cause him to amplify the physiological intensity. Then, noticing how his heart, lungs, muscle tension, etc. felt, he would *feel afraid* of that.

We would then get *fear looping around fearing itself* and everything it encountered. I've found this strange phenomenon in a number of people. Eventually they would build the strategy so that *relaxing would scare them*. Talk about a higher frame eliminating a resource from working! Here fear as a state (thinking fearful/scary thoughts) becomes so pervasive that it becomes the meta-state of choice and used to process and filter everything. This would empower it to *operate like a canopy of awareness over one's entire self-experience* and so controlling perceptions, thinking, remembering (the state-dependency factor again) and creating a self-fulfilling self-expectancy for the person. Now that's what I would call a Dragon State.

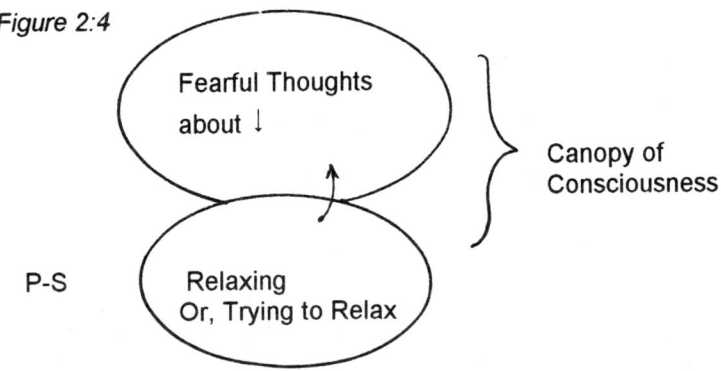

Figure 2:4

What can we do in such a case? I've learned to approach agoraphobics indirectly and to meta-state them from unawares. Why? To not activate their *fear meta-state.* Once it's activated, it can powerfully discount, disqualify, nullify, scare, and negate any and all information that I or anyone else could offer to help them *tame* that dragon.

> "And I wouldn't want you to *feel too curious* about just how relaxed you can feel as you learn to *appreciate* in a new and surprising way this wonderful ability you have of accessing an aroused body state, because as you calmly notice your excited body and fearful thoughts, it gives you true control and more control than you've ever had before, now..."

Negativism

Have you ever met a person who operated from a meta-state of negativism? From that meta-level of thinking-feeling, they believe such things as:

"Nothing will work." "Whatever can go wrong, probably will."
"People who are optimistic are unrealistic."

Operating from these *frames* will then lead them to constantly be talking about and presenting problems. They seem to have eyes programmed for them! And if you hear them talking about some problem you can expect that whatever solutions you might offer, no matter how brilliant, they will hear your solutions through (and discount them) a *pessimistic mind-set.* Count on it. Their negativism as a canopy of consciousness colors everything for them. It will effectively prevent your good solutions from being taken into account.

To get through to them we first have to alter their meta-state. Only then will they even have the ability to hear the strategies, skills, and solutions that we could offer.

Could this self-organizing nature of meta-level frames explain why you have found it near-to-impossible to make certain changes that you desire to make? Could you have some overriding meta-state at work negating those particular transformations? What meta-state could be operating and getting in your way from making some desired change?

It's our nature to build and operate from meta-states. Everybody has hundreds of meta-states about numerous facets of human existence. Further, any state that we repetitively, intensely, and regularly access involves thoughts-and-feelings that eventually become so familiar, so habitual and so regular that we *inevitably* apply them to other states. Eventually, they become a meta-state of awareness that *settles down as a canopy* over all of our other awarenesses. All of our primary states operate embedded within the meta-states. In this way our habituated primary states grow up to become meta-states. More commonly we call these meta-structures by such names as beliefs, values, assumptions, expectations, frames-of-references, etc. And yet, as meta-states, they drive all of our experiences and determine the very quality of our lives.

When Trauma States Become Meta-States

Consider the following example of how our mental and emotional states can become meta-states that encode trauma as a belief and strategy. Suppose you grew up in a home where you made the following learnings about your home, yourself, your parents, etc. First the self-talk of the person and then the *state*.

(1) "Life is so painful. I have suffered through a horrible childhood where nothing seemed to go right for me. At home I was yelled at and abused and at school I was teased and made fun of.
States: Pain, Hurt, Distress.

(2) "I'm not good at anything! I feel inadquate about everything I do."
States: Incompetence, Ineffectiveness, Powerlessness.

(3) "You can't trust people. Mom would yell and scream but never do anything. Dad would promise to do things with me, but always go back on his word.
States: Distrust, Suspicion, Disconnected to people.

(4) "Life sucks! It's just not worth all the trouble, sometimes I just wish I could get out of it."
States: Despondency, Despair, Depression.

When we *add* these states together, we have the combination of four very unresourceful, negative, and traumatic states.

Figure 2:5

#1	#2	#3	#4
Painful experience early in life as a child	I'm not good at anything! I can't do anything.	People are untrustworthy. Don't trust; People will let you down.	Life sucks! It all seems futile, hopeless disgusting.
Pain, Hurt Distress	Incompetence Powerless	Distrustful Disappointed	Disgusted Hopeless

Adding such states together creates a real mess. Yet because we can send our mind to a higher level to those learnings and create even higher level thoughts-and-feelings *about* those understandings, notice what happens when a person draws the following conclusion.

"If you've had a bad childhood, you can expect to live the rest of your life as a victim, repeating and attracting even more terrible things."

At a meta-level, this message (since it stands above the others as a message *about* the other messages), does not merely *add* to the other states, it *multiplies the other states* with this new level of pain. This creates a psychic multiplication of states.

Figure 2:6

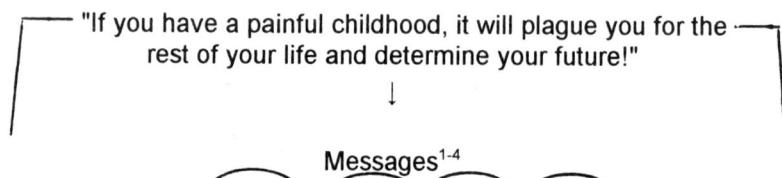

As a meta-state of belief, meaning, value, or frame this state of expecting more pain, and "I will always-be-a-victim" will filter out and negate contrary learnings at the primary state level. Send the person to a Dale Carnegie course, let her experience a positive relationship with a friend, let him read a book about effective coping, etc., these new learnings will either become negated by the meta-state or filtered by cynicism.

"Yes, that positive thinking stuff works—for other people."
"Yes, I do find Jan a good friend, but if she really knew me, she'd give up on me."

Messages, understandings, perceptions, beliefs, meanings, values, etc., at the meta-level will inevitably dominate and control thinking-and-feeling. That's the bad news. Now for the good-news. *We can meta-state our meta-state!*

Figure 2:7

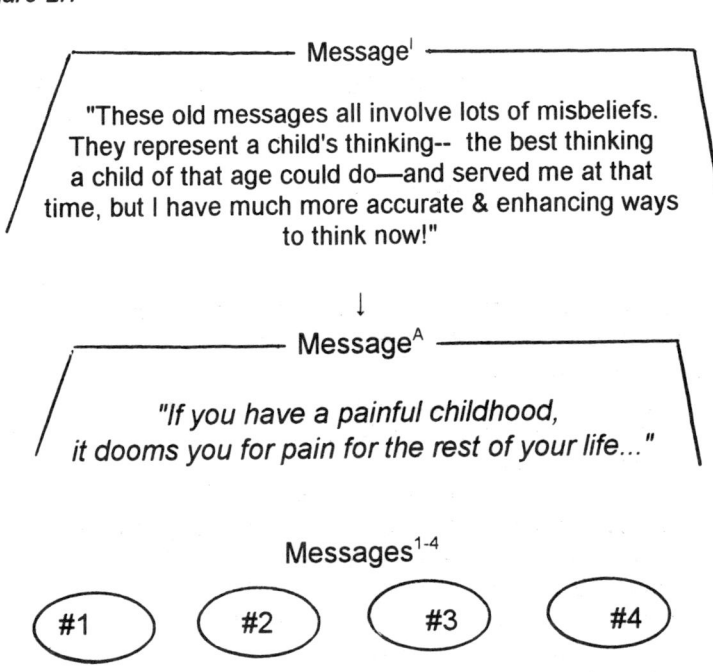

Now we can take an understanding or learning like the following and put it at a meta-level to the other learnings:

"All of these old learnings consist of learnings of a child who thought with lots of cognitive distortions, misbeliefs, and erroneous understandings—appropriate for a child's mind, but now I know better. It certainly made sense at five or fourteen, and helped me to survive then, but no longer has any usefulness."

To induce this meta-level thinking-and-feeling will induce a state of awareness and recognition by which we can then discount the earlier learnings. It discounts our former discounting. It gives us a new meta-perception that empowers us to re-classify, re-index, and re-categorize the old pain.

Figure 2:8

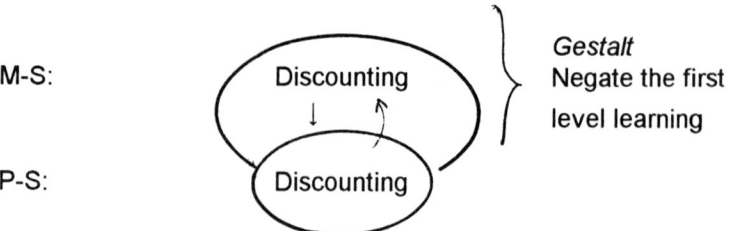

M-S: Discounting — Gestalt Negate the first level learning
P-S: Discounting

This meta-stating shows the power and importance of *setting the higher states or frames.* At the same time, it raises a very important re-directionalizing questions.

> "What meta-perception, understanding, belief, meaning, etc., has functioned in my mind as a negative meta-state *filtering out* useful solutions?"
>
> "What meta-perception, understanding, belief, meaning, etc., *could* I bring to bear on my meta-states that would shift everything and give me a new lease on life?"

Stepping aside to evaluate not only our states, but also our meta-states enables us to ask the kind of higher level questions that allows us to *Quality Control* our own mind.

> "Does this program, frame, or state help me and make things better? Does it enhance my life? Does it make me resourceful?"

These such meta-questions move us to a level *meta* (or higher) to our meta-states. We call this "running an ecology check" in NLP. This refers to stepping back to evaluate the overall ecology and productivity of our mind-body system. This gives us the ability to change things at a higher logical level, a level that will have pervasive effects throughout.

These questions also move us to a place of meta-choice. They nullify the thinking and feeling of "being a victim," as they empower us to chose how and upon what to "set our mind." Whatever you believe about a thing does not make it externally real. At best, it can only make it internally and subjectively real to the person so thinking.

The "truthfulness" and "accuracy" test is important, yet there is an even more important question. Namely, the questions about usefulness, productivity, life-enhancement, etc.

"Does this thought, awareness, belief, etc., serve me in a productive and enhancing way? Does it make me resourceful?"

Most of us think about engaging in "change work" as changing *the content* of old states. We want to go through each and every learning, belief, understanding and challenge it in order to shift each as a primary state. And given enough time and effort, that might be able to pull off the transformation. It's not guaranteed, but it might lead a person to create some new higher frames. Given enough time and effort and new learnings, people often do make enough shifts and changes that they can then draw a new meta-learning level conclusion and thereby induce a new meta-state or frame. Most psychotherapeutic processes focus on doing things in precisely this manner.

Meta-States suggests much more efficient and streamlined way to do the same. It allows us to slay, tame, and/or transform old dragons with one fell swoop. Rather than fighting at the primary state level and slaying each and every dragon that arises, we move to the level meta to the dragon frame in the first place and deal with the Dragon from on high. Then *we* can breathe down on and bear down on the old dragons that have run the show long enough.

In this way we can even allow all of the old ideas to stay intact without fearing them. Why? Because we will have drained the poison from them from a meta-level and we will have installed a more empowering meta-frame which pervasively changes the entire system. The old ideas that once induced and evoked the old unresourceful states will have no power left in them. There will be no magic in the thoughts because we will veto them from above.

"Just old ideas... the best thinking of an eight year old mind, but ultimately, outdated ideas."

This transforms what once were "beliefs" into "mere thoughts." As we make the thoughts invalid through a higher frame, they cease being "beliefs." And with no confirmation, they become just "thoughts" again. In this way, we also *index* the old dragons. Doing this puts the old fire-breathing Dragons in iron cages, from which they can't escape.

"Yes, at five years of age I thought-felt that. How silly that I drew that conclusion, yet I did. I guess I made those understandings with a five-year old's brain."

"Yes, I did find life difficult at ten. That accurately represented my perceptions back then. Funny now that I look back on how real it seemed back then, but at that time I didn't know the difference between my thoughts and feelings and reality."

Indexing the events, thoughts, experiences, perceptions, feelings, etc., of previous events to their time-space coordinates sends more truthful messages to our brain about "today." In this way, we can lock away previous hurts and put them where they belong, in the "past." And as we also *index* some new truths about our story, other thoughts and understandings that have remained "un-storied," we can set other frames that help tame the old Dragons.

"And I survived! And I lived through that hell and refuse to give in to that abuse, hurt, ugliness, etc.!"
"Therefore today I shall view myself as resilient, a survivor, assertive, etc."

This totally *reframes* things. And as it puts new frames-of-references around the old experiences, we can begin to think in new and different ways, we can attribute new meanings, and induce much more empowering states.

Getting the Feel of Meta-States

There are several key differences between primary states (P-S) and meta-states (M-S) that I'll point out in this text. One of these concerns the role, nature, and experience of *body sensations, "feelings,"* or what we call *kinesthetics*. Notice that I did not here use the word "emotion." "Emotions" differ from the sensations or feelings that we experience in the body. Emotions certainly involve such feelings, yet they also go beyond mere sensations as they involve evaluative cognitions.

Here then is a key difference. *Primary state emotions* almost always involve some fairly strong body sensations. Consider fear and anger. Where in your body do you feel such? Or what about relaxation and joy? Further, the stronger the state, the stronger the kinesthetic feelings of the body. The body really gets into the act. So when we experience anger about someone, or fear, joy, disgust, calm, stress, contentment, etc., we can usually identify where in our body that we feel these feelings and usually identify them pretty clearly. We can identify the kinesthetic components in terms of our muscle tension, breathing, movement, temperature, visceral sensations, etc.

All of this seems to change, however, when we move to meta-states. Here we typically find that our "emotions" seem to have milder kinesthetic components to them. We also typically find that we have less ability to locate such emotions in the body. These "sensations" (if we can even call them that) occur more "in the head." Consider. *Where* do you feel self-esteem? Resilience? Forgiveness? What about when you "feel judged?" "Put down?" "Okay?"

When someone says to me, "I feel low self-esteem." I like to respond,
> "Where do you feel this at?"

At first I usually get some blank stares. So I then prompt them,
> "Well, do you feel this low self-esteem down in your knee? Or in your leg? Just where do you feel this?"

Then before they can respond, I like to say,
> "It hasn't gotten so low that it's down in your ankle, is it? I hope by God that it's not down that *low!*"

Typically, we experience meta-states and meta-emotions mostly in the "mind."
"I feel put down."
Where do you feel that at? How does that show up in your body?
"I feel judged."
"I feel forgiveness toward him."
"I feel un-insultable."

While the composition of meta-states involve some body sensations, they primarily involve mental abstractions and conceptualizations. These show up as judgments, evaluations, concepts, etc., as the previous statements clearly indicate. So although we use *the linguistic phrase, "I feel..."* the so-called "emotion" word which we then stick in that phrase actually involves our *judgments and evaluations,* not our feelings.

"I feel put down, judged, down on myself, at loose ends, troubled, guilty, etc."

Now here's something interesting and insightful. Suppose that to these *"mind" emotion statements,* we now ask a feeling question like:
"How does that make you feel?"
"How does it feel to feel put down, or judged, etc.?"

What will this elicit? Typically, we will obtain a response that sounds more like a primary state emotion. "I feel judged." And how does that make you feel? "I feel upset." "I feel angry." "I feel scared." Upsetness, anger, and fear identify a primary state, "judged" reveals *the meaning of abstraction* that the person has made at the meta-level. Both occur. And both meanings/emotions occur simultaneously. And as we access meta-level thoughts-feelings, these drive and modulate the lower states, sometimes blinding us to those primary state feelings.

Understanding this helps us understand why we often find it difficult to change or transform a meta-state emotion, one of those "emotions of the mind." By contrast, if I feel stress and tension, as I relax my body and mind, I shift states. And if I anchor the neurological state of *relaxation or calmness*, and then use that when I'm feeling stressed, I can very quickly shift state and "fly into a calm." Such human "technology" gives us some very powerful interventions at the primary state level. It's one of the pieces of "magic-like" transformations that has set NLP apart from other models (see *Instant Relaxation,* 1999).

Yet such changing occurs with much less effort than changing one's evaluative understandings, beliefs, values, and models of the world at the meta-level. And that explains *why* transforming the higher levels of the mind typically involves more involved patterns.

If we want to *fly into a meta-state,* it will usually (there are exceptions) involve building it up conceptually in your "mind" and doing the work of "thinking" in a new and different way, and then repeating that new habit of thought until it becomes a *frame of mind* that you can quickly get into. To get into the meta-state of self-esteeming, proactivity, magnanimity, forgiveness, un-insultability, inner peace, etc. demands that we have set the necessary frames for such concepts at a higher level of abstraction and have built a ready access to it. In a later chapter, we'll describe the process for doing that.

Understanding this distinction between feelings and emotions at different levels will also play a significant role as we slay and tame our dragon states and meta-dragon states, and build up many positive and empowering states.

Summary
- When we speak of *Dragons*, we use a metaphor to describe the states that we experience which seem to "have" us rather than we "have."
- We can experience out-of-control states at the primary level as any primary level thought or emotion can grow beyond our ability to manage it. Mostly, however, our *dragon states* refer to higher level states or frames.

They involve those meta-states that put us at odds with ourselves, that turn our psychic energies against ourselves, or that prevent us from actualizing all of our human powers and resources.
- *Dragon states* undermine our success, effectiveness, and health. They lack an ecological balance and so do not serve us well.
- Yet they are not entities. We do not have them as Aliens or Demons living inside us, we create them out of "the stuff of thoughts and feelings."
- Some Dragon states we simply need to slay and destroy. They are comprised of thought viruses and only poison. Other Dragon states need to be tamed and transformed... we can ride the energy and power that they provide. And so, with that in mind, on to Dragon Slaying and Taming!

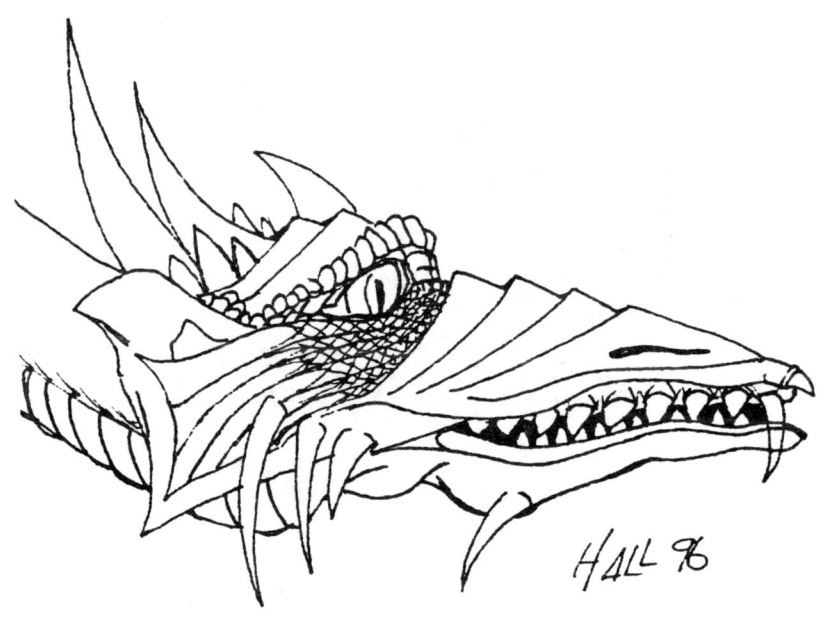

CHAPTER 3

DRAGON SLAYING
How to Slay, Tame, Transform And even Slap Dragons

With this ability to access complex negative meta-states of fear of fear, guilt about anger, upsetness about worry, judgment about "self" as inadequate, unlovable and unworthy, etc., we have the amazing ability to generate intense emotional pain in our lives. In this work, we're calling these painfully destructive and out-of-control states, **Dragon States**.

Oh, you want me to name one? Sure. *Dragon states* include guilting, self-contempting, self-pitying, revenging, reactivity, negativism, commiserating, cynical pessimism, self-shaming, victimization, blaming, etc. If we backtracked to the kind of thinking that informs these states, we'll sometimes discover some really sick thinking, toxic and morbid. At other times we'll find out-of-balanced thinking, ill-formedness in logic, childish or primitive thinking, etc.

Enough about that. What do we do about such? How do we slay a Dragon? How can we tame them? What process can we use to transform it into something much more useful?

Dragon Slaying
Scene 1. State Interrupt
Lucy frowns as she passes by Charlie Brown and orders, "Get out of my way! I feel ultra-crabby today!" Turning around to Charlie Brown in frame two, she explains, "'Ultra' means 'going beyond the usual limit, excessive, to an extreme degree.'"

She moves on down the road.

Frame four, Charlie Brown says, "I knew what it meant."

Later, on the phone Lucy comments to a girl friend, "I don't know, I've just felt crabby every since the year began." Now that's a long time for a dragon state to persist!

"Everything seems so hopeless." She explained.

"Do you feel crabby too? Why don't you come over? Sure bring her along if she feels crabby... bring everybody!"

Lucy then informs Linus, "I'm having a 'crab-in'!" This comes close to institutionalizing a dragon state.

Later that day, Charlie Brown notices several girls on their way to Lucy's place. "Hi, Girls! Where..."

They storm, "Get out of the way!!" sending him into his famous Charlie Brown backward flip.

Nancy commented, "We're on our way to a 'crab-in'!"

This hooks Charlie Brown's interest, so he knocks on the door. "Is this where the 'crab-in' is being held?"

Lucy shouts out, "Who wants to know?" sending Charlie Brown sprawling.

On the ground with his head spinning, he says, "This must be the place."

Finally, Charlie Brown gets up and seeing Snoopy says, "Don't go near that house today, Snoopy. Lucy's having a 'crab-in'."

But Snoopy knocks on the door, *kisses Lucy with a smack on the lips*, completely interrupting her state. As he walks away, he says, "That's how you break up a 'crab-in.'"

Earlier we talked about interrupting states. And that's precisely what Snoopy's actions accomplished. By kissing the crabby face, he completely violated and interrupted the pattern of crabbiness. Kissing, as a message of information did not fit Lucy's state. She didn't know how to process it. So in the process of slaying and/or taming dragons, we must first recognize a dragon state as such, then interrupt it. And planting kisses on Dragons can often work magic.

Dragon Slaying
Scene 2. Information Starvation

As Charlie Brown listens to a song on a record player with Lucy, he says, "This song always depresses me." Reflectively, he says, "It brings back such sad memories...you know what I mean?" "I've never heard another song that depresses me the way this one does..." He at least had awareness of the state that the song elicits in him.

Then in the last frame, he says, "Play it again, will you?"

At some level, he had developed an enjoyment of his depressing mood. Yet what a monster that creates! *Enjoying feeling depressed,* when it grows up, becomes a dragon state that will rob one of the energy and courage it takes to give up the depressing habit, and to find some true pleasures and joys in life.

How then can we slay or tame dragons? For one thing, we can *stop feeding them.* If you don't feed the dragon, it will tend to starve for lack of nourishment. But here Charlie Brown feeds his dragon. "Play it again, will you?"

Dragon Slaying
Scene 3. Re-languaging

Sitting up in bed late at night, Charlie Brown says, "I struck out. And I let my team down. I'm no good for anything." What state will those ideas elicit?

At a meta-level he accesses a self-despising state. **"I'm** just no good. I shouldn't ever try to do anything. I should just stay in bed for the rest of my life, and sleep." Helpless, hopeless, powerless, self-blaming, he negatively predicts his future.

Then in frame three, he laid down and tried to sleep. But sitting up again in frame four, he says, "I can't even sleep good!"

His mental looping around and around and around negative thoughts was cranking up his self-disgust, his sense of helplessness, and his insomnia. Do you know that one?

How would you slay that dragon? We must become aware of the looping, we must interrupt the negative self-languaging and self-inducing, and we must *change the messaging.* Here Charlie Brown was engaging in meta-messages about failing at a specific task on a specific day in a specific game needs. Yet he was over-generalizing and failing to index the specifics. When we fail to *index specifics* we tend to create dragon states by over-generalizing a negative event. Instead of his sentence, "I'm not good for anything" he needs to speak more accurately and enhancingly,

"I love to play ball, but today I didn't pitch as well as I wanted to..."

He could also slay and/or tame that dragon if he had brought a resourceful state (like acceptance, optimism, resilience, etc.) to bear on his primary state.

> "I accept that I failed to pitch well today, what can I learn from that so that I don't have to repeat the pattern?"
>
> "I accept my fallibility as part of my humanity. So this only reflects on my pitching skill, not my personhood."

When someone says, "My self-esteem is low" I first want to help them recognize that this state does not exist so much as a feeling, as a judgment. So, too, with the thought here, "I'm no good."

Where do you feel that Charlie Brown?

Mainly in his head. It's his judgment and his evaluation which he has made about his *self*. "Confidence" represents a feeling, so does "lack of confidence."

Next, I want to ask, "What stops you, right this minute, from esteeming yourself as having value, worth, dignity, potential, etc.?"

If the person says, "Because I don't feel confident about playing baseball" (or, meeting girls, making a speech, communicating assertively, etc.), then I can highlight the nature of self-esteeming.

> "Oh, the feeling. What *judgment* do you make about that feeling of clumsiness, not succeeding, feeling awkward with something, etc.?"

Now we have moved to a higher level of conceptualizing and evaluating.

> "Do you *believe* that a person has no value or worth or dignity if they show ineptness at some skill or ability? Do you believe that our value as human beings should rest *conditionally* upon what we can do—rather than *unconditionally* upon our human being-ness?"

The meta-states of self-esteeming versus self-contempting, self-valuing versus self-denigrating, self-regarding versus self-discounting, etc., all exist at a meta-level of belief, conceptualization, and abstraction about the "self" as a concept.

Dragon Slaying:
Meta-Stating

Of course, I think that one of the best ways (if not *the* best way) to slay and tame dragon states occurs by simply **meta-stating** them. This refers to bringing *a resourceful and effective state to bear upon an unresourceful state.*

Accessing and amplifying an intense state of calmness and then bringing it to an anger state can powerfully modify the anger. That generates calm angering. Or, how about slaying the anger dragon by appreciating your ability to become angry? Or you could slay or tame it with thoughtfulness (thoughtful and full of "presence of mind"). Thoughtful anger differs from violent and no-bars hold anger.

Accessing *an ecology-check state* wherein we can properly and calmly *evaluate* things and bring it to bear upon any other state shifts us to a higher logical level and thereby enables us to stand aside from ourselves in a calm and positive reflection. Then we can make new and better choices.

Recently, I talked with a young woman who related to me about an event in her life with which she struggled. To the story, she then said,

"I am so disgusted with myself; I hate it when I do that. When I respond in that way, it's a terrible response."

Ah, primary state of ineffectiveness and meta-state of self-disgust! So I shot back,

"Don't you ever get disgusted with that kind of self-disgust?"

That took her back. It seemed to momentarily interrupt her. The wheels in her mind seemed to spin around as if wondering, "What does that mean?" As a state-interrupt, it worked to give her a moment to break away from the ruts and habits of her mind.

Then, in that space, I coached her through the new thought a little slower, "Now stay with this idea for a moment. Do you ever get disgusted with your disgust of yourself?"

She acknowledged that she did.

"What does that feel like? Take a moment, register this deeply— what happens inside when you allow yourself to become truly disgusted with your self-disgust?"

I figured that by meta-stating her in this way, it would change the quality of her first meta-state. And it did.

She said, "You know, I feel like my self-disgust kind of evaporates when I do that."

We can slay and/or tame meta-state dragons in this way. Doubt of doubt negates the first level doubt as it sends us into a more sure state at a higher level. Procrastination of procrastination stops the putting off (since we put that off) and so it facilitates the taking of action. Disgust of disgust negates the first level disgust so that we may even esteem our self. In describing these relationships between states, we have now illustrated the often *paradoxical nature* of some (but not all) meta-states.

Frequently, what "makes sense" at one level will not at another, and what creates order and structure when sequenced between levels creates confusion and paradox when treated as operating on the same level.

META-STATING RESULTS AND EFFECTS

With meta-stating as a way to either slay or tame a Dragon state, all kinds of wild and wonderful effects can result. When people ask me, "What happens when you meta-state yourself or someone else?" I have to say, "It all depends." A wide range of interfacing effects can occur. In fact, we have identified sixteen such effects.

The number of *relationships* that can emerge when we inter-relate one state with another state illustrates the nature of a system. In this, meta-stating can create *all kinds of wild and sometimes strange effects.* Anthropologist Gregory Bateson (1972) has said that "meta-messages always *modify* lower-level messages." Yet the way they *modify* the lower-level messages depends on the unique combination and configuration of the states— the gestalt that results. The following describe the key interfaces.

(1) Meta-stating can sometimes reduces painfully intense states.
> When I feel calm about my anger, the calmness mellows the anger. When I appreciate my fear, my fear becomes a valued asset.

(2) Meta-stating can sometimes intensify states.
> Bringing some states to interface with other states will frequently amplify and turn up the primary state. If I worry about my worry, I go into hyper-worrying. If I become anxious about my anxiety, I become engaged in hyper-anxietying. If I feel calm about my calmness, I more deeply relax.

(3) Meta-stating will sometimes exaggerate and distort states.
> Dr. Wendell Johnson analyzed stuttering that broke it down into a meta-state formation (although he didn't use those words). He said that stuttering essentially arises as operating from *a state of hesitating about the primary state of non-fluency.* Johnson wrote a chapter entitled, "The Indians Have No Name For It." In his study of Indian cultures, he could find no reported cases of Native American children or adults stuttering who were raised in those cultures. They did not language that

phenomenon. When the kids expressed non-fluency and had difficulty finding the right word and perhaps started and stopped and started and stopped in their search for the right word, the older ones thought nothing about it. They didn't say anything. They didn't respond any differently. And so they did not mark out, or punctuate, that experience as we do when we label it "stuttering." (*People in Quandaries,* 1989, p. 453).

But suppose I set the frame in my *think*ing and so meta-state about my *speaking* (as a primary state) the following, "I do not want to stutter; to stop, go, stop, go in my search for a word!" What then? If I evaluate stuttering as "bad," take away permission from myself to speak non-fluently, I will more then likely *hesitate about my hesitations.* Then I will create stuttering by so punctuating my experience via the term "stuttering."

The solution to this? Practice stuttering intentionally. Intend as a meta-state to hesitate as you hesitate or talk non-fluently. This paradoxical intervention (Frankl) adjusts and tames one meta-muddle by another meta-structure.

Negative meta-states arise as Dragons, like stuttering, because the hesitating to hesitate amplifies the intensity factor (the stress) which, in turn, causes the primary state to become exaggerated so that it functions like a demon to us. We demonize the non-fluency, call it names, judge it harshly, and no wonder it then turns on us to torment us. Thus, anger about my anger, fear about my fear, sadness about my sadness (depression), etc.

(4) Meta-stating will sometimes negate a primary state.
Some meta-states actually negate the content emotions and thoughts at the lower level. In doubt about my doubt, I usually feel more sure. In procrastinating my procrastination, I take action and put off the putting off. If I avoid my avoidance, I no longer avoid.

(5) Meta-stating sometimes generates what we call "paradox."
Some meta-states create a paradox by shifting the experience to a higher level. This offers lots of possibilities for transformation. It explains powerful techniques as "paradoxical intention," as in *the "Be spontaneous now!" paradox.* Hence,

"Never say never;" "Never and always are two words one should always remember never to use." "I'm absolutely certain that nothing is absolutely certain." "You sound pretty absolute about that!"

Suppose I showed you a sheet of paper filled with statements and the top line on the sheet said:

"Every statement on this paper is a lie."

How would you process that? Do you conclude that all the following statements represent lies (for so the statement asserts)? Or do you think that since that title statement also occurs on that page, it lies? Therefore it lies about the truthfulness of all of the other statements. Therefore all of the other statements speak the truth. Paradox. It is "paradox" unless you realize that that statement functions at a meta-level to the other statements. It does not speak about itself, only about the other statements. It classifies the other statements, but is not a member of the class.

I like using this intervention with fear. "That seems like a lot of fear that you have, but, just for a moment, I want you to access even more fear—so that I can see what happens when you become even more fearful."

Unless you think in logical levels or know the Meta-States model, you might not catch the paradox. I have asked the person to turn their fear up. By implication that presupposes that *they have control over the fear* rather than the fear having control over them. It presupposes that they can access a state of control over their state of fear.

(6) Meta-stating will sometimes interrupt states.

We have noticed this before. Sometimes the state of our thoughts-feelings and neurology which we bring to bear on another state radically jars and shifts the first state so that it interrupts it. Hence, becoming humorous about one's seriousness; feeling really anxious about calmness; or feeling calmness about anxiety. Interrupt!

(7) Meta-stating will sometimes create solid confusion.

Some will create the interruption or reduction by generating confusion as various thoughts-feelings collide and "fuse" "with" each other in ways that we do not comprehend.

(8) **Meta-states sometimes create a dissociated state.**
   Sometimes the meta-state will cause one to so *step out and away from* a primary state that the person will feel disoriented, numb, and unsure of what to feel. It changes the feeling intensity. "How useful do you think your anxiety would serve you in that situation? What resources would have enabled the younger you of seven years old to have handled that situation better?"

(9) *Meta-stating frequently confirms and solidifies primary states.*
   When we bring a state of confirmation, validation, "proof," etc. upon a primary level thought or emotion, it can turn the mere thought into a neurologically charged "belief." This explains how higher level states or frames can become so "set" that we can wake up in that "frame of mind" day after day, year after year.

(10) *Meta-Stating frequently disconfirms and dissolves a state or belief.*
   Conversely, as we can solidify thoughts, we can also use meta-levels to dis-confirm beliefs and reduce them to mere thoughts again. It works very simply. Just bring thoughts and feelings of doubt, questioning, skepticism, invalidity, etc. to bear upon a belief. The higher doubt frame will eat away at the belief like an acid.

Dragon Slaying:
Scene 4. Ungluing the Language

If you want to slay or tame a meta-state Dragon— **pull apart the words,** the linguistic structure that holds the pattern or creature together. Our subjective experiences which exist at the meta-state level exist there *due to* the language that so encodes it. It exists *in* language and *through* language. The conceptual categories that our minds process and create such as time-space, causation, self, purpose, destiny, meaning, etc. only exist in the "mind" as mental concepts, and therefore as semantic states.

We cannot even have meta-states without symbols and language. Mere sights, sounds, smells and sensations (the modalities of awareness at the sensory-based level) cannot code such high level abstractions alone. We need *higher level symbols,* and especially *words* to perform that function. These "realities" only arise from out of a language reality. Yet some of our languaging creates monster (dragon states) rather than royal states that enhances life.

Listen to the languaging that drives and formats this dragon state:

> "Because my relationship is falling apart (primary state), I feel like a complete failure and reject (meta-level abstractions about the primary state). This always happens (meta-state abstraction about "time" and causation). It will always be this way (meta-level abstraction about the "future"). I'm just not cut out for relationships since I was raised in a dysfunctional home (meta-level abstractions about caution and identity)."

The very process of thinking in this way and using these words creates this meta-state "reality." If the person stopped this kind of languaging, he or she would *no longer* experience the neuro-semantics of this dragon state.

So when we begin to challenge that language, it simultaneously begins to pull the dragon apart. The dragon state becomes untangled and unglued so that it can no longer cohere as a neuro-semantic reality.

> "How did you relate to Sue that did not work? When? How do you as a person become a 'complete failure' because of this one undesirable event?"

Indexing the non-referencing words like "failure" and "reject," and such non-productive causational statements ("raised in that home *makes* me unfit") destroys the coherence of those ideas. The "ideas" as ideo-dynamic suggestions for neurology cannot continue to do their damage. The spell is broken. The old black "magic" spoiled.

In NLP we call this process of challenging ill-formedness in the structure of language, the syntax (order) of language, and the semantics of language **meta-modeling**. This refers to using the Meta-Model of language, a model of twelve linguistic distinctions that cues us regarding forms of language that represent poor (or ill-formed) maps of things. The "challenges" to these map-distortions typically has the effect of getting the recipient to the challenge back to the original experience and elicits a new remapping of things. The new mapping brings forth a fuller and more adequate way to think about things. (See *The Structure of Magic*, 1976, *The Secrets of Magic*, 1998).

For myself, the dragon state of "failure" or of "being a failure" no longer exists in my mental mapping of the world. I have eliminated such languaging from my vocabulary. And accordingly, I can no longer access such toxic states. Nor can you induce me into that state. My brain will not process that nominalization ("failure') in that way anymore.

My brain immediately indexes.

> "What do you think I specifically failed at? When? According to what standard or criteria?"

All of this, of course, warns us about the potential danger of treating words as real. They are not. They are but *maps* that we use to navigate through life. They are only as good as we find them useful in mapping our way through some experience.

As we now tune our ears about the non-reality of language, we can set the frame (as a meta-state) that language only serves as a map *of* reality, never the territory itself. Whatever we say *about* anything, our words only exist as symbols that refer to some territory, but never the territory.

We may even boldly assert, "Words are not real!" You cannot find nourishment through the words on a menu. The word "cat" cannot scratch you. The words "warm bright sunshine on a summer day" cannot give you a suntan. Such words may invite you to access memories or imaginative understandings so that you go into some state and get your neurology activated, but the process represents *a mediated process*. You used the words as symbols *about* the reality.

Yet a tricky thing happens when we so use words unless we program our brain about the map/territory distinction. We can get so much into a habit of confusing map/territory that we can begin to *identify* words with reality or the territory, and so treat and respond to words as if "real." This works wonders if your are wanting a particular hypnotic trance. If not, it will play havoc in your mind and body.

Words and symbols are *not* real in the same way as the energy manifestations that our sense receptors pick up from "outside" are "real." One deals with the world of physics; the other with the world of communication and information transfer. Yet, once we confuse map and territory, then the words and language forms that we use on ourselves automatically, immediately, and un-thinkingly create a neuro-semantic reality inside of our nervous system.

So, if you tell yourself you "are" a "failure" and a "reject," and that you "are" doomed to misery for the rest of your life because of some past event, those very words will begin to program you to so think, feel, and act. It will language you into a constructed world with those ideas as your frames of reference. It will give you a map that will keep you stuck in ineffectiveness and disempowerment.

We exist as a symbolic-class of life who inevitably use language not only to communicate ideas, but to generate internal, personal, subjective "reality." That's why we need to learn to listen to our language and to challenge it. Otherwise we can get bamboozled by language. When, however, we refuse to build *dragon states* via our self-languaging, we can rip such dragons apart and refuse to keep them alive by our misuse of language. Many of our dragons exist only as a function of our abstractions, understandings, and meanings that we have given to something.

Consider *the way we language the dragon of the "I'm a Victim!" game.*
"I had a painful, traumatic, and abusive childhood, therefore I am an adult child of screwed-up parents, and therefore am doomed to various forms of dysfunction and pain for the rest of my life!"

How about that for a piece of hypnotic induction! Would you want that one to "run your brain?" Would you want that piece of programming in your neurology? Would that make your life more of a party? Would you want to bequeath it to your children? I don't think so.

Yet, if a person represents his or her experience with those words and then **believes** those words, it will become that person's neuro-semantic "reality." And inside, it will feel real. It will feel excrucially real. But we do not have to believe that garbage. We can pull that language apart and challenge it. And when we do, we thereby slay that ole dragon. To do so, just step aside, take a meta-position, look at it, evaluate it, and slay the non-sensical, irrational, and non-productive language that constructs it.

Dragon Slaying:
Scene 5. Transform the Limiting Belief

Meta-states operate and exist as **beliefs**, that is, as linguistic structures that encode and validate some concept about self, time, causation, masculinity, femininity, relationships, purpose, destiny, etc. This gives us at the minimum of two levels. On the first level we have the thoughts and ideas which comprise the primary representations. Then we have a level of confirmation. Knowing this, we can now examine our beliefs and run a *Quality Control* or "ecology check" on them. If we find that they work in our mind-body systems as limiting beliefs, then we can begin to deconstruct them.

How much do you *trust your beliefs*? Do you now immediately recognize the state of "trusting your beliefs" as a meta-state (trust) *about* another state (a particular idea about something) and hold back on confirming it until you evaluate it? As we recognize that *automatically* trusting or believing in our beliefs puts us in the unenviable position of closing shop on new ideas, alternative understandings, and ongoing updates, that it initiates us into such states as being rigid, closed-minded, arrogantly cocksure, etc., do we really want to go there? I hope not. Believing in our beliefs tends to give those ideas an absolute power over us.

MAKING WAY FOR PRINCELY STATES

Once we have slain or tamed our dragons, we can use our power of *self-reflexive consciousness* to build ever more resourceful states that empower us in living and developing. We can use our power of self-reference to layer higher states of consciousness. These princely or royal states will then enable us to become more integrated, centered, and congruent. Then, we'll get along much better in interacting with others whether in business or in personal relationships. With this power of *self-reflexivity* we can also intentionally build and install all kinds of empowering meta-states; we can design engineer such states as self-esteeming, resilience, proactivity, forgiveness, un-insult-ability, inner serenity, magnanimity, etc.

All in all, this reflexivity process will give us a way to more effectively manage the meta-levels of our states and frames of mind. It will empower us to work much more methodically with our consciousness to "run our own brains." This will show up as we mindfully choose to become calm about our anger, insightful about our impatience, happy about our frustrations, etc. Imagine the possibilities of such princely states.

In all of this, language itself will play a central role. So here, instead of pulling language apart in order to *unglue* a destructive meta-state, we will be *putting together* forms of language to build empowering princely states. We will put together compelling belief statements that will glue our higher states together.

Figure 3:1

PRIMARY STATES	META-STATES
First-Level	Second/Third Levels, Etc.
Simple/Direct	Complex/Indirect
Immediate	Layer levels of consciousness
Modality Driven	Meta-level driven (i.e., by "submodality" distinctions)
	Linguistically-Driven
Experiences strongly Kinesthetically	Less immediate & localized Kinesth. more mental-feelings
Easily Anchored	Chains of Anchors--*glued* together by words
Primary Kinesthetics	**Meta-kinesthetics** or "emotions" Evaluative judgments coded in the soma (body)
Intense to Very Intense	Typically less intense, more thoughtful although can be very intense
Strong	Weaker kinesthetically
More Focused	Multiple-focus, simultaneous, holistically
One time learning	Less frequently subject to one time learnings; typically installed by repetition
No layers of consciousness	Several or many layers
First Position & Associated	Multiple Perceptual positions
	Consciousness expanded & transcendental
Thought	Thoughtfulness/ Mindfulness

Chapter 4

CONSCIOUSNESS & STATE MANAGEMENT

Tracking The Brain Through All Its Contortions

- Can we explain our mental and emotional states?
- Is there a rhyme and reason of our emotions and moods?
- What are the primary mechanisms that govern our states and meta-states?

Consciousness inevitably affects our states and meta-states, and typically determines them. As we think-emote, so we generate our states at all levels of awareness.

Earlier we described "two royal roads" to our mind-body states. Of these, our internal representations describes the contents and forms of our consciousness and as such, *representations and the higher frames of meaning* preeminently determine our mind-body states. If we backtrack any given state by analyzing *the contents* of our consciousness, *"what"* we have on our mind, and the *processing* of our consciousness, *"how"* we run our brain as we represent ideas, we can identify the informational components which come together to create our states.

In one cartoon strip, we see Linus out in a field of weeds so high that they come up to his head.

"I can't find the ball," he says.

"Waddya mean, pick it up?" he asks.

"How do you expect anyone to find a ball in weeds like these? What did you hit it out here for?"

By frame four, Linus has worked himself up into a real dragon state.

"It's impossible! Of course I'm looking! I said I can't find it! If I could find it, would I still be out here?" And then, "This is hopeless! Nobody could find anything out here! You couldn't find a battleship out here if it..."

From representing messages of frustration, Linus felt more and more frustration, then annoyance, then anger, and finally utter helplessness. "It's impossible!" he yells. Then he awfulizes using extremist language: "This is hopeless! Nobody... battleship..."

The Circular Loop From Thoughts to States

If we have accessed a state of fear, we have *fear thoughts* dancing around in on the theater of our mind. In a state of contentment, we will have *contentment thoughts*. **Thoughts** lead to emotions and thereby generate corresponding states. These two facets of consciousness (content and structure) determine the states that we can, or cannot, access. They also control the degree of ease or difficulty with which we access such states.

Now, **if** consciousness plays such a crucial role in state then the more we understand the principles, "dynamics," and processes of "mind" or consciousness, the more we will gain skill in managing it. Consider your consciousness:

- How does my brain move and interact and dance when I attempt to shift my thinking (or conscious awareness) and access another state?
- *Does it dance playfully, cooperate delightfully, or does it go into contortions?*

The Dancing of Consciousness

The problem with some brains (and I use "brains" to designate the entire systemic process of thinking-emoting consciousness) involves just how stubborn they can become at times. They can become highly uncooperative. They can, in fact, get into some antagonistic and contradictory moods.

How about yours?

And, why would a brain do that to its owner?

While I don't intend to spend much time on this *why* question, it may boil down to something as simple as "relationship." That is, given the way some people have talked to their brain, why would it want to take orders from them? Given the way they have repeated the insulting language that they have used on themselves, why would any self-respecting brain even care about listening anymore? Would you listen to someone who talks to, or treats, you that way? Wouldn't you first want an apology?

Ah, the meta-stating effect. When we bring thoughts-and-feelings to bear upon our thought-and-feeling generating brain, we set frames about it. And as we can create Dragons when we turn judgment on other states, we can do the same thing with our relationship to our "mind" itself.

In one cartoon strip, Snoopy lies on top of his dog house thinking. "Every night it's the same..." Then looking at two bowls, "I have supper in my red dish and drinking water in my yellow dish." In saying this, Snoopy reveals that he has developed awareness or consciousness of a pattern.

Frame three he makes a decision about a choice for some variety. "Tonight I think I'll have my supper in the yellow dish and my drinking water in the red dish."

Then he adds a comment of explanation, "Life is too short not to live it up a little!"

Here consciousness first allowed him to make a choice and to then follow through. Yet some people have difficulty in this very task of getting their consciousness to take instructions. How about you?

When I first began conducting NLP Workshops on states and later on Meta-States, people would sometimes complain that they "just can't do the state accessing," especially when I would just invite them to do that out of the blue.

"Think about a time when you felt really confident..."
"Imagine your experience if you operated from a state of playfulness..."

I had several individuals who would tell me that just as soon as I would make such a request, their mind would "go blank." If I had not requested them to obtain some information from within, they could have done it. But just as soon as I asked, now they couldn't.

Strange.

Does that happen to you? How does your consciousness respond to requests for some performance? How does your brain respond when you make a request of it?

Brains sometimes act funny about "taking information or orders." They can get into habits (i.e., habitual ways of functioning). They can develop effective and ineffective thinking patterns. They can associate and link up all kinds of strange referents so that they go to weird places when we begin to work with them in terms of accessing various states of consciousness. And upon habituation, they seem to develop a "mind" of their own, so to speak.

And yet, because we create, build, access, and induce ourselves into states by means of the processing of information in the brain, as goes the brain—so goes the state. The way we process information, and the information we process, generates the resultant state. Therefore taking charge of our brain so we can engage our consciousness in ways that allow us to take the driver's seat lies at the heart of state-management. Ultimately, if you don't (or can't) take charge of your mental information processing, you will not develop the ability to manage your states.

To effectively manage your states then we have to learn to "run our own brain" in the sense of learning to effectively manage our consciousness. And to manage consciousness, we will need to know some things about how consciousness works and how to engage it effectively.

Understanding Consciousness as a Process

By way of review, the following points about consciousness summarize some of the key factors we need to know about brains and mental-emotional functioning if we want to take charge of our mind and "run our own brain" for fun and profit.

(1) Representations drive our brain and the world it creates for us. We present to ourselves the sights, sounds, sensations, smells, and tastes that we first encountered and then we use these sensory-based representations as symbols for higher level "ideas," "thoughts," "understandings," "concepts," "beliefs," etc. Representation obviously occurs at the primary level. It also occurs at the higher levels. There we represent the previous thoughts using more abstract thought: words, language, symbols, linguistic structures, stories, etc. We "present" to ourselves information via these modalities (modes) of awareness.

This power of consciousness provides us the ability to induce ourselves into all kinds of neurological states. We can make ourselves happy or miserable apart from and sometimes, in spite of, the events around us. We do this by both *the content of what* we represent at any given moment and by the *form and structure* of our thoughts. Our representational world at all levels provide signals to the rest of our body about how to feel and act.

(2) Our body also drives our brain. Consciousness also has a biological / neurological basis. As we avoid the dualistic thinking that separates "mind" and "body" as if they were disconnected and unrelated phenomena, we speak about mind-body consciousness or "neuro-linguistics." We *embody* our thoughts and so *incorporate* our higher concepts. We are, after all, a semantic or symbolic class of life, and hence have a neuro-semantic consciousness. We not only "think" with and in our heads, but also with and in our bodies. In fact, my fingers now "know" the computer keyboard whereas my consciousness "mind" no longer "knows" the placement of the keys.

(3) Our brain works like a three-pound bio-computer to process information. While consciousness operates primarily as an information processor about the world, it does more. It interacts with the world, and uses its biology to co-create the world that we experience.

What "instincts" do for animals in terms of providing them the "programs" for living, functioning, and being, consciousness does for us. Abraham Maslow (1954) noted that we have, at best, only *"instinctoids,"* that is, instinct-like biological drives (i.e., hunger, thirst, safety, survival, love and affection, etc.), but no specific details about how to fulfill those "drives."

This explains our need for consciousness in the process of building our "programs." It provides us our primarily mechanism for survival, for navigating in the world, for figuring things out, for taking cognizance of our environment, for mastering our environment and situation, etc.

What does consciousness primarily seek to accomplish? Representing information about the world to ourselves as well as access our own internal needs and constraints. Consciousness functions as a clearinghouse for sensations, perceptions, feelings, ideas. Afterwards, we use awareness to evaluate that information, to establish priorities regarding those evaluations, etc.

In a cartoon, Sir talks aloud to Snoopy while processing some unpleasant information. "Marcie and Chuck have gone off to camp while I have to stay home and go to summer school... I'm so jealous I can't stand it!"

She (Sir) here made a comparison, thinking about what they have that she wants but doesn't have, and what she has that she doesn't want. Looking at Snoopy she then asked *why* questions. "Why am I so dumb in school? Why can't I get better grades?"

Next frame: her brain searches for answers to those unresourceful questions and came up with an answer. "Sometimes I think maybe I tore all the ligaments in my head."

(4) "Language" (or symbol manipulation) drives and controls the higher functions of your brain. Human consciousness has a linguistic structure to it. This realization led linguistic Norm Chomsky to assert that we humans come hard-wired for language acquisition and use. Our highest consciousness emerges in and with words, sentences, language, and stories. We transcend the sensory-based consciousness of sentient animals who see, hear, feel, smell, taste, etc. because we say words **about** those sights, sounds and sensations. We develop meta-symbolic levels.

(5) We typically buy our bio-computer programs from the people we hang around with. Human consciousness operates from and in *a sociological context.* We learn language, and therefore the structure of human consciousness, from the cultural environment in which we grow. First of all, others language us. Then we begin to language ourselves, totally and naively accepting the structures, limitations, forms, and presuppositions of the language. We absorb our language consciousness from others.

(6) Our brain knows itself as a brain. This means that our brain can think about itself. It can think-feel about its thinking-feeling. Human consciousness, which processes language (a meta-sense), operates *self-reflexively.* This enables us to not only know, but to know that we know. When we become conscious of our consciousness we then begin to direct our consciousness rather than just letting it float along its stream of consciousness. *Human consciousness, by definition, exists as a meta-state* and as a meta-meta-state.

Without our form of human consciousness we would only know what exists and what goes on around us and then respond to such instinctually and reactively. But now, with a consciousness that can represent things-not-present, we can weigh, measure, evaluate, choose, etc., how we want to think about what we observe, what meanings to attribute to it, and how to respond to it. The closest experience we have to the consciousness non-reflexively occurs in dreaming. There we still have conscious content -- but it happens to us, and we (for the most part) can't direct it (there are exceptions such as "lucid dreaming").

Self-Reflexivity, in fact, represents the most powerful element in our form of consciousness. Becoming conscious of our consciousness

empowers us to *direct* our consciousness and to over-ride stimuli (external/ internal) from that position. This provides several very powerful and uniquely human powers:
- Intentionality and goal-directedness
- Disconnectedness to "instincts," forces, influences, impulses
- Circularity of consciousness (instead of linear)
- Self-direction and self-control

What does this mean? It means we do not have to live as victims of our own thinking. Becoming conscious of our consciousness enables us to use our higher logical levels of awareness to control and manage the lower levels. This enables us to make quantum leaps in self-management. Many have said that we only use a small portion of the brain's capacity, that vast and enormous untapped potentials exist in our "mind" waiting for us to tap. This model gives us the ability to begin to tap into those potentials.

Figure 4:1

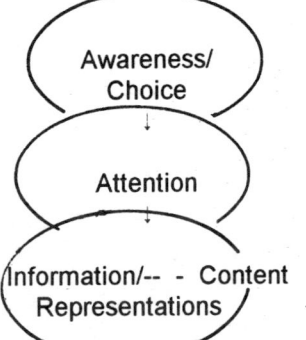

(7) Our mental mappings about the "future" drives our brain. With self-directive consciousness, then our awareness becomes "intentionally ordered information" (as one cognitive psychologist defined consciousness).

What does this mean? It means that we inevitably use our brain to set our direction and determine where we want to spend our future. We not only process and represent information, but we manage it, order it, and intentionally focus it. **Intention** gives us the power of controlling consciousness. By it we can "pay attention" and use our intentions to keep information in consciousness ordered so we don't have to suffer from un-ordered consciousness or an out-of-control consciousness. Our intentions show up as "wants," "desires," "focus" so that we get our "mind" organized in hierarchies of goals which creates our mental focus.

DIFFERENT BRAINS FOR DIFFERENT PEOPLE

The previous seven statements describe how our brains function generally. Let's now shift to notice how our brains differ. After all, *all brains do **not** run alike or in similar ways.* This gives us an eighth thing which we can say about brains.

(8) Human brains differ in that they develop different information sorting styles. We can, and do, buy and install different "software packages," so to speak, in their brains. The NLP model which specifies the different ways that we "run" our brains as we sort for information as *Meta-Programs.* These processing styles as "programs" occur at a meta-level, hence the language of "Meta-Programs." Each operates as a different *frame of mind* in how it handles and processes information.

Like a computer, our brain, processes information as it cognizes the world. And like a computer, it uses software to organize and structure that data. Our brains utilize various "programs" or software in order to filter, organize, structure, and make sense of data. These processing styles at meta-levels formulate the very mental structures that govern *what* we pay attention to, *how* we pay attention, *the direction* of our attention, and *how we make decisions* regarding the data (important / unimportant, interesting / dull, meaningful / meaningless, etc.).

The following list of distinctions (Figure 4:2) offers a checklist of the various styles for how brains operate with different frames of mind. These Meta-Programs give us a way to understand "the mental software" that others run which determine the way they process information. And in the same that if you didn't know the specific software which a computer uses, how would you know how to communicate with that computer, or the meaning of its output? So with humans. To *not* know a person's mental software or Meta-Programs prevents us from interacting, communicating, understanding, etc.

Begin by noticing the sorting or filtering style of your own software program. What frames of mind do you typically use? Do those frames or Meta-Programs serve you well in a given endeavor? Check the ecology of such. Quality control your style of sorting and processing. As you do, recognize that you are far more than your brain. You "are" more than just a thinker. Processing information merely describes one aspect of your experience and one of your core personal powers.

Even in the process of stepping aside for a moment to assume a meta-position to your frames and Meta-Programs, you are thereby developing an increasing *flexibility of consciousness.* This will, in turn, allow you to shift your conscious awareness back and forth along these processing continuums which thereby increases your choice about how to run your own brain. Given this, you can now ask, "Which side of the continuum or choice would offer me more resourcefulness?" These meta-processing styles, as frames of mind, also describe how we can *order* our consciousness.

(9) Brains can and will run any mental software that we give them.

Meta-Programs: *Awareness Scene 1.*
Charlie Brown, with rake in hand, knocks on Lucy's door and says, "Ask your mom if she'd like one of her leaves raked."

"One?!" Lucy asks. "We have a whole yard full of leaves!"

Charlie Brown explains, "Well, I'm kind of new at this..." "Why don't we just start with one, and see how it goes?"

What Meta-Program does this indicate? How is he sorting? What frame of mind does he seem to be coming from? Ah, the Meta-Program of "Specifics, Details."

When he began processing the data about "raking the leaves" of the yard, his mind went to "one at a time." He didn't entertain any larger picture than that. His self-image of lacking confidence contributed to this frame of mind and this way of filtering.

State Accessing Exercise Using the State of Appreciation
Let's now do a "thought" experiment to see how your brain actually runs (or jumps, dances, or contorts).

> *How often do you visit the state of appreciation?* Do you find appreciation a common state to which you have lots of easy access?

Well, let's see. First, access for yourself a state of appreciation. Think about a time when you really thought-felt a strong sense of appreciation toward something. See what you saw then. Hear what you heard. Feel what you felt. If you fully and completely accessed an appreciation state, how would you need to shift your body and breathing and muscle tension? Begin to put your body in a state that accords with appreciation now.

Figure 4:2
Meta-Program Distinctions

Allow yourself to move around in your chair until you find the right physiology that fits with *the state of appreciation*. What do you need to do with your facial expressions? Feel honestly appreciative of something. What do you appreciate, something small and simple, yet valuable and precious, something you truly appreciate? Perhaps a sunset or full moon. Perhaps a newborn baby. Allow your unconscious mind to scan through a list of things that when you think of those things it elicits in you a sincere appreciation—appreciative thoughts, appreciative feelings. And you can allow yourself to feel more appreciative about these things than you ever have before... now...

Good. How did that go? Did your brain cooperate with you? Did it bring forth to your consciousness items that helped you *go into state*? Or did your mind "go blank?" Did your mind jump around from this item to that item? Did you elicit a little voice inside, "But this isn't really it." Where did your brain go? It went somewhere? Even if it went blank—you had some thought.

Tracking Down Thoughts

When I did this exercise recently, one lady said, "I'll tell you what happens to me, when I try to think of something like that, *my mind goes absolutely blank.* Nothing! I mean nothing!"

So I asked, "So where did your brain go?"

She said, "Meditating. Just meditating."

"Good, let's track down those meditation thoughts in terms of the sights, sounds, sensations and the words that your mediation took?"

She then said, "I lost focus."

"How do you know that?" I inquired.

"Because I said to myself, 'I can't do this!' 'What's wrong with me?'"

"Ah! So you start saying words to yourself—doubting words which questioned your ability, your skill level, your competence..."

"Yes, that's what I do!"

"And what would happen if you then said something appreciative about your brain's ability to do this?"

"I wouldn't want to do that." she said.

"Yes, that's obvious. I know that you wouldn't. I didn't ask that. I wanted only to know *what* would happen **if** you did it, *if* you said something affirming and appreciative about your strong mind—your mind that wants to have it's own mind about things?"

And inasmuch as this completely interrupted her, I continued.

"Some people's brains get into a very powerful habit of resisting and rebelling against 'being told.' In fact, now they 'can't tell' their own brains anything! They have a strong-willed part of their consciousness and can't impose or force information upon themselves. I would guess that in your past you have had somebody (probably a parent) who tried to 'tell' you things, give you orders, and impose on your consciousness, and you developed this fabulous ability to resist taking instructions from anybody and about anything."

An ear-to-ear grin spread across her face.

"And how much do you now *appreciate the strength of your mind* when it does this?"

"Well, not at all;" she said. "It makes me feel stupid."

"Ah! So you access a meta-state of feeling stupid about thinking-feeling in a strong-willed way?"

"Yeah."

"Does that serve you well in terms of resourcefulness?"

"No. Of course not."

"So now you have thoughts-feelings of 'ineffectiveness' to thinking-feeling 'stupid' about thinking-feeling rebellious."

She said, "What?"

I repeated my statement slowly...helping her to recognize the primary state of rebellion, the meta-state of judging that state as stupid, and the another meta-state of evaluating that process as not serving her well. "So now, how do you feel about it?"

She said, "Like I want to learn a more effective way to manage my consciousness."

"Excellent! It sounds like you now know that *you* as a person, as a human being, exist as much more than your brain? (She nodded.) And that you do not have to over-identify with the rejection of information, but can cue yourself to receive information."

"Yes, I think so."

"So let's see how you do about appreciating your brain. Appreciating that you can stand firm and reject information and that you can equally open yourself to receive and accept information."

As long as she had turned her psychic energies against herself with name-calling ("stupid"), she became locked in the strong-willed, polarity mental response and so became stuck in that one way to run her brain. As soon as she attained a meta-position, ran an ecology check on it, she began to free up that program. She began to create more flexibility of consciousness for herself.

How have you used your self-reflexive consciousness in thinking thoughts about the way you typically think thoughts? If we entertain not-so-very-nice thoughts about our thinking, we can put ourselves in conflict with ourselves. If we condemn, reject, taboo, blame, or contempt ourselves we get ourselves stuck in negative emotions. By contrast, when we appreciate and validate our thinking-feeling, we free up that energy and discover we have more power to manage it.

So do this. Go inside and say this words to yourself, "I give myself permission to appreciate the way I have learned to run my brain up until now. I will allow myself to appreciate not only the way my brain dances, but also the contortions it can get itself into. This shows its power and range of motion."

When we meta-state ourselves with the resource states of *appreciation and acceptance*, we powerfully unshackle many of our self-rejections and self-contortions. Now imagine the effect of applying appreciation to other states. Imagine feeling appreciation about your fear, anger, grief, sadness, etc. This process can free us from various Dragons, from taboos, blaming, judgments, and other self-imprisoning processes.

THE POSITIVE INTENT BEHIND STATES

There's yet another thing about brains that we have to take into account.

(10) Brains always aim to do positive things. Yes, of course they do not always succeed in achieving positive outcomes, but they try. They operate from good intentions. They attempt to succeed and fulfill things that we consider of value. When they end up creating pain, foolishness, hurt, ugliness, sin, violation of values, etc., this highlights their fallibility. But their aim? They intend to do good—always.

This understanding expresses a basic and powerful presupposition that governs NLP regarding human nature.

"There's a positive intention behind all behavior. All behavior attempts to adapt to the world to achieve something of value."

In saying this, we distinguish between a positive *intent* and the effects or products that often result from behavior. Obviously, all behavior does not create positive results. Yet every behavior (e.g., action, emotion, response, communication, etc.) makes sense to the person generating it. It may not make sense to us on the outside, but it does make sense to the person. Everyone acts to create something of value even though the thinking at the time is often misguided, downright wrong, and ignorant. Conversely, we do not do "bad" things in order to do "bad" things or to be evil. We do so to accomplish something we think will improve our situation.

Philosophically, this premise offers a positive ontology about human behavior. It enables us to look beyond the immediate effects of hurtful actions to the person's *intentions*. Doing so allows us to enter into their world and align with them. This builds rapport and enables us to then offer better ways to achieve those positive intentions. This perception also establishes the basis for all of reframing models inasmuch as it allows us to separate person from behavior, intention from result.

Therapeutically, this perceptive gives us a motivation in reframing negative behavior as it allows us to set a positive frame.

> "What positive intention can I find in this or that particular behavior?"
>
> "What positive intent could drive this or that expression?"

Demonstration

Think about some state that you experienced this past week that you didn't like and which you didn't experience as enhancing, resourceful, or productive. Then give that state a name. What would you call that state?

"Irritable and frustrated."

And what behavior did you produce while in that state which you didn't like and wish you had not produced?

"I fought with my son."

What positive value did you seek to accomplish by fighting at your son?

"Well, nothing. It was totally negative. It hurt his feelings and I felt like a witch doing so."

Precisely. That describes how you experienced your state and the behaviors that resulted. You did not experience them as positive at all, but negative. So what were you attempting to achieve that would have been of positive value to you as you fought with him?"

"I was trying to get him to *get his school work done*."

Good. A part of you wanted to help him accomplish his school work?

"Yes. Sure."

Now allow yourself to think about that part of you and as you do, what would you have liked to have accomplished with him that you would evaluate as even more positive and even more important than just getting his school work done?"

"Well, I wanted to help him to stay on an even keel, instead of seeing him flip out as he does so often, and then become stubborn and refuse to do his work at all."

As you think about seeking to positively help him stay on an even keel, if you got this result from him in just the way you want it, fully and completely, what would you want ... through having that ... which you would find of even more value and of more importance? If he had stayed on the even keel, how would you find that a positive value?

"I don't know. I guess I would feel a sense of *self-satisfaction* about seeing him get his homework done—a sense of accomplishment as his mother."

And what would you feel of even more importance by feeling satisfied about that accomplishment?

"It would *free my energies and time* from having to deal so much with his studies."

Now as you think about these higher intentions that you have as you seek to achieve freedom from those responsibilities that really belong to him, what would you find even more important than that?

"Knowing that he is going to be okay."

And what value does that serve you?

"I'd know I was a *good parent*."

What an incredible set of positive intentions driving her primary state that seemed so negative, as she got into a "fight" with him over homework! Above and beyond fighting, she had many other objectives in the back of her mind. She wanted to—

(1) help him get his school work done
(2) help him to stay on an even keel
(3) feel self-satisfaction about completing a task
(4) gain a sense of freedom in time and energy from his responsibilities
(5) feel like a good parent.

Figure 4:3 charts these outcomes-of-outcomes up the levels of mind in terms of the Meta-States model. Begin reading the chart from the bottom at the primary level.

It all began with her initial disliked "behavior" and the state out of which it came. Yet using the levels of mind model, we kept tracking up to the higher level states from which she was operating, eliciting and teasing out her higher intentional states. We did that in order to specify the larger level value frames and belief frames which also played a role in driving her primary state.

Figure 4:3

    MS: Being a good parent
                 ↑

    MS: Sense of freedom from his responsibilities
                 ↑

    MS: Self-satisfaction about finishing task
                 ↑

    MS: Helping son stay on even keel
                 ↑

    MS: Get school work accomplished
                 ↑

    P-S: (Irritation / Frustration —>)   Behaviors of "fighting" with son

Having done that, we can now just for a moment, start with the highest meta-states, her highest *intentional states* and use them as a resource.

That's what I did with her. I asked her to simply "access her highest state as a resource, as a highly resourceful place from which to operate. Imagine, completely and fully how you experience the mind-body state of 'being a good parent.' Take a moment to reacquaint yourself with how that feels, what that means to you, how that's so important to you, and just notice the thoughts that dominant your mind when you just step into that state, and how your physiology shifts when you operate from that frame of mind... And you can take an even deeper breath as you do...

Now as you access this state even more fully, **how** does this enrich and enhance your ability to feel satisfaction as a parent? Don't answer aloud... just become aware of it inside. And when you fully and completely *feel that self-satisfaction* as a parent in just the way you like to feel, *how does that enrich and enhance your ability* to help your son to stay on an even keel?

Beginning from these resourceful states of "being a good parent" and feeling self-satisfaction, now imagine fully yourself as helping your son stay on an even keel and *how does that enhance your ability* to help him accomplish his school work? ... And suppose you operate from these resourceful states completely, how would they transform your "fighting" behaviors? ...

This process reverses the basic procedure most of us use in living our lives. We generally start at the primary state level *trying to accomplish something of positive value* for ourselves. But given our states, like irritability, anger, fear, upsetness, etc., we may not find our actions very effective. We usually act *in order to* fulfill a value (being helpful) *so that* we can access another value (good parent) *so that* we can access another value (a caring, loving person), etc.

This process reverses that by suggesting that we simply begin at the top and simply *access the resourceful meta-state* in the first place and then put it to good use. If we imagine it fully and completely so that we access the thoughts-and-feelings, the supporting beliefs, and all of the other frames that are involved, then we can let it modify the lower states all the way down to the primary states. In this way, we bring our highest resources from our meta-states down to our everyday level.

Once we discover the meta-states that we truly seek and work for, our highest intentions and dreams, we can begin to live our lives from that frame of mind. We can use our highest and ultimate value states as *the basis of our inner life.* Would that create a new orientation in life? Would that give us a new way to navigate? Using our highest experiences of resourcefulness would them become our highest frame of reference.

Now we can simply begin by accessing the high level meta-states, step into them, and *operate from them.* After all, they are just "states." Just mental and emotional states and as such they are made up of the same "stuff" that makes up any state—a set of internal representations and corresponding physiology. Now we can amplify them until we have them fully and completely enough to use as our way of being in the world. We can commission all of our higher frames to let those higher intentions transform all of our primary states.

This facet of the Meta-States model was derived in part from the "Core Transformation Process" that Steve and Conierae Andreas developed (1994). It uses the same meta-questioning that you'll find in Core Transformation as it asks the reframing question about "what positive intention" do you have at one level that's even more important.

It differs from Core Transformation in that it utilizes a very different metaphor, a *height metaphor* that corresponds with *going above and beyond* ("meta") one level to yet a higher level. "Core" Transformation uses a "depth" metaphor and conceptually takes one down and talks about various "parts" of one's person.

Meta-States goes up and sees each higher level as a higher *frame of reference ... and higher frame of mind.* With each self-referential and self-reflexive move up, we layer or laminate our mind so that it becomes textured with yet higher values and understandings. This meta-stating process first teases out the levels and then it invites us to let them coalesce into our one holistic mind as we keep all these higher values in mind as we face the world.

The process operates also from an empowering *assumption.* It operates from assuming that we can *start* with resourcefulness and bring such higher experiences down into our everyday states. This makes a significant break and shift from how we ordinarily operate.

Suppose we used this same process with regard to self-esteem. Imagine for a moment that you have accessed a state of high level self-esteeming and self-respecting of your innate dignity based upon no conditions, but unconditionally appraising your *self* as having value, worth, respect, dignity, love, potentiality, etc. Now suppose you accessed this fully and completely. How would you feel? Breathe? Hold yourself? Act when you walk out of here? Suppose further that you began to operate from that state of mind, using the frame of self-esteeming as you went to work tomorrow?

Imagine someone talking or behaving rudely. How does your rich and expansive sense of your innate dignity transform that experience? Do you buy into the rudeness or take offense at it very quickly? Probably not. As you imagine *the You* for whom the expressions of rudeness would be a piece of cake, let this reinforce the power and elegance of starting everyday from your highest and most resourceful meta-states.

Summary

- You now know some basic facts about how brains work and how to use your consciousness to take charge of running your own brain. Knowing these principles of your brain provides a foundation for learning to manage your mind at all its higher levels.
- "But what if I don't?" Well, left to its own, your brain will run its programs as the default programs with whatever ideas that it has picked up. It might even torture you by playing old "B" rated movies to keep you up at night and induce you into loops of thinking-feeling the same thing over and over and over again.
- The question is, Do you "have" your brain or does it have you? Do you process information productively or does it "have" you and make you have thoughts-and-feelings even when you don't want to have them? The choice lies with you.

Chapter 5

META-STATING

Setting the Mental Frames
At Higher Levels To Bring Out Your Best

We began this exploration of our mental and emotional *states* by recognizing them as *neuro-linguistic* states. That is, our mind (linguistic) and body (neurological) states operate by means of how we *think* (internally represent things, believe, value, understand, conceptualize, etc.) and by means of how we use our physiology (i.e., how we hold ourselves, act, breathe, move, eat, sleep, etc.). It's as simple as that; it's as profound as that.

Simple ... because all of the "stuff" of our states arise from how we use our nervous system to think-and-feel. While we give the higher level experience fancier and more abstract names ("beliefs, values, paradigms, concepts, identity, etc.), we build them out of the same "stuff" as the simplest thought. This gives *representational power*. It puts into our hands the ability to *represent* and map things as we chose.

Profound... because with each self-reflexive jump, with each layering of self-referencing, we build up more complex and complicated states of mind. And as we do, each higher frame begins to operate as an attractor in a self-organizing system. This gives the sense and feel of "stability" at the higher levels. It also creates the system dynamic that we call *state dependency.* This means that once in a state, the *state* operates as if it has a "mind" of its own. Then all of our learning, memory, perception, communication, behavior, etc. reflects and reinforces the state.

In our exploration through the previous chapters, we have looked at the processes by which we put ourselves into various states. We have that power. We can *induce, evoke, and elicit* states. We can do this in ourselves and in others.

These "states" that we elicit, however, are not static. Although the very word "state" may convey that to some, a *neuro-linguistic state* actually refers to a very dynamic set of interactions and processes of our thinking and acting. For this reason, we mis-speak and inaccurately language ourselves with a false-to-fact map when we speak of states using nouns. Nouns, if you remember, designates things and tangible objects; "persons, places, or things." You can put real nouns on a table or in a wheelbarrow.

We cannot put a neuro-linguistic *state* in a wheelbarrow.

Because "states" refer to processes (mostly internal), we should map them using *verbs*. Therefore we more accurately linguistically map our referent if we shift to talking about how we *put* ourselves into various mind-body states, *induce* a state, or even "state" ourselves (even though that sounds strange when you first express it that way).

We "state" ourselves via how we use our *language* (the linguistics of sensory based representations as well as words) and our *physiology*. These mechanisms enable us to cue our brain with various messages which then elicits our states. Since this terminology sounds stilted and artificial, I shall talk in terms of "accessing" and "inducing" states.

Our Everyday Mind-Body States

Everyday we experience many "states" of consciousness. We find some of these helpful and resourceful, some unhelpful and unresourceful. Some give us a sense of purpose and vitality; others seem to suck all the vitality out of us. Yet every one of these "states" inevitably operates from our thinking-and-acting. As we *think* (internally represent information) and *move* (act, behave, respond, emote, cope) so we create our states. Ultimately no one "makes" us have or experience any state; each and every state we have is ours. We create each and every one of them.

This doesn't necessarily imply that we know *how* we do so. Yet our internal *state of mind, emotion, and body* belongs to us. The state that we experience and feel arises as a systemic process from hundreds of thousands of internal factors that all contribute to it.

Given this realization, we now can recognize the empowering insight that—

As we learn how to *alter the way we think-and-act*, we can transform our states.

We "are" not a victim of our states. Not really. Sure we can sometimes find ourselves in various *states* and wonder, "How in the world did I get into this state?" We can develop habits of *not* paying attention to our states, *not* learning how to manage them, but none of that means that we are ultimately or existentially *a victim* of our states. Unlike animals, we have *choice* about our states because we can make a meta-level jump to *awareness and observation about our state* and to awareness about the mechanisms by which we can take charge of them. And that changes everything.

Of course, we can also *believe* that we are victims of our states. Many people so believe. And as long as they remain in *that* frame of mind, they think, feel, and act like victims. It's not a pretty sight. It doesn't lead to empowerment. But it makes perfect sense given *that* way of thinking.

Conversely, when we *decide* to use our *self-reflexive awareness* and *observe* our states, *notice* how we can alter them by our thinking and responding, and then develop the skills for state management, we begin the journey to becoming *masters* of our states. And, in a way, that's what this book is all about.

> **As we have created our internal Dragon states, we can tame those dragons, slay them, or transform them. We can elicit higher and more empowering states that make us the Masters of this neuro-linguistic magic.**

On Becoming Neuro-Linguistic Magicians

The *magic* that lies at our command for taking charge of our states lies in *the communications* that we send ourselves. It lies in the frames that we set for our thinking-and-feeling. It lies in the meta-states that we create for ourselves.

- How do you signal your brain about what mind-body state of consciousness you want to experience?
- How much *awareness* do you have that you perform *signaling communications* to your brain?
- How do you use your representational power?

You, like me, already use your powers for representing things in order to signal your brain-neurology about what to experience. Given that we are a semantic class of life and do this, we now want to develop more conscious awareness of this so we can take charge of these powers and use them more intentionally in running our own brain.

In view of that, we begin then by increasing our understanding and appreciating of the languages of "mind" by which we signal our brain. These comprise our sensory based representations, all of our linguistics (i.e., words, symbols, concepts, etc.), and all of our physiological responses (i.e., breathing, movements, muscular tension, posture). This is the "stuff" that endows us with our primary state-management tools. Using these *languages* of the mind, we can re-language ourselves in new and different ways. Then our brain will receive new and different messages and will comply by generating new and different neuro-semantic states. It's that simple.

And, of course, the way we think-and-act will habituate. It always does. And repetition thereby empowers our thinking and acting to becoming increasingly more powerful to quickly re-induce us into the corresponding states. Eventually, in fact, *this process will streamline so that we will "fly into"* the given state. You already do this, do you not? You can "fly into a rage" pretty quickly while driving, can't you? How about "flying into a down?" We do this pretty naturally with the unpleasant emotional states. How about learning to "fly into a calm, confidence, joy, etc.?"

The habituating of our states does not make any state any more "real" in any external or objective sense. And it certainly does not necessarily make the state particularly useful or true. It only makes the state more probable, more typical, and more "in character" with the directions and pathways that our brain has learned *up until now.* That's all it means.

We now want to break those mental-emotional-behavioral **patterns** (interrupt them, turn them down, push them away, etc.) and **build empowering patterns** that will induce the kind of positive and resourceful states wherein we can "be at our best" and produce our best.

This highlights another thing about brains. They don't seem equipped with any built in *"Quality Control"* mechanism. Have you ever noticed that? Our brains just process whatever we feed them. Whatever thoughts we sit with, nourish, attend, and repeat will give our brains something to chew on. So unlike our stomachs which come with a built-in vomit response to garbage, our brains don't seem particular about *what* it feeds on. Give it mental garbage and it makes a meal of it. It will process toxic and morbid thoughts as it will healthy and nourishing thoughts. If we want our brains to *Quality Control* the information that we feed it, we're going to have to teach it to do so and set that as a frame of mind (or meta-state) for it.

State Awareness: *Scene 1*

Linus handed Charlie Brown a picture that he drew. To that Charlie Brown commented, "This is a very nice drawing of a man, Linus." Charlie Brown seemed to be in a friendly and complimentary state. He continued, "I notice however that you've drawn him with his hands behind his back..."

What state does this indicate? Perhaps analytical as well as attentive. Explorative and curious.

Charlie Brown then said, "You did that because you yourself have feelings of insecurity."

Ah, now we have some mind-reading! And as most of us don't take to mind-ready very well, Linus didn't either. A bit angry, he said, "I did that because I myself can't draw hands!"

State Awareness: *Scene 2*

Linus stands up to the school podium. He announces to the entire student body, "If I am elected school president, I will purge the kingdom!"

Then raising his fist and his voice, he proclaims, "My administration will release us from our spiritual Babylon!"

In the third frame he gets biblical, "My administration will bring down the false idols in high places! My administration will..."

Cartoonist Schultz, in frame four, zooms in on the front row where Charlie Brown asks, "I wonder why the principal looks so pale?"

So what state or states would you call the one out of which Linus was speaking? Zealous, ambiguous, positive, intoxicated with a sense of power? He certainly got carried away. And how about the principal? Embarrassed, shocked, confused? Such is the power of language to evoke states.

State Awareness: *Scene 3*

On the phone, Charlie Brown excitedly says, "A baby Sister?" Then running out the house and passing by Lucy and Linus, he shouts, "I'm a father!" "I mean my dad's a father! I'm a brother! I have a baby sister!! I'm a brother!"

In the final frame of the cartoon, Linus looks at his older sister and commented, "You didn't act like that when I was born!"

What states do we have here? Excited, proud, confused in Charlie Brown. In his excitement he became confused so that his tongue didn't seem to work very well. He mis-spoke and had difficulty finding just the right words. And the state of Linus?

The Meta-States Model

In *Meta-States* model, we work with not only primary level states, but higher level states as well. The model allows us to use the process of stepping aside from our thoughts-and-feelings and *going "meta"* (i.e., above and beyond) to our primary state as we access another state of thoughts-feelings. Doing this allows us to access various positive and useful states (such as acceptance, calmness, realistic evaluation, appreciation, joy, curiosity, etc.) which we can then *apply to* the primary mind-body state. When we do such, we have engaged in perhaps the most unique human pattern, one that we've designated as *meta-stating.*

> **When we use the Meta-States model positively, "meta-stating" as a verb, refers to accessing an enhancing state about ("meta") a previous state.**

Whether we experience that first state as enhancing or not, does not really matter. By *going meta* to that prior state, we thereby treat that state as a lower logical level order of experience. Doing this enables us to thereby *qualify and/or modify* the primary experience *by* the higher level state. By *transcending* the lower and going to a higher state of mind, we thereby *set a frame* for the lower. This allows us to bring the resources of the higher states to bear upon the lower states.

> [I know this paragraph is semantically loaded, so you may want to read it several times. It is key to understanding Meta-States.]

What results when we pull off that maneuver?

> **The higher order level or frame (the meta-state) then begins to operate in such a way that it drives, modifies, tempers, and manages the lower states.**

I'm now describing *a systemic function.* As we use our *reflexive consciousness*, we move up levels, logical levels. Each higher level is "logical" because it classifies and categories the lower level.

For example, if we feel out-of-sorts in response to being at work on a Monday morning, and then we think, "God, I hate this job. Why do I have to be here?" We have just jumped a level *in reference to* our mood and classified or categorized that out-of-sorts feeling as a function of "having to do a job that we don't like." It's like a mental filing cabinet.

Where do you put the feeling of "out-of-sorts?"

Let's put it in the file called, "Monday morning blues."

And where do we keep all of the thoughts and ideas about "Monday morning blues?"

Why, in the file labeled, "Having to put up with a job that I dread."

How different things would be for the person who "just noticed" the initial feeling and filed it under, "Not the Most Resourceful Feeling," and filed that under "Awareness and Choice about How to Cope with Emotions," and filed that under "I'm in Charge of my Attitude."

Each higher level or frame controls the lower. Each higher frame *determines the meaning* (and hence the derived emotions). Each higher frame Catalogs how to think-and-feel about life. Each higher frame, as a meta-state, layers and textures the very quality of our life. These meta-stating processes play *that crucial a role* in our lives!

At What Level Are You Thinking/Feeling?

All of this highlights something else about meta-level states and frames.

> *It is not only what we think or even how we think that determines our emotional states, it is at what level are we so thinking-and-feeling?*

There's nothing wrong at all with the thought or the feeling, "I'm feeling out-of-sorts today." That happens. We may just be feeling tired or worn out. We may see nothing exciting or thrilling in some of the upcoming activities that week. Such thinking-and-feeling may very accurately map and describe one's situation.

In fact, *at the primary level* such thinking enables us to forthright look the facts of our life situation in the face without blinking. At the primary level also, all of our unpleasant ("negative") emotions operate as wonderful and highly useful messages. We need them. They register for us *the difference* between our Map of the World and our Experience of the World.

It's at the *meta-levels* that we then set the frames for *how to think* and feel *about* the primary state. And it is at that level that we begin to create our semantic structures, from which come our neuro-semantic states. What frame (or meta-state) do you have above your primary level experiences of "negative" emotions? How have you *outframed* the emotions that we find unpleasant?

   Acceptable or Unacceptable
   To be welcomed and valued — To be rejected and despised
   To be celebrated as signals — To be hated as being "wrong"
   To be used as information — To be pushed down and denied

Our frames *about* our everyday experiences sets the stage for *the meanings* that we experience. It sets the stage for the quality of our life. In meta-stating then, we build, establish, and load up the semantic meanings that then govern our lives.

In meta-stating, we then have the ability to radically *transform* our primary states and to endow them with some very new and different qualities. We can *texture* our everyday mind-set as we set frames of references, categories and classes of understandings, beliefs and values, etc. which serve us well, which enhance our experiences. In this way, Meta-States as a model provides us a highly generative mechanism for generating all kinds of empowering states.

Because *meta-stating* deals with phenomena which involves logical levels, it can lead to some very practical applications for living our lives. And because higher levels always drive and organize lower levels, we can now establish higher executive levels of ideas and beliefs that will support our resourcefulness. We can now even design engineer all kinds of positive resources. Consider the attitude of "joyful optimism." We now have a way to tease out the structure in that attitude and recognize the components that go into the mix. The adjective *joyful* tells us about the highest frame— *joy.*

Optimism, however, isn't a primary state, but already a mixture of several levels. What goes into the ability to look at things in terms of opportunities and possibilities. The belief that we can make a difference. The thought that things can change and be transformed. The awareness that we can tap into resources, learn, cope effectively, etc.

Figure 5:1

Meta-Levels of States and Frames

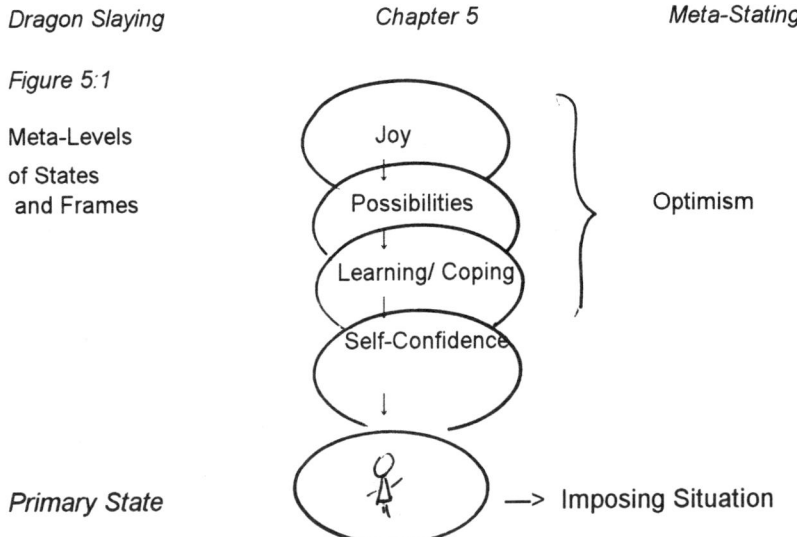

Primary State → Imposing Situation

When we so meta-state ourselves up against the experiences of everyday life, we can create within ourselves the kind of *quality of mind and emotion* that allows us to have a strong calming effect. It allows us to temper, modify, and qualify our primary states so that we no longer experience "raw" fear, anger, stress, joy, relaxation, etc. We experience such primary emotions in a richer way. Meta-stating thus gives us new frames-of-reference by which we can experience primary states in much more resourceful ways.

The Driving Power Within Meta-States

What power or factor in consciousness creates and drives our meta-states and our ability to move upward to set new frames?

Our ***self-reflexive consciousness.***

This describes perhaps the most unique characteristic of the way human consciousness works. We can, conceptually and mentally, *step aside from* ourselves and construct thoughts and feelings about our thoughts-and-feelings. We can then step aside again to entertain even more thoughts-and-feelings about those thoughts-and-feelings. And as our consciousness *recursively reflects back onto itself,* with each jump our consciousness moves up to yet a higher level of abstraction. This self-referencing ability or power enables us to meta-state any state, to outframe any frame, and this ability never ends. As a semantic class of life we can always use other symbols to reference previous symbols. Language itself shares in this same self-reflexivity.

This power also puts into our hands (or minds as the case may be), the power of *transcendence.* That is, it enables us to forever *transcend* our thoughts, our feelings, our state, our beliefs, our identities, etc. Whatever we say or think or conceptualize, we can say yet something else, think something else, conceptual something else. There's no end point. There's no "final word." There's always more. Our mapping of reality and of ourselves never comes to an end.

This *symbolic transcendence* endows us with *an existential awareness and freedom* that no other creature shares. It allows us to operate symbolically upon the world and upon ourselves. We can rise above or transcend our emotions, our thoughts, our situations, our life experiences, our hopes, our visions ... in a word, everything. This obviously gives rise to philosophy, theology, existential questions and states, "spirituality," ontology, epistemology, etc.

If mis-handled, it can create some of our greatest hells. If we fail to negotiate the higher levels of our mind well, we can create all kinds of toxic Dragon States that create pathological structures— the disordering of personality itself.

Yet when handled effective, this transcending power enables us to prevent getting locked up into mental and emotional prisons. The consciousness of animals lack this transcendence. The most intelligent animals can jump one and perhaps two levels, but then they stop. Mostly, they see, hear, feel, smell, and taste the stimuli that their sense-receptors (eyes, ears, skin, etc.) give them knowledge of and live in *this moment.* "Time" as a higher awareness of previous events, ongoing events, and events yet to occur and the relationship between such events doesn't enter into their minds as far as we can tell. They live in the now. They haven't "lost their minds and come to their senses," they only live in their senses.

Not so with us. We humans can develop such higher levels of "mind" that we can actually lose touch with our senses. We can see and not see, hear and not hear, feel and not feel. We can create such higher levels of mind and live so much in those worlds, that we can miss the external world. We can live in mental worlds of hate, prejudice, fear, superstition, self-contempt, grandiosity, delusion, etc. that we cut off awareness from the outside world.

Animals seldom create such pathological states. It takes an animal psychologist generally (or a sadist owner) to create neurotic anxiety in animals. Animals generally live in primary states. They think-and-feel fear and anger, sad and glad, relaxed and stress, aversion and attraction, etc. And when they enter into such states, they tend to be controlled by such states. The states "have" them; they do "what comes natural" to them. Even the most intelligent of animals seem to have little awareness of having states, much less the ability to manage them. They mostly live in a Stimulus—>Response world.

Their's is a much more simple consciousness. They live primarily at the level of perception, rather than concept. And what they perceive, they feel. Distract them and you can pretty easily and quickly break their state. They may have difficulty in getting back to that state. In this, their consciousness has much more fluidity and movement than ours; it doesn't *cohere* as ours do. They don't carry mental concepts with them about time, self, gender, authority figures, meaning, etc. and torture themselves with such ideas on a daily basis. And so having much fewer states-about-states, they don't experience complicated and looping states in the way we do.

The Driving Factor Behind Reflexivity

If *reflexivity* and the self-referencing nature of thinking-feeling describes the mechanism within meta-stating, what factors or mechanism drive this power that we have to transcend our own mental and emotional states?

Symbols. We can use arbitrary symbols and thus develop language beyond *the sensory-based representational systems* of sight, sound, sensation, smell, and taste. Animals have *signals*, but not full-fledged *symbols*. Language, as a symbolic system, enables us to create an abstractions *about* what we see, hear, and feel. Language enables us to say words *about* previous words. It enables us to classify, categorize, frame, and construct concepts.

Korzybski (1933/ 1994) asserted that language gives us the ability to continually *abstract without end* inasmuch as we can always say more words about whatever we have just said. The process goes on infinitely.

As language therefore drives our meta-states, it shows up as the primary difference between primary states and meta-states. Sensory based representations (i.e., visual images, auditory sounds, kinesthetic sensations, the VAK of NLP) mostly drive our primary states. We can almost always identify specifically located and felt kinesthetics (sensations) in our primary states. So we can ask:

>Where do you feel fear?
>What does excitement feel like?
>How do you feel anger in your body?

But try to identify where in the body you feel a meta-state. Good luck!

>Where do you feel self-esteem?
>Locate the physiology of proactivity.
>Where do you experience un-insult-ability?

For the most part, you will not find or locate a specific and discreet sensation in your body for such states. (There are exceptions, which I'll mention shortly.) Rather than localized in our bodily kinesthetics, we typically experience meta-states in our head and in our language.

Why? What explains this?

Because our meta-states exist as abstractions *about* sensations, or *about* sights, sounds, etc. or *about* other words, and so exists as our mental *judgments* or evaluations about things. Notice the pseudo-feeling assertions that we can make. We can use the words *"I feel..."* and then add a *judgment* to that phrase and so create lots of pseudo-emotional statements.

>"I feel dumb."
>"I feel put-down."
>"I feel unprepared."
>"I feel low self-esteem," etc.

Yet these are not *feelings.* This represent *judgments*. More fully and accurately, we are actually saying,

>"I am judging myself as dumb."
>"I evaluate her words and actions as putting me down."
>"I don't think that I have prepared enough."
>"I esteem or evaluate my concept about my 'self' as not valuable or worthwhile according to the standard that I apply."

If we want to tease apart some of the semantic components within these pseudo-feeling statements, we only have to ask an *"about"* *question.* Typically, when we ask what we feel *about* that psuedo-feeling, we will get a response that takes us down to a lower level where

we might get an actual feeling or sensation.
"And how do you feel about feeling dumb?"
"I feel *angry*" (an actual emotion).
"How do you feel about feeling put-down?"
"I feel *upset*" (another actual emotion localized in body sensations).

So what? What are you leading to or suggesting?

This means that in order to build a meta-state, we have to use symbols, which typically means language. We need language to *glue together ideas, concepts, understandings, beliefs, values,* etc., so that they will solidify and cohere as a stable frame-of-reference that will then create an internal order or structure at the higher levels of our thinking-and-feeling.

Slaying the Concept of "Failure"

Conversely, when we want to slay a Dragon, we can go for its throat by finding the language (usually some toxic and morbid language). This will be the language that runs the program. We can then begin questioning the symbolic system and so pull it apart so that the old structure can no longer cohere. We can un-glue the linguistics.

I have done that with the term "failure." As a meta-level Dragon, the higher level thoughts-and-feelings that make up this state of "failure" no longer exists as a possibility in my neuro-semantic world. I have unglued the linguistics that once held the mental-and-emotional concept together. Once upon a time, "feeling like a failure" was a semantic possibility for me. But no longer. I can no longer go there and make that judgment. And so I can no longer create that neuro-linguistic state.

I certainly can *fail* ... I can fail to achieve a goal. I can fail in a business venture. I can *fail* to run a seven minute mile (especially as I get older!). But I can no longer experience this pseudo-thing of "failure" as if it was an entity or real "thing." Nor can *"I,"* as a person or self, cannot experience my self as a "failure." Having unglued that nominalization (i.e., a verb turned into a pseudo-noun), my mind no longer "makes sense" of the word "failure" as a reference to my *self*. I no longer allow that as a legitimate and referencing concept. So the linguistic symbol in England, "Failure," has become a pseudo-word and a non-referencing word in my dictionary.

When Meta-States Coalesce into Muscle

Earlier I mentioned a way to distinguish primary and meta-states. This involved examining the kind of emotions involved in each. I suggested that, typically, most meta-states involve weaker kinesthetics than what we find in primary states. Yet there are exceptions to this.

My first conscious encounter with such an exception occurred the day that I asked someone who said he "felt like a failure," where he felt that in his body. He grabbed the mid-section of his stomach as if in pain and said, "Right here. It feels like a gut-wrenching pain right here."

At that moment, I really didn't know what to say or do about that. I had not anticipated that response. Later, as I considered some of the things he told me and read through my notes, I suddenly realized what it meant.

When I had inquired as to *when and how* Fred had learned to sort for "failure," he related a number of stories. He told about flunking a particular test in the third grade, of not being picked for a baseball team, of being yelled at for being stupid, etc. When I inquired about his feelings at such times, he said that he had "felt sick to his stomach." When he was not picked for the baseball team, he "felt like he had been punched in the stomach."

Such were his referents for failure. Like all of us, he had taken these experiences and used them to map out his unique *model of the world*. In his case, he drew up a series of frames or meta-states about the concept of "failure." He concluded that "there was such a thing as 'failure,'" that "it's terrible to experience failure,' that "failure creates pain in the stomach," etc. He even knew what kinesthetics to use and connect with the sense of "failure," the gut-wrenching muscle tighting pain in the stomach.

With frames of reference like that about "failure," and some strong kinesthetics linked to it, a person would only need few repetitions to habituate that meta-state. It would then quickly coalesce into his muscles to give him a *strong and undeniable felt sense* of "failure."

Summary
- Now that you know about *Meta-States* and *meta-stating*, you can now move to a higher level and begin to run your own brain in intention and mindfulness.
- *Meta-stating* operates as the natural functioning of our minds because we can reference ourselves, our thoughts, our feelings, etc. We call that self-reflexive consciousness.
- Reflexivity operates as it does because as a semantic class of life, we can use arbitrary symbols to stand for things other than itself. As such symbols represent a development beyond *signals*. We not only signal each other, but can use totally arbitrary signals *to stand for* something else.
- Meta-stating allows us to set higher levels of awareness that become our frames of mind and which texture our everyday awareness.

Chapter 6

FLUSHING OUT OLD DRAGONS

FOR NEW META-STATING

We now know some crucial things about Dragons. For one thing, we know the process that creates them. We know that when we bring one state of thought or emotion to bear upon another (the meta-stating process) we thereby establish our higher *frames of mind* and so initiate our neuro-semantic world. And it lies within this every process that we also create all kinds of toxic and sick Dragon states that undermine our effectiveness, peace of mind, and sense of empowerment. Now that we have recognized this very mechanism and structure of what undermines our happiness and sabotages so much of our personal success, we can do something about it.

No longer do we have to live under the dominion of Dragon States if we don't want to. No longer do we have to put up with and live lives of quiet desperation due to morbid frames of mind that color our thinking and feeling. No longer do we have to act out the old programs in our head installed unwittingly by parents, playmates, cultural norms, or the magical thinking of childhood. That's the good news.

The bad news is that Dragons hide. They lurk. Most of all they love to lurk in the hidden recesses of the mind at higher levels. Up there they seem invisible. Up there they don't seem like Dragons at all; they seem more like reality, like "well, that's just the way it is." So first, we have to flush the Dragons out. First we have to put the spotlight on them and prevent them from lurking in the shadows of the mind. First, we have to go on a Dragon Hunt.

Dragon Hunting

We have lots of ways to chase out Dragons from their hiding places. The mere awareness of "ideas" (i.e., concepts, understandings, beliefs, identifications, etc.) as mere *maps* and not externally real gives birth to the several empowering realizations. Now we can know that just because we think or believe something, and just because our body responds to such beliefs with appropriate emotional an somatic responses, none of these validates the ideas as real. Korzybski (1933/1994) initiated neuro-linguistics early in the twentieth century with his classic engineering metaphor that distinguishes nervous system product and the world of energy manifestations "out there."

> "A map *is not* the territory it represents, but, if correct, it has a *similar structure* to the territory, which accounts for its usefulness. ... If we reflect upon our languages, we find that at best they must be considered *only as maps*. A word *is not* the object it represents; and languages exhibit also this peculiar self-reflexiveness, that we can analyse languages by linguistic means...." (p. 58)

Begin by simply noticing the words (i.e., adjectives, adverbs, and descriptive phrases) that you use to characterize or qualify your states. These indicate meta-states. *Joyful* learning tells us something about how one may characteristic learning. The adjective *joyful* points to the quality one experiences about learning. Someone has put the experience of "learning" within the frame or category of *joy.*

Our words tell on us. They tell about the mental and conceptual worlds we live in. So take any experience and begin to listen to what you say *about* it.

- What do you call it?
- How do you experience it?
- What do you say about it?
- What qualifiers do you use to describe it?

Oftentimes the simple *naming* of an experience flushes out and vanquishes the semantic dragons that roam the plains of our mind.

> "Ah, the self-pity dragon because I didn't immediately get my way" Dragon!
> "Ah, the Grumpy when I feel tired" Dragon!
> "Ah, the Get Totally Outraged when people take 'my' space when I'm driving in heavy traffic" Dragon!

Self-Expectancy Dragons

A very powerful Dragon Hunting process involves an exploration of self-expectancies. And doesn't that make sense? After all, an *expectation* refers to a very special kind of mental state... a state that anticipates what will happen in the future as a result of something. As such, it represents a meta-level frame of reference. When we *expect*, we organize ourselves, mentally and emotionally, in relationship to some future event.

So, what do you expect about yourself?
What do you expect about others?
What do you expect about work, success, fitness, etc.?

Our expectancies operate as higher level beliefs, ideas, perceptions, judgments, understandings, worldviews, etc. about various facets of our everyday experiences and so cue our body about various meta-feelings. As such expectancies color and texture our everyday states with higher level frames. No wonder they play such a crucial role in effecting and determining our responses, feelings, communications, etc.

There's even a field of psychology that focuses and studies this domain of human experience. It's called *self-expectancy theory.* This describes the extensive role of self-expectancy in human experience and nature (Kirsh, 1990, *Changing Expectations,* Kelly, 1955, *The Psychology of Personal Constructs*).

Figure 6:1

Meta-State: *Self-Expectancy* "I expect that I will respond, think-feel..." when X occurs...

Primary State: Thoughts-Feelings → Some Event

To summarize, self-expectancy theory say, *"As you expect—so you create and get!"* This reflects a statement Jesus made millennium ago, "According to your faith, be it unto you." In terms of Meta-States, self-expectancy operates as a meta-state that drives and modulates our primary states.

If I expect people to reject me and hurt me,
If I expect people to respond thoughtfully and playfully, if I expect people to behave in mean and malicious ways, or good-hearted and basically compassionate,
If I expect to make a fool of myself when I try to ask for a favor or make a public speech,
If I expect that I can't use my brain when under pressure,
If I expect myself to not assert my thoughts and feelings to an authority figure, etc.,
—> *so shall I receive.*

When you flush out your own self-expectancies, you put the spotlight on the operational self-fulfilling prophecies which are currently governing and running your life at a meta-level. Since you can't *Quality Control* them until you recognize them, *flush them out.*

Once you identify some of the self-expectancies that create your realities, then examine them to see if you have any that work like a negative vicious cycle. Vicious cycles describe an expectation that generates a Dragon state that plagues your life and impoverishes your experiences. And every time you see such, *your typical endeavors* for fixing it tends to make it worse.

Use the following *sentence completion exercise* as a way to blow the whistle on some of your non-enhancing self-expectancy meta-states. Grab a blank sheet of paper and write any or all of the statements. Then generate at least five or six and as many as ten or twenty completions to each sentence. The quicker you respond, the better. It allows you to access the higher levels of your other-than-conscious mind.

"I can expect..."
When disappointments occur (primary state), I can expect myself to think-feel (the meta-state that results)...
When someone rejects me, I can expect myself to think-feel and respond...

When someone criticizes me...
When I recognize some limitation or fallibility in myself...
When I feel angry...
When I feel afraid...
When I feel grief, loss, sadness...
When I feel guilty...
When I feel weak, vulnerable...
When I recognize that I've made a mistake...
When I feel disappointed in myself...
When I experience three disappointments in a single day ...
When I order myself to do something...
When someone else orders me to do something....

Dragons Ahoy!
- What kind of typical states-about-a state do you produce and access when you experience these undesirable states or experiences?
- How do you *outframe* the experience in terms of the meanings that you attribute to yourself or others or life at such moments?
- Can you expect that response of yourself?
- Has your thinking-feeling response become that habitual and that patterned?

Then you have identified some of your higher level frames and if they do not enhance your life and bring out your best, then you have flushed out a Dragon State. You now can recognize a self-expectancy which operates as a toxic self-fulfilling prophecy.

Typically, when we use this *Sentence Completion Exercise* in our trainings, most people are able to flush out and discover numerous Dragon States. Many who didn't think they had any Dragons have flushed out those lurking in the corners.

Almost any *negative* thought-and-emotion *about* any other state can create a Dragon State. There are exceptions, but for the most part, *any time I bring a negative judgment or negative emotion back onto myself or my state, I bring psychic energy against myself.*

Consider that. I first experience a basic disappointment, or limitation, or difficulty, or some unpleasant negative emotion *and then I turn my* psychic energies **against** myself through some judgment or negative evaluation. It felt bad enough feeling rejected, stressed, guilt, disappointed. But then I added to the misery by contempting, hating, despising, guilting, and angering myself about it!

Will that help? *I don't think so!*

How will generating more angry and rejecting emotions *about* the primary experience of hurtful thoughts-emotions and turning them *against oneself* make things better? It usually will not. And yet, if this represents what you can *expect of yourself*, then you can count on this, can you not? You can predict with better than average odds that you will do this to yourself again and again. You will do it regularly, systematically, and methodically! And further, this self-expectancy will put you in a place where you will then tend to get the very things you don't want. None of this draws a very pretty picture.

Doesn't this now explain *why* we began and continually practice the meta-stating of *appreciation?* By building and developing acceptance and appreciation as resources, we can then use them to build various meta-states of self-acceptance and self-appreciation, other-acceptance and other-appreciation, life-acceptance and life-appreciation, job-acceptance and appreciation, reality-acceptance and reality-appreciation, etc.

Imagine making a mistake, a big blunder in life, and feeling embarrassed about it ... Imagine it fully ... and now feel a simple and matter-of-face *acceptance* about that mistake ... and notice how that textures your feelings... And now allow yourself to go further, and to appreciate, fully and completely appreciate, the fallible you. The you who can so skillfully make a mistake... You can even enjoy this fallibility knowing that you have the motivation to not repeat this pattern.

I can now both accept and appreciate my anger. I can allow myself to get angry about things which violate my values and to which I respond with displeasure. And as I feel my feelings of anger and displeasure, I know that these feelings enable me to sense injustice when it occurs. I appreciate the informational value of this emotion. I can also recognize the importance of just accepting this fact without any need to hate or despise my anger, because as I appreciate it honestly, I will be texturing my anger as a valuable resource, and one that I can choose to act on or not act on. I can also temper it with other resources, calmness, respect, dignity, etc. This will empower me to "have" my anger, rather than it having me. And knowing that, then I can trust myself that the anger will never get out of control. In appreciating my anger, I welcome it and bring it to me so that it comes under my control. I no longer need to fear it at all.

People who fear their anger tend to push it down and away from awareness. As they set a frame of *unacceptable* and *not-to-be recognized*, they frame it so that it becomes increasingly outside-of-unconscious. And yet as they do this, they don't make anger go away, they only make *themselves blind* to it. So when they feel angry, they don't notice. Eventually, they take so much of it and get to a point where they then feel they can't take anymore, and so they explode. Then they say things like, "You wouldn't like me angry!" Their fear-of-their-anger works as a Dragon State to them. The very way they cope with their anger, i.e., by hating it, fearing it, and contempting themselves for it *makes the anger* worse and more demonic when it does surface.

Obviously, such persons have not yet learned the delicious art of appreciating their anger. But what if you not only appreciated your anger, but felt calm and relaxed as you recognized your anger and brought it into your awareness, so that you could respectfully communicate it while the sense of injustice still feels small and manageable? Imagine that.

I can now also accept and appreciate my sadness, my feelings of grief about loses and hurts, and about things to which I feel disappointed. I can accept and appreciate these negative emotions rather than become angry at my grief, or embarrassed, or ashamed, or weak, or whatever. So I don't have to feel afraid of my grief, reject my grief, hate my grief, or grieve-over-my grief (depression).

By now I hope you have caught a vision of how we can *meta-state ourselves for health and vitality* by simply using two very simple resourceful states: acceptance and appreciation. I've seen magic happen in personalities tormented by negative emotions by just a little touch of acceptance and appreciation. Dragon States can't endure the power of such.

Self-expectancy: *Scene 1.*

Lucy stoops to look at a bug on the ground. "Look at that bug, will you?" she says to herself.

Then mind-reading that bug(!), she says, "He thinks he's better than that other bug."

So bending down to yell at the bug, she says, "What makes you think you're so great?!"

In the final frame, we see Lucy walking away smugly commenting, "I enjoy putting his kind in their place!"

Let's backtrack from her words to the implied states which she must have been experiencing. What states drive Lucy here? What about the meta-states of superiority, insecurity, control? Thinking-feeling superior *about self* over others obviously describes a meta-state, as does insecurity *about self* which would then drive her bullying behavior. "Controlling" speaks about behavior (an expression of a state) which might arise from feeling a need to take control.

When Dragons Fill the Skies
Meta-States as Canopies of Consciousness

- Is it possible to build up so many layers of meta-states that our entire mental atmosphere becomes full of Dragons?
- If every layer of thought and feeling that *turns our psychic energies against us* becomes solidified into our way of being in the world, do we become the Dragon?

As we self-reflexively think and feel about our states we generate layer upon layer of meta-states. With each layer, our consciousness becomes richer and more "full" of higher level concepts. These coalesce into our very perceptions and so become our perceptual filters (or Meta-Programs in NLP). Our meta-stating creates the conceptual contexts or frames that we use to create meaning and so the entire matrix of our frames operates as our overall *canopy of consciousness*.

In using these images, I'm speaking metaphorically of course. These images, after all, are only ways of talking about and modeling the structure of our higher levels of mind. And yet... and yet they do provide a way to imagine and work with our self-referential awareness.

As our levels of meta-states develop, the overall effect is to create a canopy of consciousness or a matrix world of frames within which we live. Each higher state, metaphorically speaking, *engulfs* the lower states and surrounds it. As it does, the canopy filters all incoming information as well as outgoing perceptions. As this *canopy of consciousness* increasingly surround us, they generate more and more state-dependency of our learning, memory, perception, communication, and behavior.

They eventually become our internal *atmosphere* within which are embedded all of our other states. We experience our primary states in terms of as the mental-and-emotional contexts encoded by each layer of meta-states. As we build up meta-states upon meta-states, our overall canopy of consciousness function as a pervasive psychic force pervading all facets of life. As our "reality" strategy, we just assume that "this is the way it is."

This larger level structuring of our contextual frames work in both positive and negative ways. Imagine putting this to positive use. For example, imagine embedding all of your states in the macro-structure of *acceptance*. If you made *acceptance* your largest mental canopy, your highest frame of reference, then you would have it as your overall mind-set and it would automatically apply to your self, your negative emotions, your positive emotions, your fallibility, etc. You wouldn't have to activate that program. It would be your operational way of being in the world. *Acceptance* as a belief, value, frame of reference, etc. would color all your perceptions. It would operate as one of your more permanent character traits and Meta-Programs.

When we build and layer our highest meta-states as canopies of consciousness, our meta-states organize and structure our very personality. It installs "attractors" in our neuro-linguistic system which then initiate self-organizing influences. No longer do we have to access the state of acceptance or appreciation. Such become an innate part of the structuring of our consciousness, the way that we see, hear, and feel the world. We no longer have to access the state of respect for people, respect as a canopy of consciousness would simply govern all of our thinking-and-emoting.

That this describes the workings of our neuro-semantics states already, we can readily see. The only difference is that we usually don't set meta-states of appreciation, acceptance, respect, dignity, etc., we do it with contempt, blame, fear, anger, dread, skepticism, pessimism, etc. We reflexively set layer upon layer of negative judgments and emotions. Doing so installs perceptual filters of pessimism, anger, fear, resentment, bitterness, skepticism, etc.

If we now want to address such limiting meta-states, we must recognize the Dragons they create and the Dragon-like conceptual atmosphere that they generate.

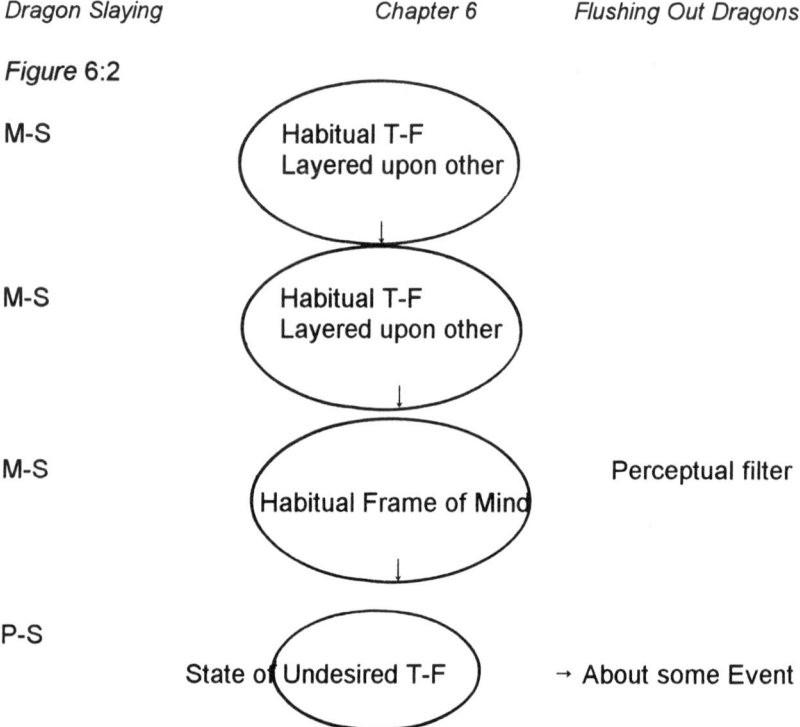

Figure 6:2

Wouldn't this explains why we have so much difficulty helping someone who operates out of a meta-state embedded in *a canopy of pessimism?* Imagine that. How do you help someone when everything you say and do gets colored and textured through a perceptual filter of pessimism? Utter all the optimistic, hopeful, encouraging, and helpful suggestions at your disposal and what good will that do? The person hears your words *in terms of* his or her mental atmosphere of pessimism.

When we deal with someone in a state of pessimism, our difficulty lies in getting through. We may have to interrupt the state and shake the person out of it. The person's state dependent learning, memory, perception, etc., will hinder communicating with clarity. And this becomes all the more difficult with every additional layer of pessimism. When the whole canopy of consciousness is colored dark by pessimism, the negativism becomes pervasive and thick. Typically, we experience such a person as "thick-headed," hard to get through, etc.. But the problem isn't the person, it's his or her meta-level frames.

Summary
- Dragon can be sneaky little devils, hiding and lurking about in the dark shadows of our mind. They do their most damage there.
- But we can flush them out. We can use the mapping nature of language to analyze and detect them. We can observe how we use self-reflexive language in our everyday talk to detect the frames and frames-within-frames that we build.
- Naming the Dragon is often sufficient to make them vanish. They don't like being named. Naming them puts the spotlight on them and this often spoils their nasty little tricks.
- We can flush Dragons out by simply examining our self-expectancies.
- We can also step back and observe the overall canopy of consciousness that we've constructed and recognize that the entire perceptual construct poisons and sickens.
- Ultimately the meta-level states and frames that imprison and defeat us are only made of *the stuff of thought*, of symbols and language. That's why the problem is never the person, at best it's only a distorted map.

Chapter 7

DESIGNING & INSTALLING EMPOWERING META-STATES THAT TAME OUR DRAGONS

Knowing that our conscious mind will forever set higher levels of frames or states (meta-states), the question for us simply becomes the question of—

How do we take charge of this self-reflexivity in order to make it do our bidding?

If we operate with a lack of awareness regarding *how* we meta-state ourselves into Dragon States, we remain blind to how we turn our psychic energies against ourselves. If we fail to reckon with the ever reflexive nature of mind and how it jumps levels at a single bound, we keep ourselves confused with regard to how we can create misery and double-binds for ourselves and others.

So how do we mindfully meta-state ourselves for greater health, wholeness, effectiveness, and enjoyment?

How do we meta-state ourselves so that we tame and transform our Dragons?

We begin with the awareness that we have *levels* in our thoughts. This very awareness itself describes a meta-state and initiates the beginning of a higher level of *mindfulness*. It allows us to start noticing and observing *how* our powers of thinking and feeling create our states. And *just noticing this* moves us to a higher level of awareness. *Just noticing the structure and form* of our thoughts moves us up yet another level. Do you have a picture as you think about that? Is it in color or do you have a black-and-white picture? Is it a movie or a snapshot? How close is it? How clear? What about a sound track? Is the volume soft or loud, close or far away, in what tonality, etc.?

This begins how we learn to "run our own brain." Recognizing the features and components that affect our brains, we begin to learn what makes a difference.

THE SHORT VERSION OF DESIGN ENGINEERING WITH META-STATES

Meta-stating really is not anything new to how we use our brains, yet to do so intentionally, mindfully, and strategically probably does describe a new and uncharted step for most people. Prior to recognizing the levels of mind that comprise our meta-states and prior to appreciating how each meta-stating jump sets the next higher frame of reference, we engage in meta-stating processes, but we really didn't know what we were doing, how it worked, or what results we could expect. Then our meta-stating was pretty much hit-and-miss and haphazard.

But now that we know *what* we're doing, we can engage our self-reflexive thinking-and-feeling in a much more intentional way. Now we can master this art of using our self-referential awareness to build up the kinds of frames that truly support us.

How then do we specifically design and install empowering meta-states with intentionality?

At a generic level, we know that designing a new enhancing meta-state will involve accessing various thoughts-and-feelings and kinesthetic body responses and then relate them to another state of thoughts-feelings and physiology. In this, meta-stating can be as simple as *access and apply*. *Access* some thought, feeling, or physiology and *apply* it to another mental or emotional state.

Would you like to *feel calm* when you express your anger? Then *take a deep breath,* relax your arms and hands, soften your gaze and tone and lower the volume of your voice... (*accessing relaxation),* and now feel all of that ... as you describe something you feel upset about and want to address (*apply to anger).*

Meta-stating can be *that* simple. That describes the short version. A bit longer version that we use in our trainings involves:

Access the resourceful state.
Amplify so that it has enough amperage to effect your mind-body system.
Apply to the targeted state or situation (the primary state).
Appropriate and *activate* into your future.
Analyze the overall effect to make sure it works in a balanced and ecological way for you and others (quality control).

THE FORMAL VERSION OF DESIGN ENGINEERING WITH META-STATES

If *access and apply* gives us the briefest description of meta-stating, the following describes in far more detail the long version. The following steps articulates a precise pattern for mindfully engaging in self-refelxive design work. Use the following as steps to walk yourself through the process of custom designing state-upon-state structures that will enhance your life.

A long time ago, Alfred Korzybski (1921) envisioned the development of human technology which would allow for "human design engineering" that would handle reflexivity. In the later chapters, we will flesh these steps out as we describe the meta-state strategies for resilience, proactivity, un-insultability, etc.

1) Identify the empowering meta-states which you desire to experience and use as your frame of mind.

You can begin with the following list as a way to prod your thinking and dreaming. Checklist the layered states or meta-states which you want to have a lot more access to. These may include those which you do not now have any access to as well as those which you have some access to, but would like to invoke at will. Which ones do you want? Which ones would empower your life? Feel completely free to add and invent other states. Identify the five most important ones which you would first want to add to your repertoire.

Primary States	**Meta-States**
Fun, Joy	Forgiveness
Celebration	Enjoyment
Pleasure	Resilience
Relaxation	Self-esteeming
Acceptance	Proactivity

Appreciation	Self-appreciation
Delight	Un-insultable
Playfulness	Defenselessness
Humor	Creative
Flirtatious	
Admiration	Mindfulness
Respect	Self-respect
Love	Undefeatable love
Care, cherishing	
Contented	Inner Peace/Serenity
Energy and vitality	Bold Courage
Sensory Awareness	
Confidence	Self-confidence
Tenderness / Gentleness	Magnanimity
Assertive	Courageous forthrightness
Releasing	Forgiveness
Decisive	Committed to Decisiveness
Positive	Optimistic
Curious/ wondering	Playfully curious
Awe, worshipful	
Loyal/ Faithful	

2. Design with well-formedness conditions.

After working with states for some time, inducing them, refining them, building anchors for them, creating languaged inductions for them, etc. it dawned upon me one day that **not** every thought I think puts me into a neurological state. Though we have *the internal representations of mind* as one of the royal roads to state, merely representing something does not necessarily induce a state.

"Thoughts put us in state, but not every thought. Hmmm. So what kind of 'thoughts' do evoke states? What kind do not?"

Actually we ought to thank God that every thought does *not evoke* a state! We'd be living continually in a precarious position if every thought that passed through our heads elicited a full neurological state! It's an act of grace that we can think lots of thoughts without being thereby "induced" into a state. "Mere" thought, un-energized thought, dissociated thought, analytical thought, doubtful thoughts, negation thoughts, these and many other kinds of thoughts do *not* evoke states. Somehow they lack the "juice" for state induction.

Imagine the situation we'd be in if every "thought" elicited a state. Just considering that for a moment indicates that we would be bouncing all over the place! We would experience our emotions as sending us on the wildest kind of emotional roller-coaster ever. Plus, we would find ourselves using our fingers to put up a cross sign to anyone who begins talking to us. We'd move through the world fearful of being talked to! "Don't talk to me!"

Thank the heavens then that all "thoughts" do not put us into state. We can try on thoughts and think about them *without* having our neurology activated. This speaks about the power of thinking in a way that keeps us from fully associating into every imagine, sound, suggestion, etc. We can *just observe* our thoughts. We can manipulate and play with them. We can play and question them. These meta-states allow us to know and use our thinking to try them out before fully stepping into them.

This realization also raises another crucial *question*:

What kind of thoughts do induce, access, and/or create states?

The answer to this lies in thoughts that we energize and empower with certain energetic qualities. We need the kind of thoughts that we find so compelling, so meaningful, so vitalizing... that to *think* them immediately invites us to *step into them and feel them.*

In NLP, we have a process for designing desired outcomes so that they are well-formed semantically and structurally. This allows them to work in us and on us in a compelling way. The pattern also suggests how we can *energize* our *thoughts* to make them strong state-inducing cognitions. To do so, do the following:

- *Choose valued content* which you find important and significant.
- *Make them vividly real:* rich in detail and graphic.
- *Give them enough completeness* so that it pulls on you.
- *Value its significance* in your life by generating reasons for valuing them.
- *Increase your desire* and passions for it
- *Directionalize your mind* to automatically go to the *thought:* swishes your mind in the direction of that thought.
- *Language it* in succinct and compelling words.
- *Symbolize it* using dramatic and graphic symbols.
- *Get your neurology into the act* by doing something

        • *Repeat* until the actions and thoughts become automatic.
        • *Feel the thought* by dancing and moving to it.
Doing these things endow our thoughts with strong enough emotions so that it has sufficient power to quickly induce us into its corresponding state. At this point the thought and its linguistic label or description will function like an auditory anchor for re-accessing the state.

State-Intensification: *Scene 1.*
Linus comments to Charlie Brown while philosophizing on the wall, "When I get big, I want to be a great doctor." "I want to be a doctor of doctors, a physician among physicians."

He moves energetically in the next frame as he raises his arm above his head, "I want to be the Willie Mays of medicine!"

Charlie Brown comments, "How ambitious can you get?"

Linus here energize his "thought" of his life vision by using intense, compelling, and graphic words. He also energizes the "thought" kinesthetically through his movements.

State-Intensification: *Scene 2.*
At his desk in school, Charlie Brown sighs, "There's that pretty little red-haired girl..."

He then begins to meditate vividly and graphically, "I wonder what would happen if I walked over to her desk, put my arm around her and gave her a big kiss?"

In the next frame he springs out of his chair and falls on the floor saying, "Wow!"

Back at the desk, all embarrassed and blushing, he comments to himself, "I've gotta stop thinking about things like that!"

Charlie Brown here discovers just how much *graphic vividness* can energize one's thoughts. At the same time he discovered his own representational power.

State-Intensification: *Scene 3.*
Linus in front of his class, reads a report. "The title of my theme is 'Experiences at Summer Camp.'"

Then he began reading, "As I got off the camp bus that day, I sensed that the woods were full of queen snakes! Queen snakes to the left of

me... Queen snakes to the right of me... Queen snakes all around me! I..."
   Suddenly a loud "Klunk" startles Linus as he looks up.
   "Poor Miss Othmar... I keep forgetting she has a thing about queen snakes!"

Building Well-Formed Designer States

Begin by eliciting a state of appreciation. Suppose in designing our states (or actually meta-states), we consciously chose to engage in the process with an attitude of appreciation. That would certainly create an appropriate tone for this task. Once we have set that goal, the question would then become, "What specifically do we need to think about to elicit the feelings of appreciation?"

In eliciting states to use as resources, especially when meta-stating, it almost always helps to pick something small and simple. By identifying a referent that's small and simple it assists us in elicit a more discreet state. Avoid thinking about something big and emotionally loaded. Doing that will more typically create confusion and *not* give you sufficiently precise signals about the state.

When I want to access a simple and discreet state of appreciation, I focus in on something like a beautiful sunset, a newborn baby, a playful puppy dog, a cup of hot coffee and a good book.

Next, do whatever you need to do in order to represent the outcome state in your mind so that it elicits the strongest feelings in you. What qualities do you need to use to amplify your state? Run a checklist on your internal representations in terms of the "submodality" distinctions.

   Have you encoded it so it it looks, sounds, and feels "real?"
   Do you have enough *vividness* in your pictures, sounds, and sensations?

Run through the movie that you have playing in your mental theater and edit in every quality that makes it compellingly vivid for you. Richard Bandler talks abut making it "Sensorama Land." When you *think* about the desired state, make sure you can fully see it, hear it, smell it, taste it, and feel it. As you step into that three-dimensional world, make a 360 degree examination all around you and notice how things look when you are there fully.

The next item on our checklist is: *Complete enough to pull on you.* Well, does it? Does it compel you, draw you, and make you drool? If your mouth hasn't begun to drool, then you have yet made your internal representations dramatic enough.

Value: What significance does this content hold to you? What rich meanings can you attribute to it? Perhaps relaxation, human dignity, meditation, personal enrichment, etc. What other values can you endow it with? Do so! How strong does your desire for it feel? What other reasons, motives, or understandings could turn up your passion for it so that you feel more ferocious about it?

Directionalize your mind: How many times do you need to run this rich compelling internal movie until your brain and neurology becomes completely directionalized by this "thought?" Vividly run through your representations five times. Let it entertain your mind again and again until it becomes automatic. How many times makes it automatic in your brain?

Language. What words do you hear in your movie that help code all of these understandings? For appreciating a cup of coffee you might say, "Ummm, good to the last drop!" For appreciating a newborn baby, "Ohhh, you cute precious thing!" As you fully recognize and appreciate that *words glue meta-states and meta-level frames of mind together, play with your words until they become succinct and memorable.* What other words can you use? What words make your thought more colorful, succulent, that drips with sweetness, rich, etc.?

Physiology: Now connect it to your body and neurology by acting, moving, and sensing it. Connect it to your breathing, posturing, gesturing, moving, smelling, tasting, etc. Find some rhythm or music or kinesthetic sense that facilitates your moving into that state. Use your hands and body like a mime to give kinesthetic movement to your thoughts. What do you need to do with your face and eyes to convey this state? How would you look out on the world with "eyes of appreciation?" What would comprise your "posture of acceptance," "the breathing of self-esteem," "the face of proactivity," etc.?

If you have problems coming up with the physiological correlates to the state, use the NLP modeling process. Go interview people until you find several who can easily and quickly get to the desired state you want. Then explore the structure of their experience:

"What do you appreciate?"
"When do you respond really assertively?"
"What brings out a deep sense of love or compassion in you?"
As they begin to respond and access state, deepen it for them with *a how-question.*

"**How** do you know that you *really* feel appreciation, assertiveness, compassion, etc.?"

This will typically coach them to access the state with even more intensity. As they do, *pay attention* to their physiology: breathing, muscle tension, posture, facial expressions, gestures, etc. Calibrate to these analogical expressions so you can try them on. Put your body into those forms and let your body lead your mind.

Letting your body lead your mind provides a marvelous and powerful "technology" for change and transformation. Act that way until your mind and neurology catch up. Pretend. Pretend vividly and graphically. Think of yourself as an actor learning a new part, and you will.

Earlier we described the fact that meta-states typically have *weak kinesthetics*, and some exceptions to that. Here's another exception. Once we have designed and sequenced a meta-state structure, and then habituated so that it becomes part of our very canopy of consciousness, it tends to coalesce into our muscles and become part of our muscle memory. In fact, intentionally linking the higher frame to a body part and process facilitates this natural process. "Let me see the eyes of self-appreciation." "And give me the walk of proactivity..."

In this way, we can actually kinesthetically anchor a higher frame of mind with all of the linguistic and symbolic representations involved in it. Doing so allows us to link it to some kinesthetic expressions so that it becomes encoded there.

To begin using the well-formed conditions on your own meta-states, take one of your highly desired states that will enhance your life, and run your design through these indicators. This will enable you to ensure that you have enough neuro-linguistic energy in your "thought" so that just thinking about it will elicit the state for you.

In the movie, *"Hook,"* with Robin Williams, after the lawyer Peter discovered his true identity as Peter Pan, he couldn't fly. Tinkerbell, his personal fairy, explained the reason. He had to think "happy thoughts" if he wanted to fly. So she encouraged him to think some happy thoughts, to find his happy thoughts. And if we want to get into happy states where we can really fly, we too have to create and vividly imagine some happy thoughts. What *quality thoughts* do you specifically need?

3. Sequence the States and Meta-States with Compelling Linguistics

At the primary level, the simple "language" of our see-feel-hear representations drive our primary states. Crank up the sensory-based nature of our pictures and sounds, and presto, the state becomes strong and has more neurological "juice."

This changes when we go meta. Now we need a *meta-representational system*. And, we have one, *the symbolic nature of language* itself. So that which ultimately creates and drives our neuro-semantic states is *language*. We do our most human and conceptual thinking in and with language. We use abstract words to create various human "realities" that we experience as understandings, abstractions, and concepts that we generalize from experiences. "Concepts" at this level do not exist "out there," they arise as the products of our nervous system and brain. And by these more conceptual abstractions, we are able to map out logical systems like science, mathematics, geometry, architecture, physics, etc. All of this arises from our power to manipulate symbols.

This also explains why we need words and other symbolic systems to navigate those areas that most concern us. After all, the majority of our lives are spent with such conceptual concerns as indicated by the following list of concepts and the semantic states that they create for us.

Time	Past, Present, Future
Masculinity/ Femininity	Gender
Cause (Causation)	Self
Self-Esteem/ Self-Concept	Authority
Relationship	Morality
Motivation	Values
Life's Meaning	Consequences
Human Destiny	etc.

You have never stepped out your front door and stumbled over any of these "things." They are not "things." They have no external tangible reality. They exist at meta-level phenomena— mental concepts that exist in the mind-and-heart of a meaning maker. Herein also lies the heart of our humanity. The "things" that we consider of most important to our human experience involve these kinds of higher level abstractions.

Immanuel Kant thought that these comprise *a priori categories*. He viewed them as innate to human consciousness, concepts that we were born with, concepts prior to actual experiences in the world. Whether that's so or whether we just map them from our experience with the help of various cultural frames, such meta-level phenomena arise mostly due to language.

When we "lose our mind and come to our senses" (Fritz Perls), we do not think or experience such conceptual states in our primary states. At the primary level, we know nothing about the abstraction of "time." Conceptual "time" does not exist there. Time-awareness (as in Through Time) doesn't exist there. At the primary level, we get lost in time. We are in the eternal now. We have to *step aside* from the primary state to even *notice* "time," that is, to notice the sequencing of events. At the primary level, we experience events happening and don't measure them in terms of other events. We have to *step back* and *out of that kind of time* in order to do that.

So with our ability to think and process *causation.* That abstract semantic state doesn't exist at the primary level. Sure events happen that lead to other things. But *to be aware and conscious* of the concept of cause-effect, contributing influences, consequences, etc. involves a meta-level awareness. So with our awareness of other categories that we use to think and feel, gender, masculinity, femininity, authority, right and wrong, etc.

As we process these higher level concepts, we have to use a higher level set of symbols and language to represent such abstractions. And to do that, we have to go into *semantic states of consciousness* where we attribute meaning, think *in terms of categories,* use higher level domains of understanding as a frame of reference, etc.

And, as already noted, our self-reflexive consciousness does not stop there. We always and inevitably then think and feel other things *about such* Kantian categories, linguistic concepts, abstractions of abstractions, etc. This leads us on to even higher level consciousness as we order our awareness in such levels, classes, and concepts. We not only develop the abstract idea of "cause-effect," we then develop thoughts-feelings *about* causation and the cause-effect world. And such meta-level concepts also induce us into various meta-states.

Now usually, or at least often, we do not even notice this process. Why not? In part because these meta-states typically (but not always) involve weak kinesthetic components. Using the higher levels of the cortex, we do not construct the concepts so that they send commands to the lower nervous pathways of the brain. Because we code and represent these thoughts-feelings *about* other thoughts-feelings primarily in language, this shifts us from primary sensations or feelings (actual body sensations, kinesthetics, internal visceral experiences) to secondary sensations or "emotions" (made up of "part cognition and part feeling"), and then onto a third-level order of sensations, or abstract emotions or mental judgments about the emotions.

This explains why *we feel primary states so immediately in our bodies* (e.g., relaxation, calmness, tension, anger, fear, pleasure, etc.). When we move to the first meta-level, *we feel meta-states partly in our mind and only partially in our bodies.* And when we move to higher meta-levels, *we then feel those yet higher meta-states almost exclusively in our "minds."*

What does self-esteem feel like? Forgiveness? Proactivity? These speak of *more abstract semantic states rather than more immediate feelings in the body.* We experience this as more mild or weak kinesthetics.

So as we move up the levels of mind, we move up a ladder of more abstract language. The first language we use in "thinking" and accessing states involves (1) sensory based language. Such language empirically describes the world using see, hear, feel terms. (2) We then use more abstract language as we encode the see-hear-feel referents using arbitrary symbols (language). (3) Next we use language that becomes more evaluative as it classifies and categorizes concepts. (4) And so on it goes as we develop and use ever more abstract generalizations about previous generalizations.

All of this underscores the importance of language in creating and solidifying meta-level phenomena and meta-states. As it is by language that we can *unglue* toxic formulations, so it is by language also that we can glue together empowering meta-states.

By language we can induce, elicit, and access states. By language also we can detect and uncover states. We can actually learn to hear states and meta-states as we listen to language. If you listen to how people talk, you will hear them expressing and revealing meta-states. If you tune your ears linguistically, you will hear the canopies and meta-frames from within which others live, breath, feel, perceive, communicate, and behave! We can even specify many of the linguistic cues for meta-stating (see Glossary).

4. *Eliminate Any Incongruencies You Find*

If feeling congruity about an idea, outcome, or self-definition gives us the sense of personal power, then feeling incongruity about a newly designed meta-state structure can feel dis-empowering and conflictual. The sense of being incongruous then works against us since it prevents us from experiencing the new state in a powerful way.

Imagine that I set a frame that values relaxation as a healthful response and so I begin to relax my mind-body. But just as soon as I begin, I also start in with criticizing myself, "I'm not doing this right! I should relax more. What's wrong with me that I can't relax?" My tense, stressful, critical, and judging thoughts-and-feelings will counteract my thoughts-and-feelings of relaxation. The incongruity of the two states will interfere with each other and prevent me from accessing the resourceful state.

The same applies for any other meta-state that counters or conflicts with yet another higher frame. If I want to become more proactive, and believe in it as an expression of maturity, and a means to developing more skill and competence, but simultaneously fear taking a risk, and over-value safety and security, these conflicting meta-level frames will not allow me to engineer an empowering meta-state of proactivity.

To check for congruity / incongruity, we need to establish a baseline. You can easily do this by thinking of something that feel totally congruent about. Think of something small and simple which do you think, say, or do with the full alignment of every part of your mind and body.

"Because I care about my health, I regularly exercise."
You do?
"Yes."
Consistently and faithfully?
"Yes."
Does any part of you object to doing that?
"No."

Upon accessing a clear and congruent *yes* that validates the referent, just feel it and notice how you feel, speak, hold yourself, etc. Now contrast that with something you are not congruent about. Think about something that you would kind of like to experience, but also don't care all that much about. "I'd like to help straighten out local politics by running for a local office."
You would?
"Yes... well, I think it would be good."
So will you?
"No, I doubt it."

Once you have contrasted and compared congruent with incongruent, quiet yourself as you relax with an internal focus about the desired meta-state. As you then imagine stepping into that meta-state and using it, notice if there any part of yourself that seems to object to it. Give yourself permission. Go inside and say, "I give myself permission to fully have and experience this state as a resource." Again, simply notice your internal responses to that statement. For example, "I give myself permission to go operate from a state wherein I trust and accept people..." Stay quiet. Let it settle. What happens? Do you hear any voices? See any pictures? Feel any kinesthetic sensations in response to that statement?

If you do get a sense of objection, thank the part of your mind which produced it, and then explore further. "What objection do you have against me accessing this state fully and completely?" Then, use that information by incorporating it into the state.

If a part of your mind says, "Well, I fear that people will take advantage of me if I trust and accept them." Now use this additional concern to further qualify the state so that the new meta-state becomes even more specialized. "I give myself permission to use the state of trust and acceptance of people, namely those persons who have showed themselves honest and trustworthy, and I will recognize such when I saw X, Y, and Z behaviors."

As we learn to welcome, utilize, and learn from our own *internal objections, concerns, and fears,* we stop fearing it or despise it as if there was something wrong with us. This reframes objections as *vital information* which we need for balance. We can then put our objections to good use as we build up the kind of meta-states which respect the ecology of our value and belief frames. Continue to check on the inside until all of your inner parts fully and congruently accept accessing the state. This process allows you to use internal objections to build in necessary resources.

Sometimes the objection expresses itself as a feeling of discomfort because we anticipate feeling weird, strange, or uncomfortable with the new resourceful meta-state. The incongruency only indicates that we're stretching beyond our former comfort zone. Use permission for this. "I give myself permission to accept the feelings of finding this new response strange and uncomfortable because it means I'm stretching and will do so until it becomes familiar."

5. Step into the meta-state and rehearse the process.

Meta-states typically differ from primary states in that they need lots of practice, rehearsal, repetition, and "walking" oneself through the sequence in order for them to cohere and to become habitual. Frequently, primary states need very little practice. Driven by basic sensory modalities and kinesthetics, we typically find that we have ready access to our primary emotional states (i.e., fear/ anger, joy/ sadness, tense/ relax, attraction/ aversion).

Driven by language and comprised of layers of thoughts and feelings in a specific sequence, meta-states more generally need lots of rehearsing in order for them to habituate. How many times do you need to get angry before you can quickly "fly into a rage?" How many times do you need to fully experience calmness about your anger before you can fly into a calm-about-my-anger state? Since this represents a more complex structure, it will take more rehearsing to get the feelings and thoughts ordered in this way.

Stepping into the meta-state and experiencing it and building it up, using the "As If" frame, imagining when and where and with whom you like to have this resource in your tomorrows, these rehearsal processes train your brain-neurology to go in this direction. Now just keep doing it until it "takes."

6. Symbolize your language with compelling symbols

Once you have used your linguistic skills to accurately and completely describe and formulate the semantic structure and significance of your desired meta-state, just close your eyes and begin to allow your unconscious mind to *pick a fitting symbol* for it. For your concept of "justice" and all that you say and believe about such, you might see a balancing scale as a symbol. For your state of "adventurously moving into the future with courage and foresight," and all that you believe and value about that, you might use a visual image of an eagle to symbolize it.

Symbolizing our conceptual ideas which we have formulated in language gives us *a non-linguistic form* of it which we can then use as a single symbol *to stand for* the entire concept. This symbolization can take the form of a visual image, a diagram, a cartoon figure, a color, a sound, melody, song, or even a feeling or piece of physiology. It could take a non-propositional linguistic form as in a poem, proverb, koan, riddle, joke, paradox, etc. These provide yet another kind of symbolic language for coding abstract understandings.

Nelson Zink and Joe Munshaw (1996) have described this shifting from a linguistic coding of our generalizations to a symbolic, icon image for of languaging of our generalizations in their NLP pattern, "Collapsing Generalizations" (*NLP World*, #3). Robert Dilts (1994) used a similar process in his Einstein strategy for problem-solving and creativity (*Strategies of Genius*, Albert Einstein).

7. Step fully into the meta-state and put it into your future.
What specific contexts, environments, people, situations, etc. would define where and when you want to experience this meta-state? Imagine these parameters for this new frame of mind vividly as you step into it fully. This "future pacing," for so we call it in NLP, also has the effect of installing the strategy.

As you also remember that meta-states inevitably drive and modulate your primary states, take a moment to think of your newly designed meta-state as a canopy over your primary state, a canopy that engulfs all of your other thoughts and feelings. Imagine this as you think about it becoming your perceptual filter and letting it orient you as you move through life.

FRAMES TO AVOID MESSING THINGS UP

You now have all you need in order to go out and meta-state yourself and others for fun and profit, for increased joy and effectiveness. So go and enjoy yourself in the process.

"But what if I mess someone up?"
"What if I encounter some difficulty I don't know how to handle?"
"What things could possibly go wrong that I should know about?"

Can you mess someone up with meta-stating? Sure. You could easily create even worse Dragon States if you're not careful! After all, anything as powerful as the layering of state-upon-state and frame-upon-frame that constructs and deconstructs *meaning* is not only powerful enough to open up possibilities and enhance lives, it's also powerful enough to limit, imprison, sicken, and create pathological states.

In introducing the Meta-States model here, we have repeatedly described how complex and layered forms of conscious awareness can create *Dragon States* which can torment and make life a living hell. Negative pathological states can and do arise in human experience. People can and do use their self-reflexive mind and meaning-making powers to create toxic and morbid meta-states all the time anyway! We have not *invented* meta-states, we have just *discovered* them and offered a description of how they work, the mechanisms that drive them, and how to manage them for health and empowerment. The meta-level states that we experience are not new and unique. This model primarily gives us a way to talk about these experiences and a map about how to handle them.

To meta-state yourself for working effectively and productively with people (or yourself), remember the following. Use these as meta-level frames that will enable you to work with others in a sane, loving, and respectful way.

- *All of your mapping, at whatever level, is just that—mapping.* None of it is real. It's all a way of running your own brain. The map is not the territory. The menu is not the meal. Talking about sex differs from experiencing sexual intimacy.
- *Lighten up with healthy respectful humor... it's not that serious.* Set a frame for fun and playfulness. We start a disease and toxic process when we meta-state yourself and others with *seriousness*. Laughter is good medicine.
- *The problem is always the frame, never the person.* In your mind separate person from behavior so that you don't confuse yourself and over-identify a person with his or her maps or states or behaviors.
- *Loving respect enables us to honor the experiences of others.* Not only is laughter inherently therapeutic, so is respect, empathy, and love. Set these as your frames about people so that you can enter their realities gently. They may be as wrong as hell about things, but they have the right to be wrong.
- *Run a Quality Control check frequently.* Get into the habit of stepping back from things and running a sanity check, a reality test, and an ecology check to make sure that you're not doing harm.

- *Enjoy your right to be wrong.* In avoiding the disease of seriousness, you'll need to develop a good relationship with your own fallibilities. If you make a mistake, proactively catch it and apologize. Then back up and do something else. Don't set a frame that making a mistake "is the worst thing in the world." Of course, you'll make mistakes ... and if you are *open* to them, you'll *learn* from them, and keep improving your skills.
- *Bathe yourself and others in acceptance, appreciation, and awe.*
- *Pay lots of attention by being in sensory awareness.* More often than not we will elicit or create unenhancing meta-states when we don't pay attention. So set a frame for noticing and calibrating to people.

TROUBLE-SHOOTING META-STATE DESIGN WORK

If in the process of working with current meta-states or building new meta-states you need to *troubleshoot* difficulties, use the following suggestions as a basic orientation.

(1) Identify the specific difficulty that you're experiencing.
- Incongruency between meta-state and primary state?
- The lack an intense or compelling enough representation of the outcome?
- The lack of well-formedness in the languaging of the meta-state?
- The lack of sufficient rehearsal in order to install it fully?
- The lack of clarity about when and where to use the meta-state?

Use the strategy model and track down the steps and stages of the process (what we call "the strategy") as you walk through the design. Once you have the strategy of the meta-state, especially notice the jumps to meta-levels that occur within that strategy.

(2) Index the Meta-State. When do you want this meta-state, *where, in what context, with whom, to what extent,* etc.? Such indexing of the specifics of the meta-state enables you to make sure that the meta-state will work ecologically. Indexing in this way enables you to send specific directions to your brain as you create a cognitive map that lets

your neurology know when and where to use the meta-state, and where not to use it.

(3) Check and Distinguish for Multi-ordinality. Korzybski (1933/ 1994) defined *multi-ordinal words* as those which could operate at many different levels of abstraction. As such, they carried no specific meaning, only a general definition (i.e., science, love, knowledge, state, understanding, etc.).

Most nominalizations (as verbs turned into nouns) operate multi-ordinally because they point to no specific referent, but take their meaning from the level of abstraction. The test for multiordinality is self-referentiality. Can the term refer to itself? Can use the word on itself? If you can reflexively or recursively use the word on itself, you have a multiordinal term on your hands. And multiordinal language always lies behind, and within, meta-states.

Love: "I *love* Jill," "I *love* loving Jill."

(4) Interrupt negative meta-states to stop old meta-level strategies. Sometimes you will discover that the very intensity of a state makes it difficult to deal with or even stop. Frequently a person will access some unresourceful or even traumatic state and the only thing we can do at that point is to interrupt the state. This applies to both primary and meta-states. What state interrupts (pattern interrupts) do you have at ready access by which you can interrupt a dis-empowering state?

If, or when, a meta-state starts looping unresourcefully onto itself, it becomes a vicious cycle in a closed system and so doesn't have a way to exit. For example, when someone feels angry about your anger and angry at the anger at the anger, etc.! Talk about a formula for unending misery and self-torture that evokes an inner Dragon.

> Feeling guilty about feeling guilty and then guilty for feeling guilt about guilt!

In situations where a state keeps looping in on itself and going nowhere, things will only get worse. Persisting in a process like this which doesn't work only causes the process to cycle faster and faster and generates what in systems thinking is called a run-away system. Since this isn't good, we have to interrupt it dramatically.

(5) Distinguish and separate the "logic" which occurs at different levels. Frequently what will work as "logic" at one level will become illogical, and even contradictory, at another level. This explains the way "paradox" works. We suffer from category errors when we fail to

distinguish levels. "I want you to show me your panic. Now just panic all over the place so that I can see if you really have a problem with fear getting out of control."

Summary

- You've been *meta-stating* all your life. But for most of your life you've been setting frames without conscious awareness of what or how you were doing it. Now we can take charge of this empowering process and use it to quality control our lives.
- Meta-stating tames dragons as we set frames that manage, control, and contain our psychic forces. This allows us to no longer fear ourselves, our thoughts or emotions, but to welcome and accept with appreciation our God-given powers.
- Meta-stating can be as simple as *access and apply* or as complicated as involving a whole strategy for design engineering human excellence.
- Meta-stating also increases our level of *mindfulness* about the messages and states that we've grown up with and have habituated. Now we can catch our self-inducing meta-state languaging in order to run much more wholesome programs in our mind.

Chapter 8

DRAGON SLAYING #101

Dragon Taming,
Transforming and Slapping
The Science & Art of Handling Dragons

I hope that by now you have shifted from perhaps someone who once lived in fear and dread of Dragons to someone who feels totally masterful and skilled in Slaying, Taming, and Transforming Dragons?
   Are you now a Masterful Dragon Tamer?
   To what extent have you become an expert Dragon *Slayer*?
   How much confidence have you now developed using *Meta-States* that you can take on and handle any Dragon that presents itself to you?
   How much more resourceful would you like to become as a Transformer of Dragons?
In this chapter I want to summarize and discuss the range of Dragon Slaying, Taming, and Transforming tools and skills. We will touch on your own training and internship as a Dragon Master.
   Dragons, you remember, metaphorically describe the energy fields and states that we experience from our thoughts and emotions. It's a nice metaphor. I like playing with it. But it's just that—*a metaphor.* We are not *really* slaying Dragons. No endangered species are being eliminated from this planet. It's just a way of talking about the neuro-linguistic *energies* that build up from the way we think and feel and that we experience as our neuro-semantic states.
   As a metaphor, Dragons refer to any neuro-semantic energy field. We typically talk about the unpleasant Dragons that arise from our "negative" emotions such as fear, anger, grief, sadness, disgust, pain,

shame, guilt, regret, etc. Although we can just as well talk about the Dragons that can emerge in our personalities when our passions, lust, love, joy, humor, power, drive, etc. get out of balance and seem to "have" us rather than we having it.

With that definition, let's pose the central Dragon Slaying and Taming question:

How do you slay, tame, or transform a Dragon state?

1) Catch the Dragon

Before you can slay or tame a Dragon state, you have to locate them. And sometimes this will not be an easy job. Why not? Because many Dragons like to lurk in the shadows. Others adopt *invisibility* so that they can move about without being detected. Dragons will frequently lie to you and tell you that they are *not* Dragons, but faithful watch dogs there to serve and protect.

So with Dragons disguising themselves and hiding, what's a Dragon Master to do? How can we ever address, challenge, attack, slay, or tame a Dragon that we can't even see it? For this reason, we have to first flush the Dragons out into the open where we can see them for what they are. As long as they slink around in the dark shadows of the mind or in the dark chambers of the heart, we may feel that something's amiss, but not know what.

Here *the "Dragon State" Meter* might provide you a helpful tool (see the charts at the end of this chapter). Use the meter to register your states, to register both the *kind* of state you're experiencing and its *intensity*. When you have done that, step back and evaluate the state in terms of its health and ecology. Does it serve you well? Quality control the state. What are its qualities and characteristics? Explore it's *intentions*. That will flush out some of it's meta-levels. What intentions drive the state?

Such questions will typically flush out hiding Dragons and even numerous Dragon babies.

What *Dragon thoughts* have you entertained today or this week?

What seeds have you been conceiving and planting that will eventually hatch into a Dragon?

How do you have your thoughts encoded? Which of these feed the *Dragon*?

Suppose you find that you have a self-critical thought in your head, one that accurately evaluates something in which you want to improve, but you have those evaluative thoughts coded in a loud, harsh, insulting tonality. How well do you respond to that tone and quality of voice? Or suppose you find that you have an accurate and useful thought of sympathy for yourself, yet it's coded in a little whinny voice, "I wish I could get the breaks that others do." Dragons often arise from such things. A painful and unproductive energy field arises when *how* we inwardly talking to ourselves doesn't fit with *what* we're saying.

While you're at it, check out the higher level meta-states and frames that you have your primary state embedded in. When you experience *an undesirable primary state* (i.e., a negative emotion such as anger, fear, disgust, guilt, embarrassment, etc. or an undesirable experience such as rejection, criticism, disappointment, weakness, fallibility, etc.), what state do you go then experience *about* that emotion or experience? What state would your closest friends expect you to go into?

To what extent do you turn your *psychic energies* **against** yourself? Whenever we do that, we put ourselves at odds with ourselves and with our powers and frames of mind. You can see and hear such when we say such things as:

"I hate my anger."
"I feel disgusted with my fear."
"I feel angry at my guilt."

All of these judgments and negative evaluations turn our own psychic energies of thoughts, values, emotions, etc. *against ourselves* which then puts us into internal conflict. We then feel and act out the incongruity.

And when you catch this kind of thing in yourself, or another, you now know that you have a Dragon by the tail, a meta-state Dragon! So hold on tight, it might be a rough ride for awhile.

> Have you adopted any thoughts-or-feelings that reject, criticize, and/or denigrate yourself?
> Do you have any self-talk that quickly goes into judgment mode against yourself?

When we language ourselves in that kind of a way, we inevitably build Dragon states. Perhaps someone else has languaged you in a judgmental way so that you've learned how to be rough and harsh with yourself.

"What's wrong with you? Are you stupid or something? Can't

you use your head?"
"It is so disgusting when you tear up that way and look like you're going to cry!"
"I feel like smacking you around when I see you angry like that!"

Later on, people who receiving this kind of mental programming can simply continue to talk to themselves in this way.

What *Dragon thoughts* do you entertain that puts you at conflict with yourself or some facet of your human experience (i.e., your human drives for safety and security, love and affection, recognition and status, power and achievement, fun and adventure, self-actualization, worship and awe, etc.)? What *ideas* do you entertain that rejects your experiences, mock you for having them, and declare them off-limits to you?

Questions like these enable us to throw our net around the Dragon. This enables us to see the Dragon and its destructive energy. We first seek to catch the Dragon so that we can then slay or tame it. Whenever we engage in negative evaluations on our own experiences and states, we seed the ground that allows all kinds of baby dragons to arise and begin running around undetected in the corridors of the mind.

For many people, even full grown, fire-breathing, life sabotaging, and misery mongering Dragons operate pretty much at unawares—totally invisible and/or misidentified.

"I don't know what comes over me when I get like that!"
"It's my Irish blood—that's what it is; we're Irish..."
"It's just a woman thing—we're more emotional than you men."
"It's a guy thing—we just like to see results and so we take hold of things and make things happen."

Some people *think* they see the Dragons that torment their lives—in others. And so they accuse and blame others for their own Dragons. Talk about a Dragon Delusion. The Dragon has really pulled the wool over those people.

"You piss me off!"
"You make me angry, depressed, upset, stressed-out, etc."
"She always puts me on a guilt trip."

This kind of languaging not only indicates that the person's Dragons are operating inside them at unawareness, but that they have also pulled a ventriloquism trick on the person as they project the Dragon out onto someone or something else.

Now many dragons do simply vanish once we turn the light on them. Expose them to the light of day and they cannot continue. Other Dragons, once we have spotted them and have thrown our linguistic net over them, become easy targets for a quick jab to the heart. Frequently, all we have to do is to Name the Dragon.

"Ah, Self-Pity! I see you!"
"Ah, the Dragon of Discounting the Good!"

In the dark, outside conscious awareness, Dragons seem ferocious, wild, untamable, and powerful. Yet once we turn on the light and see that *they exist as languaged entities* (as linguistic-semantic ideas and constructs), we can get out our Dragon-slaying sword and quickly put them out of their virtual reality misery.

2) Evaluate the Dragon

Run a *Quality Control* evaluation on your thoughts and the emotions that they produce. If that doesn't slay or tame the Dragon, it will surely put the spotlight on the *quality* of your thinking and mapping.

Previously I mentioned that our brains don't seem to have any innate quality control functions. Our brains don't seem to care what information we feed it. You feed it a "thought," an idea, a concept, data—and it will just "process" it. Brains don't seem very smart about the quality of the content that we feed it, unlike our stomach. At least the stomach has enough sense to vomit when it gets garbage. The brain doesn't seem that intelligent!

That's where *we* have to come in and take charge of the quality issues and criteria. If we don't set some standards for quality, our brains will accept and process toxic thoughts without seeming to notice. Give your brain false and erroneous ideas and it will just take it in, process it, and put your neurology into some corresponding garbage state.

So run an ecology check on the quality of your thinking. The following items provide you some of *the basic ecology checks* to run on thoughts. Use them as a checklist to determine the quality of the ideas you feed your states.

Accurate / Inaccurate:
  Does my mental mapping accord to the territory? Does it have a structure similar to the territory?
  How much precision or vagueness do I use in my languaging? Does that help or hinder? Confuse or clarify?

Useful / Unuseful:
> Even though some thoughts may correspond accurately to reality, do they truly provide a useful service?
> What value will this thought provide me? Will it enhance my life?
> Yes I felt that I had a rotten and abusive childhood, but does it do me any good to keep focusing my mental-emotional energy on it?

Cognitive Distortions:
> Have I exaggerated, personalized, awfulized, emotionalized, used black-and-white thinking, etc.?
> Have I checked for any thinking errors that might be undermining my critical thinking and reasoning skills?

Enhancing / Unenhancing:
> Does this thought or way of thinking enhance my functioning and feeling as a human being?
> Yes, five people have rejected me so far in my life, but do I give this fact enhancing or unenhancing meanings?
> As I think about any given event, do I represent it in a way that promotes my sanity, humanity, and productivity? Or does my way of representing it keep me reliving and re-feeling it and degrading my level of resourcefulness?

3) Take the Dragon's Temperature

Track back from the Dragon state to the physiological and emotional intensity of the state. How intense is the Dragon State? The *"dragon-ness"* of some states arises due to the inappropriate intensity rather than the content of the state.

The state of anger, for example, describes a perfectly healthy state. It's perfectly healthy *if* the thinking-and-feeling energies of that state relate to a displeasure that signals an injustice in your value system which needs signaling, and regarding which you can then take appropriate action. But if you anger yourself about the existence of traffic, human limitations, and injustices about which you can do nothing, you will only generate inappropriate anger and has no where to go.

For example, "I feel anger about the way he implies I'm lying." This thought and its resulting feelings might indeed represent an accurate assessment of displeasure about something you may want to address with the other person. Yet if your anger level reaches the boiling point so that when you open your mouth, you breathe fire and spit out hot retorts, you probably won't get very far with the other person. That person will more than like *not* even be able to "hear" what you've got to say. You have far too much *intensity* than you need. So, you may want to first tame that Dragon a bit by calming that Dragon with some calming thoughts.

"I dislike the implications of his tonality, but before I jump to conclusions about this, I need to check it out with him."

"It rather bothers me that he doesn't have better management over his tonality. I think I shall model a better use of tonality."

Inappropriate content and representation can, and will, create inappropriate intensity. Every cognitive distortion (Ellis, 1973) tends to generate too much physiological response and that can then lead to an out-of-control emotion. So as we track back to our physiological intensity, we can then begin to explore the various factors that increase this physiological readiness that we feel. As a result, this will typically bring up some contributing factors as our eating and exercising habits, our sleeping patterns, our relationship to "time" and scheduling, our stress level and stress management skills, lack of delegation skills, inability to politely say "No" to requests effectively, etc. Whenever we push ourselves to our limits and activate the old brain Fight/Flight responses, we can easily trigger Dragon States.

4) Name the Dragon

This is a fun one. I really like the art of *Naming the Dragon*. Doing this puts into your hands a pretty powerful Dragon exposing, slaying, and taming technology.

One man named his "problem with anger" as "The Temper Tantrum Dragon."

I thought that was great and so asked him a series of questions about the ole Temper Tantrum Dragon:

"When does this beast sneak upon you?" I asked.

"Have you ever felt this dragon breathing down your neck just prior to his attack upon you?"

"What does this beast say, that is, what dragon-talk does he spew out?"

"What can you say to this dragon that would immediately shrink him down to size so that you can put him in your back pocket and keep him well contained?" (Talk about Dragon taming!)

As he gave thought to such dragon-management questions in response to his Dragon Naming, it enabled him to develop a greater vigilance for the Dragon as it increased his own personal sense of power over it when it arose.

With this maneuver, you throw your linguistic net around the neck of the ol' Dragon. This provides you a marvelous way to contain and manage the dragon.

"Ah, the Anger Dragon!"
"The Self-Pity Dragon!"
"The Grouchy, or I-really-need-a-nap, Dragon!"

This accords with what the developers of *Narrative Therapy* have developed in that field. They describe the Naming the Dragon process as *"externalizing the problem."* White and Epstein (1990) tell of a case of a little boy who had a problem of messing in his pants. They ended up calling the problem *Sneaky Poo,* which then enabled them to ask questions about when and how Sneaky Poo would sneak up on him and how and what processes have helped, or would help, him to fight off *Sneaky Poo.*

So, in that vein:

"Ah, so Snowballing Emotions took you on another roller coaster ride this past week?"

"So Rigidity showed its appearance again after having worked so hard at keeping an open mind when in conflict?"

"And what did Sourness of Attitude tell you this time?"

Dragon Naming— try it. I think you'll like it.

5) Interrupt the Dragon

There's nothing like a *pattern interrupt* or *state interrupt* to halt a Dragon in its tracks! I have referred several times to interrupting states and developing reliable mechanisms that you can use to interrupt the states which don't serve you well.

State interrupts occur all the time. The phone rings, someone knocks on the door, a desperate thought bounces uncontrollably into your stream of consciousness, someone shifts the subject suddenly, etc. and we find ourselves in a different place. A little later we wonder, "Now where was I?" "What was I thinking?"

Given this interruptability of states, we can now put this mechanism to good use by developing some reliable state-interrupt patterns. Then, when we need to interrupt a Dragon from carrying on his Dragon business as usual, we have a way to do that.

How can we interrupt our state? Breathe deeply and count to ten. Wear a rubber band on your wrest and snap it so it stings whenever the Dragon arises. Stand on your head—few Dragons can continue when you shift your relationship to gravity. Try it out next time the Depressive Dragon or the "I'm So Bored" Dragon enters the scene. Turn around and around in one spot as you did when you were seven-years-old and do so until you become so dizzy you can't stand up. That will interrupt your state and the state of those around you! Take one hundred long, deep breaths while trying not to imagine Elvis Presley dancing with twelve wild blue monkeys.

6) Starve the Dragon

Dragons are a hungry bunch. They have a rapturous appetite. They need for lots of food just to keep them up their fierce stomping, heavy fire-breathing, and roaring. Given that, it's amazing how tame a Dragon can become when you kick away the food tray and force them on a diet. Many of them will almost immediately begin to shrivel up.

And, what do dragons use to fuel their metabolism?

> Internal representations and physiology (the two components of state, the two royal roads to state, remember?).
>
> Ideas, especially sick ones. Exaggerated emotional demonstrations—blaming, accusing, awfulizing, dramatizing that no one loves them. Toxic beliefs.

Starve your Dragons of the languaging that you have fed them. What words, statements, and ways of representing those thoughts cause your dragons to grow? For anger Dragons, use some "soft answers" and you will "turn away wrath" (as says an old proverb). For self-pity Dragons, re-languaging yourself with your response-abilities tends to tame or slay them. For stressed-out Dragons who feel burned-out, eliminating all of the "pressure" words about what you "have to" do brings about a calming effect.

Dragons most of all like to feast themselves on toxic, poisonous, and morbid thoughts. Feed your Dragons sick ways of thinking, and they'll love it and they'll expand and become quite ferocious.

"I can't stand criticism!"
"Why do bad things always happen to me?"
"This will be the end of me!"

"What she did ruined any chance I had for happiness."

As you track back the Dragon state to the "thoughts" that feed and nourish the state, you will find *Dragon Food* in the form of toxic thoughts. After all, we create our neuro-linguistic states from what we think and the way we think. This gives us two categories for quality controlling our thoughts: content and form.

Content refers to **what** we think. What Dragon thoughts inform your states?

"What ideas dominate my mind?"
"What dragon thoughts have I given free reign to?"
"What internally represented thoughts keep inducing this Dragon state?"

The thoughts you typically entertain induce your Dragons. Behind the state of fear we will always find *fear thoughts*. Behind the state of anger, you can count on *anger thoughts*; behind and within states of joy, *thoughts of joy*.

If I look at you crossing your arms across your chest and I attribute a rejection meaning, then I can use this content to go into a rejection state whenever I see someone crossing the arms. In spite of the fact that he may cross his arms to relax himself, or she crosses her arms to stop herself from biting her fingernails, or to quiet himself so that he can pay more attention while listening, etc., our *meaning attribution* about that behavior will elicit a state of feeling rejected. In this way, I can upset myself and go into a Dragon of Rejection state most inappropriately.

Form refers to *the structure of **how*** we think.

"What codings have I used to represent something that creates a Dragon-like mental or emotional state?"

How do you think about the content? Step back and notice your visual, auditory, and kinesthetic representations and instead of paying attention to *what* you have in the picture, notice the cinematic features of the picture.

How close or far have you coded the picture or sound?
How clear or fuzzy?
In three-dimensions or just as a black-and-white picture?

By checking the "submodalities" distinctions, we can often discover the qualities that actually *over-drive* the Dragon state and make our thinking out-of-proportion. The sounds may be too intense, the tones too harsh, the pictures too close, pictures right "in my face," etc. Many

Dragon states only need to be tamed by altering how we have encoded our thoughts. Look and listen then to the ideas that you are representing, the ideas that seem to bother you, and before you reframe it, examine the cinematic features. The problem may not be in the movie that you're watching at all. It may be that you are standing right at the 40-by-100 foot screen with the volume blasting at a deafening volume. You may just need to move back 20 rows.

You can also *starve your Dragon of the physiology that nourishes their morbid states.* For example, I'm sure you already know how that the depression Dragon glories in slouching shoulders, eyes zoomed in on dirt, a slow tonality, and other depressive ways of breathing, moving, talking, and acting. Victimization Dragons need a whinny little worthless tone.   Stressed out Dragons need sleep deprivation, stimulus overload, and no time for relaxation or exercise.

In one Peanuts cartoon, Charlie Brown demonstrated the physiology of depression to Peppermint Patty. Bending over with head slumping forward, he says, "This is my 'depressed stance.'"

He explained, "When you're depressed, it makes a lot of difference how you stand."

Then, lifting his head way up and looking skyward, he says, "The worst thing you can do is straighten up and hold your head high because then you'll start to feel better."

So slumping again, he says, "If you're going to get any **joy** out of being **depressed** (a meta-state!), you've got to stand like this." Lifting your head and looking upward will starve the dragon of the physiological components so important for a good state of depression.

7) Say, "On Guard, Dragon!"
And Then Put Your Sword Through the Dragon

When we discover structure, we can engage in *structural changes and transformations.* That's the purpose for exploring the sensory-based components of our internal movies (i.e., sights, sounds, and sensations) which form, order, and structure our Dragon states. As we identify the specific features or qualities of the images and sounds (the so-called "submodalities") along with the linguistic structure or meta-state frames, we then have the unique opportunity to alter the structure itself. And that's the heart of *Dragon Slaying.*

Remembering that we construct our neuro-linguistic and neuro-semantics from the various languages of the mind, we can now *unglue* these constructs. We do so by shifting the "submodality" distinctions and meta-modeling the linguistic forms of how we have languaged the Dragon into existence. Nothing will break the spell of a Dragon as robbing it of the language of its "magic."

Dragon taming and slaying excellence begins then as we backtrack to the language and languaging that we use to formulate our thinking-and-feeling *about* some primary state or experience from which the Dragon State arises. We can now begin to realize just how much *language* itself operates as a function of our personal *psycho-logics*— the logics that govern our "mind" at all of its levels. While these psycho-logics are not externally "real" and have no actual existence outside our nervous system, inside our neurology they rule. There language, representation, and information dominate as they functions as our symbolic systems for navigating the world. With words we create mental maps about the world, about the meanings of things, and about our frames of reference. The words that we use in that world create our "sense of reality," our reality strategies, and our felt experience. Yet just because we use particular words there do not mean they necessarily have some correspondence in external reality. We can use words to language things that have no actual reference anywhere.

It is by language and linguistic symbols that we make mental maps for navigating the external world. Of course, the road test for any map ultimately comes down to *testing it out* to see if it will take us where we want to go. The fact that we can create a map does not guarantee its usefulness at all. It doesn't even guarantee that any referent on the map actually exists.

What this means in practical terms is that we ought to get into the habit of *reality testing our languaged maps* about things. If, ultimately, our maps only truly serve us when they have structural similarity to the territory, then we can begin evaluating our maps in terms of structural similarity. In addition, we can evaluate them in terms of their usefulness in getting us where we want to go. Maps don't have to be perfect; they don't even have to be completely accurate, they only need to be good approximations that provide sufficient direction.

Mapping validity and usefulness becomes true with a vengeance when it comes to the *words* we use to describe *our neuro-semantic states*. Here we are mapping higher level ideas, beliefs, and concepts. Here we are mapping out our recursive and reflexive consciousness. Here the words and language forms which we use and invent as we "think" about a previous state of mind-body and track the recursive loops of our thinking only exist as symbols of our own psycho-logics. They have no real referent outside our nervous system. All such words exist only as higher level abstractions of abstractions. No wonder we can easily lose track of where we are, what we're talking about, and invent unproductive and even toxic maps. Here also our language actually does double-duty. We not only use language to map the pathways that we or others have taken in conceptualizing things, but our language also creates and generates new concepts. Our mental realities or psycho-logics are therefore highly influenced by our words. They arise as the meanings that invent along the way. It's in this way that we sometimes inadvertently create Dragon States that not only do not serve us well, but begin to make life a living hell for us.

In Neuro-Semantics we distinguish the language of primary states from the higher evaluative language of meta-states and the emergent gestalt states. In primary states most, but not all, of our words refer to things "out there," things beyond our nervous system that exist in the world of physics. We can think of these as *"world words."* These see-hear-feel words have sensory-based referents. Such language shows up as empirical and descriptive.

Now one of the neatest things that arise regarding world-words is that it's pretty hard to mis-communicate when using such language.

"This stool stands about three feet high, made of four wooden legs that culminates in a brown leather covering for a seat."

Words like these make it easy for others to internally picture. They don't even have to have ever seen anything like the particular referent. The see-hear-feel description provides symbols that we can easily take and generate a facsimile in our own "mind" that corresponds to the reality.

But what do you do in your head when I use non-descriptive evaluative words:

"There's an old ugly stool over there in the corner."
"I have a beautiful and delightful stool to sit on while presenting."

The reference of "old," "ugly," "beautiful," and "delightful" does not exist "out there" in the world. These words do not map such, they rather map the categories, classes, and ideas that I have inside my mind as part of my internal world of evaluations.

We can refer to these kinds of words then as *"mind words"* in conrast to the *world words.* And why would we do so? Doing so provides us a constant reminder of my own mental evaluations and abstractions as we engage in meaning-making about things in the world. Doing so reminds me that I'm referring to, and coming out of, my own psycho-logics: my own thinking, processing, valuing, etc. They arise as operations of my own framing, mapping, and meta-stating. And as they do not exist apart from my "mind," they lack any external or objective reality.

Words "work" as *symbols* of meanings, that is, symbols that transfer and create contexts and frames of meanings. They "work" as they enable us to represent a way of mapping things in our "minds. Words "work" for communicating (co-communing meanings back and forth between two minds) as they enable us to transfer meanings with approximate accuracy. Yet the more abstract and evaluative the words and language, the more opportunities we have for mis-communicating. With greater abstraction and higher frames we also have more opportunities to create non-referencing and non-productive semantic "realities."

NLP began in 1975 as a linguistic model when its two co-founders, Richard Bandler and John Grinder identified *twelve linguistic distinctions* that identify *map ill-formedness.* By studying and modeling the expert language skills in three world-class therapists, Virginia Satir, Fritz Perls, and Milton Erickson, they noticed the way these therapists would specifically address and challenge the ill-formed language of their clients. They noticed also that through the process of challenging the deletions, generalizations, and distortions in the client's language, the client would be enabled to create a fuller, richer, and more complete linguistic expression. This would then enrich their internal world. It would then seem almost "magical" in the way the clients would become unstuck. Suddenly various semantic pains would disappear. Suddenly they would come up with and invent more well-formed structures or maps for navigating life. And with that they would have maps for developing better skills, competencies, and resourceful states.

It all seemed so "magical." And in a way, it was. Curiously exploring and challenging the way we language our world alters the psycho-logics of our higher neuro-semantic states. And so while it may seem like "magic," Bandler and Grinder (1975, 1976) specified the *structure* of the magic. As a result, they generated a model of twelve linguistic distinctions by which we can challenge or meta-model language. The seeming "magic" in this linguistic process describes *the wonderful transformation* that occurs when we create different linguistic structures. This shows up in the transformation of our meanings.

8) Wield Your Dragon Slaying Sword With Power

I took that discursion into describing the NLP Meta-Model of language because, without doubt, it offers the greatest Dragon Slaying tool at our disposal. With the Meta-Model, you can cut into the heart of toxic Dragons and rip asunder the sick constructions that undermine your own resourcefulness.

After all, if language itself and our languaging of ideas can create and drive our positive and toxic meta-states, then when we *use the meta-model challenges* as a weapon against ill-formed ideas, we can thereby tame and/or slay tame the internal Dragon that would undermine our very sanity. You can count on the linguistic distinctions of the Meta-Model to enable you to pull apart the old unproductive, destructive, and self-torturing ideas that, left to their own devices, will self-organize our entire mind-body system for unsanity.

Now without teaching the entire Meta-Model as a linguistic process for making our language much more precise and well-formed, the following distinctions will offer you some really central *Dragon Swords* that you can use at this point.

> (For the original Meta-Model, see, *The Structure of Magic*, Bandler and Grinder, 1975 and 1976. For an expanded version of the Meta-Model, see *The Secrets of Magic* (Hall, 1998), which includes additional linguistic distinctions from Korzybski.)

Nominalizations: *Beware of turning processes or verbs into nouns or static snapshots of invariable reality.*

When we turn a process and set of actions (or verb) into a noun and treat it like a tangible "thing," we call the result a "nominalization," and the process of doing that, nominalizing a verb. Wreaking this kind of havoc on a "process" greatly distorts our understanding as it deletes the entire sense of action and movement and over-generalizes things so that we create a really ill-formed construct, a Nominalization. At that point, it looks like a Noun, sounds like a Noun, behaves in language like a Noun—but it isn't a Noun.

A good example of how a process dresses itself all up to look like a noun shows up in the phrase, "self-esteem." *Self-Esteem,* why it sounds

like a thing, a real, actual, and tangible object.
"I suffer from low self-esteem."
"My low self-esteem is getting me down. If only I had good self-esteem like John has."

When I hear that kind of nominalizing, I like to tease it out by asking, "Well, *just how low* do you feel this low self-esteem? Is it down in your thigh, or your knee?: Surely it's not all the way down to your ankle yet? Your self-esteem hasn't fallen down that low?"

I like doing that in order to humorously interrupt and confuse. And it usually works.

"What? What do you mean?"

"You said you had *low* self-esteem, I'm just wondering *how low* have you gotten."

Sometimes I will say, "That's interesting. You do know, don't you, that self-esteem does not exist?"

That always seems to get eyes to glaze over. People will stop dead in their tracks, not quite sure where I'm going to go with that one.

"Well, you've never walked out your front door and stumbled over a hunk of self-esteem, have you? People just don't leave self-esteem around like that, neither high esteem or low esteem. It just does not exist as a thing in the outside world, it only exists as a process of valuing or thinking, and so always occurs in someone's head, as someone's judgment based upon some standard. Now upon what basis do you judge yourself as having *low* value?"

Ah, nominalizations! As noun-looking and noun-sounding words, they create the false-to-fact impression that we're speaking about a real thing, as something you can point to, see, hear, touch, handle, as something that comes in various quantities. Yet these pseudo-verbs actually describe a process, a movement, an action, or as in the case of "self-esteem," it describes the mental processing of valuing. So to *"thing-ify"* (or more technically, to *reify*) refers to representing a process as if a static reality. And that, in turn, by implying something permanent, static, and unchangeable, dis-empowers us.

So we need to *de-nominalize* the nominalization of the pseudo-noun in order to recover the verb hidden deep inside. By de-nominalizing we can then point to some process and take charge of that process.

With "self-esteem," this means waking up to the fact that to **esteem** myself highly is to recognize my value as a human being. When we recode it as a verb, we recover *the process*. I experience "self-esteem" when I think in a valuing and respecting way about myself as a person. This allows us to change, alter, or stop *a process*. I can stop contempting myself and learn to esteem myself with more appreciation and respect.

Representing *processes* as if they were things misleads our thinking-emoting and so triggers inappropriate states. It builds an ill-formed idea and that then induces a sick neuro-semantic frame. No wonder we then begin to feel that we have no power over the statically-represented reality.

"I *have* low self-esteem. Therefore I must just accept it. It's what I *have*."

This illustrates the danger of turning verbs into nouns. As you therefore explore your Dragon states and expose their linguistic structures, tune your ears to hear the language forms and particularly this form of ill-formedness. You will find lots of nominalizations. Most "value" words, "state" words, etc. come wrapped up in a nominalized package.

William Glasser pioneered Reality Therapy and then later developed "Control Theory" (1983). In doing so, he adopted a very similar stance to pseudo-nouns. He said that we should phrase emotion words and most psychosomatic terms as *verbs*. As a medical doctor, he felt that after one has eliminated physiological cause for psychosomatic states, the ongoing processes that create such are best coded when we talk about them as *verbs*. As a psychiatrist, he recommends that we no longer tolerate such terms as "depression," "anger," or "guilt." He recommends that we immediately translate them into verbs: hence, depressing, angering, guilting. Accordingly, "headache" becomes headaching, "stomachache," becomes stomach-aching, panic becomes panick-ing, etc. Doing this puts *process* back into the picture.

Unspecified words: *Beware of unspecified words.*
When we talk in terms that are unspecified, it invites us into the ill-formedness of speaking too generally and in too much of fluffy language. Then what state will that induce in you? Will it not put us into a state where we experience vagueness, imprecision, and the lack of clarity? Will it not undermine our ability to speak in speciic and precise ways?

Suppose I use an unspecified verb, like "reject," "rejected," or "rejecting." I can then generate some representations of pain as I say things like:

> "I had a terrible childhood due to how my dad constantly rejected me."

Notice all of the unspecified words in that statement: "terrible," "childhood," "constantly," and "rejected." The lack of specificity shows up in the over-generalization words ("constantly," "childhood") and in the non-referencing word ("terrible"). The statement programs terribleness! It describes something full of unremitting pain.

We can challenge such non-specificity by simply *indexing* these representations by asking questions to explore the when, where, what, who, which, etc.

"How, and in what way, did your dad reject you?"
"For what?"
"Under what circumstances?"
"How often?"

Such *indexing of referents* will then bring clarity and precision out of the unenhancing generalizations. It will enable us to stop over-generalizing and drawing unresourceful abstract concepts.

Indexing the lack of specificity in this way will corner Dragons that otherwise would get magnified out of proportion. *Specificity enables us to identify and tame the Dragon.*

"My dad said he felt ashamed of me for getting into trouble at school and for not getting good grades."

"So it sounds like your dad thought that by shaming you that you would perhaps study harder and do better?"

"Yeah, he always took that negative approach."

"So he would use his own Dragon State of intimation and shame in order to try to shape you up? But you really just wanted him to understand you, validate you, and unconditionally support you."

"Right!"

"So what you experienced as 'rejecting' behavior and 'rejection' probably consisted of his 'ineffective parenting methods.'" (Ah, reframing itself also works wonders when it comes to taming Dragons!)

But as long as we represent *fluff*, it's easy to assume that our vague generalizations is reality. And doing so over time invites a Dragon to arise. Vague fluffy language, in fact, empowers our internal Dragon States as it simultaneously dis-empowers us from taking effective action in dealing with them.

Name-calling falls into this category of unspecified words—

unspecified nouns, adjectives, etc.
"I'm a loser."
What did you lose? Lose in what way? When did you lose it? When did you over-generalize from some loss and take that action as your identity?

Equation Language: *Beware of the language that generates "meaning equations."*
The Meta-Model describes the languaged constructions which equate one thing with another as a "Complex Equivalence." When we take words and equate one level of reality or abstraction (like an external behaviors, E.B.) with another level (like an internal state, value, significance, etc., I.S.) we thereby confuse and mix logical levels.

Figure 8:1

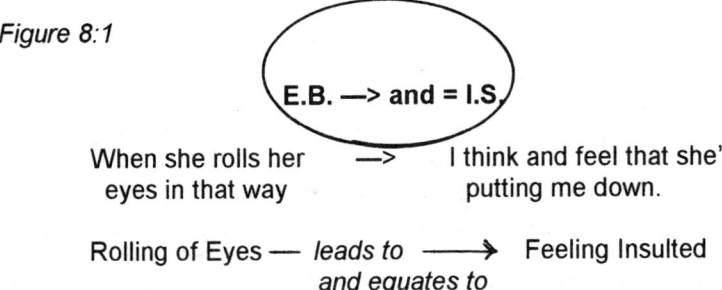

When she rolls her eyes in that way —> I think and feel that she's putting me down.

Rolling of Eyes — *leads to and equates to* ⟶ Feeling Insulted

In doing this, we have created *a meaning equation* between these levels (external happenings, internal states) so that we build a mental map that equates an external behavior (i.e., some see-hear-feel actuality) with some internal states (some emotional state). Once we do this and it becomes habitual, this way of thinking as a frame of mind gets programmed into our very mind-and-neurology. Then this *"complex equivalence"* (or meaning equation) begins to runs the show as computer software determines what shows up on a monitor. Then, regardless of how powerful, rational, or expensive the computer, if we run garbage software that has a computer virus, then the computer will compute that and output accordingly.
For example, suppose as we confuse logical levels, we create the following Dragon State based upon any of the following maps.
"His harsh tone of voice means, 'is,' or equals to the fact that he

doesn't like me."

"When he folds his arms across his chest that means he disapproves of my ideas and rejects me."

What then? Do we not need to really watch for this kind of languaging? I think so. Whenever we take some external behavior and load it with internal significance or value, we thereby create our semantic (or neuro-semantic) reality. For weal or woe, it becomes our neuro-semantic frame of reference and so our human "program" for responding to the world in thoughts-and-emotions.

When we give external stimuli *meanings* (and as humans we cannot do otherwise), we create *meaning equations* which then, in turn, *programs* us and induces us into various states. Eventually these semantic equations will drop out of conscious awareness and we will then experience the external stimuli as directly "causing" our subsequent states. States, after all, always and inevitably reflect the meanings that we attribute to things. Yet once habituation takes over, we lose awareness of this process. Then we only know that this or that event, word, experience, look, gesture, etc. *"Is"* an insult, and *"makes"* us experience the thoughts-and-feelings that we do. (This leads to *causation words* which we will discuss in the next section.)

Korzybski (1933/ 1994) repeatedly warned about the unsanity in *the "is" of identity*. This offers us yet another description of equation words. These *"to be"* verbs (i.e., is, am, are, be, being, been, was, were) most subtly sneak in identities and equations.

"He*'s* a jerk."
"Losing this job *is* terrible."
"If only she *was*n't such a nag."
"To apologize *is* to make myself look like a fool."

Since our states operate as our somatic experience of meaning (hence, semantic-states and neuro-semantic states), once we have set up some meaning equations, then we can easily, quickly, inevitably and automatically "go into state." We do so by just exposing ourselves to the external stimuli.

If to the external condition of a rainy day I give the meaning, "nasty day," "limitations on what I can do outside," "unpleasant," "uncomfortable," etc., then as this becomes internally installed so that it drops out of consciousness, I can feel bad (unpleasant, limited, nasty, etc.) quickly and automatically. What a skill! If I give it the meaning "wonderful reason for staying in and enjoying the indoors," "time to cuddle with a loved one," "time to snuggle with a good book," etc. then I can quickly and automatically go into feeling "domestic," cuddling, etc. General-semantics calls these "semantic reactions."

The emotional states that we regularly and unthinkingly access *tells about the meaning equations* at work within us. It tells about the meanings we have given to things. Recognizing this can enable us to beware of our meaning-attributions, because, ultimately, it only exists in our mind. This explains, to a great extent, why two people can experience the same event and walk away from it feeling radically different things about it. It means one thing to one person, and so induces one state. It means something else to another person, and so induces a different state. States reveal meanings.

If someone doesn't talk to me and I think, "She won't even answer me, she thinks I'm stupid," then as I internalize these meanings, I put myself into a state wherein I feel insulted and put-down. I will access a "feeling stupid" state. And yet *"stupid,"* as a non-see-hear-feel word, does not exist "out there." It only exists as a category of someone's brain. Whatever meaning we give to things, so we experience. It becomes that to us.

Causational words: *Beware of causational words which set up and create cause-effect statements.*

Words about causation present belief statements regarding *how things work in the world* (in contrast to the meaning equations that describe what things mean). Causational words include: "make," "cause," "force," "determine," "lead to," etc. "She makes me angry" functions as a mental map to explain *what* activates my emotional state of anger. It implies by presupposition (next section) that

"I don't do anything to get myself into the anger state. It just happens. It comes over me. She runs the keyboard and 'makes' me angry."

My causational statement, "Dennis makes me angry," maps the idea that "I don't have charge over myself, Dennis does. And he misuses his power when he 'makes' me angry." And, of course, I do have some responsibility— I need to stop him from making me angry! What a set of Dragon States this can evoke!

Causational words obviously describe a very powerful process. They describe a state inducing process. Yet such words operate at a much more covert level than these overt cause-effect words. The more covert way of expressing causation without just coming right out and saying something causes something else involves simply using *present tense active words*: "The sunshine feels so good today." Or use passive constructions that highlight some adjective: "We experienced a most delightful dinner last night." "John scares me." "It isn't working."

Presuppositions: *Beware of presuppositions as carriers of Dragon States.*

These refer to the silent assumptions behind our words and statements. Every sentence carries with it all kinds of loaded presuppositions, the beliefs, understandings, and perceptions that we assume as true. This means that we can sneak in all kinds of belief systems, values, world-views, understandings, etc., via presuppositions without ever having to overtly articulate them. We can imply them, assume them, and operate as if they simply exist as givens.

> "Jim and Jane recently got divorced. I expected it, after all Jim grew up in a dysfunctional alcoholic home."

What has the speaker presupposed in this statement? What has to exist as a given, or be true, in order for this statement to make sense? It presupposes that growing up in "a dysfunctional alcoholic home" (did anyone hear lots of unspecified words there?) somehow causes, determines, or fates someone to marriage problems later. It presupposes that it makes the person a victim, that he or she can't help themselves, and has no or little responsibility. A lot of presuppositions! Yet the speaker did not just come right out and say any of these things.

This is how presuppositions generally work. You can say things by presupposing them without ever actually "saying" them. I can presuppose the superiority of men over women, "This task demands a man—someone who won't get hysterical." I can presuppose that a person's past determines and controls their future. "If you had been molested as a child, you wouldn't have any self-esteem either."

"I can't listen to him when I'm upset. I just get too upset." What do these lines presuppose about the speaker? The speaker assumes that he or she just *can't* control their emotions, that the emotions predominate and that they cannot take charge of them. Limiting assumptions! (This one also includes another important linguistic distinction, the modal operator of impossibility, "can't.")

The Dragon States that we can suggest, imply, and assume by presuppositions can become every bit as destructive and devastating—

and **invisible**—due to the covert nature of presuppositions in language. "Watch out when she gets angry; you know what they say about the redheaded Irish."

What Dragon-like ideas lurk behind your languaging of yourself and others, sequestered away in presuppositions? We have to tune our ears to hear these covert messages and flush them out by "reading between the lines" and regarding the silent assumptions that make the statements feasible.

Beware of the "job" Language can do on you

As we recognize the non-reality, non-referencing, and non-productiveness of various words and language forms that we commonly use in talking, we can prevent ourselves from getting bamboozled by words. The mental mapping that we do via language can generate all kinds of unresourceful Dragon States if we do not take care in our use of language as our meta-representational system. Conversely, we learn how to effectively *challenge the linguistic constructions* we hear and utter to ourselves (our self-talk), we can take charge of our own languaging. Consequently, we can prevent various Dragon States from arising in the first place and we can slay/tame many a dragon state in the second.

Think about the Dragon State induction that someone engages in who says to a friend,

"*I'm suffering* (unspecified verb) *from depression* (nominalization) *because* (causation) *my relationship* (nominalization) *doesn't work* (causation) *very well* (unspecified) *so I feel so unmotivated these days* (causation) *so that* (causation) *my self-esteem* (nominalization) *has hit bottom* (unspecified metaphor)."

What does that one line presuppose? What state do you think it will induce?

That line could bamboozle someone into feeling like a victim, like a helpless and hopeless victim. Such bamboozling by words can then get somatized into the body in the form of ulcers, headaches, neckaches, stomachaches, fatigue, inability to concentrate, etc.—symptoms of Dragons.

9) Meta-State the Dragon

Finally, we can *meta-state Dragons*. We can induce a state of calmness and experience that resource with regard to the Dragon, We can feel acceptance about the Dragon, appreciation about the Dragon, etc. We can bring lots powerful and enhancing mind-body states to bear upon the Dragon State. When we do so, the higher resource will operate as a frame that will modulate, modify, and drive the primary state. And, whenever you meta-state a Dragon, it becomes a very different beast, sometimes a fun loving and playful Dragon.

Summary
- Some Dragons we need to just outright slay. We don't need the particular ordering of thought-and-emotion because it's toxic and morbid through and through.
- Other Dragons we can Tame and Transform into highly useful states as we balance and texture them with various resources. Doing this enriches our lives and empowers us for new adventures.
- Now that you know the ins and outs of Dragon Slaying/ Taming #101, how much closer are you to becoming a Dragon Master?
- Oh, yes, about Dragon Slapping. I did mention that in the title of this chapter. Once upon a time a young woman walked into the Institute of NLP and Neuro-Semantics in Austin Texas and saw the first edition of this book. She thought it said, "Dragon Slapping" and so asked Jeisyn Credour, the director what that meant. Well, I suppose we can Tame some Dragons with a nicely placed Slap ... and so if it has to come to that, then please feel free to engage even in *Dragon Slapping*.

Chart 1

DRAGON STATE METER FOR ANGER DRAGONS

Based on a Displeasure Continuum

Violence
Out-raged

Rage
Wrath

Fury
Ire

Anger

Indignation
Offended
Stress

Frustration
Agitated

Upset
Vexed

Irked

Dislike

Annoyed
Bothered
Peeved

Take your "mental" and "emotional" pulse by assigning a numerical value from 1 to 100 for the intensity of your state. Let 1 stand for "none" and 100 for "total."

Chart 2

DRAGON STATE METER
FOR FEAR DRAGONS

Based on an Apprehension of Danger Continuum

Utter Terror

Terror

Exaggerated Fright

Agoraphobia

Phobia

Fear

Dread

Apprehension

Negative Thoughts

Take your "mental" and "emotional" pulse by assigning a numerical value from 1 to 100 for the intensity of your state. Let 1 stand for "none" and 100 stand for "total."

Chapter 9

SEMANTIC

DRAGONS & META-DRAGONS

Meaning—the Mechanism that Feeds Dragons

Before I turn you loose to fight with Dragons, to tame, transform, and slay them (Part II), I want to prepare you for *the transformation process* itself. As you slice apart the toxic meta-states of self-contempting, Reactivity, Victimization, etc., and as you cast spells for self-esteeming and proactivity, you will be dealing with Neuro-Semantic reality.

To become a full fledged Dragon Master, you have to know how to work with the mechanisms that make transformation from Dragons to Princes possible. What are these mechanisms? What do we need to know and what skills do we need to have in order to handle neuro-semantic reality effectively? When you know that, you'll be ready to go forth and slay or tame Dragons!

Becoming a Neuro-Semantic Dragon Slayer
Consider these questions:
- What is the role or relationship between meaning and mind-body states?
- How do you describe the relationship?
- How does meaning (our semantic attribution of significance to things) induce, create, identify, and explain states?

- Where do we put "meaning" when we diagram states of mind?
- If the two royal roads to state involve mind as internal representations and body as physiology, where do we put "meaning" in the NLP model?

Figure 9:1
A Neuro-Linguistic State

State of Consciousness

The Levels of Meaning

What what does *"meaning"* mean? *"Meaning" describes the interface between mind-body.* Generally we use the term "meaning" to refer to the significance that something holds to us. It describes *a relationship between* some thing (i.e., a person, event, term, language, object) and *our full neuro-linguistic experience* of that thing.

If, in our history, we experienced school, sports, talking, hanging out with friends, a dog, fishing, a bike, etc. as fun and pleasurable, that event or thing comes to "mean" fun or pleasure to us. If we experienced pain with it, it "means" pain to us.

At the first level, meaning operates as *the association or linkage* that we have experienced between two things. The external event or behavior (E.B.) having lead to and resulted in a particular feeling, state, evaluation, or significance (I.S.) now seems connected together. In this way, our neurology (i.e., brain and nervous system) has abstracted and constructed a "meaning." In this way, we link up a stimulus with a response. Eventually we forget that how this came about and so we treat it as real and not constructed. We assume, "That's the way it is." "That's what that *is.*"

This gives us the first level or dimension of human "meaning," the meaning of association. We also talk about meaning in this way. Someone says something that we may not immediately understand, so we ask, "What are you talking about?" "What are you *referring* to?" In asking these questions, we're wanting to know what a person is using as a reference point. This allows us to know what he or she "means."

As this habituates, it streamlines so that we talk about meaning using "cause-effect" statements. "He makes me feel so good when he says those things." It's a short jump from causation meaning to equation meaning. "He *is* thoughtful."

When such "meanings" become referred repeatedly and become our mental "frame of reference," we begin using it in a more complex way than just association. We begin using it as *contextual meaning.* Now it becomes our mental system or framework, the conceptual context for our thinking and feeling. This moves us up a level. Now we have a higher frame or a meta-state and hence, "meaning" as a neuro-semantic construct.

Nor does meaning stop there. Every time we jump a level and create yet another meta-state, we set another conceptual frame. We build an entire neuro-semantic system or network of concepts. Many are nested inside of other concepts. This creates symbolic networks of connections, associations, and frameworks.

"Meaning" then does not describe merely an intellectual defining of terms, it involves much more than that. It involves the ordering of our neurological responsiveness as we take various ideas and concepts and "hold them in mind" (the literal meaning of *meaning*).

This explains why "meaning" does not exist outside of, or apart from, the human nervous system. It arises from the thinking processing, and functioning of a mind as our mind-body system encounters and relations to a word, sentence, event, person, etc. For these reasons, "meaning" is always uniquely personal, psycho-logical, and when we share meanings with others, it becomes socio-historical and cultural.

Since we never get into our car and sit on a hunk of meaning and yell at the kids, "Who left this meaning here?" *meaning* must be a mind-word. It must operate as a facet of our neuro-semantic nature. And yet while we do encounter "meaning" itself in concrete forms in the outside world, we do encounter manifestations of meaning.

Our states inevitably and prolifically manifest our meanings all the time. You can see a person's neuro-semantics if you look closely enough. After all what we encode in our "mind" by sensory representations and linguistics, eventually leak out into our lives by how we talk, what we say, how we act, what we do, etc. It pops out in our neurology and our physiology.

Sometimes we have to say to each other, "Excuse me, sir, but your *neuro-semantic state* is showing. You might want to wipe that sarcasm off your face." Or, "You might want to get rid of that bitter and hateful look before you go talk to the boss."

We do reveal our states and the ideas that we "hold in mind" (our meanings). Sometimes our mental meanings show up in psychosomatic expressions: headaches, neckaches, strained looks, blushing face, tight muscles, fast breathing, panicking, etc.

Because every state of consciousness operates as a neuro-semantic (meaning) state and carries with it not only one layer of associative meanings, but multiple layers of contextual meanings and conceptual frames, we most intimately deal with meaning, and we inescapably deal with meaning, whether in ourselves or others.

Insight Into the Meta-Stating Process

In the next couple chapters, we will first explore the Dragons of Self-Contempt and Whiny Victimization. Meanings drive and inform those states. People in those states feel put-down and defeated. They think of themselves as contemptful, worthless, and hopeless. You will find these kinds of associative meanings in them, you will also find convoluted toxic conceptual meanings in them. And when you shall cast a spell and transform them into royal states, into Self-Esteeming and Undefeatable Resilience, you will do so by transforming the meanings.

We focus on meanings here because that's what Dragons feed on. You can't have a Dragon stomping around and going berserk unless you've been feeding it its necessary dragon-food. Conversely, when you know some of the non-sense and morbid things you've been thinking and saying, the things that feed that Dragon, you thereby discover the very neuro-semantics to forbid the Dragon.

Lots of Dragon Slaying and Taming occurs from the deceptively simple process of asking questions and curiously exploring the meanings that a person has created. This has the effect of *ungluing the linguistics* and undermining the semantics that comprise the Dragons. They hate that! So be careful. Be sure you have good rapport with the Dragon. Then ask those wild and wonderful questions that untie the webs of deception and non-sense and that begin to spin the webs that will make for some empowering neuro-semantic states (i.e., self-esteeming, resilience, etc).

When we work with neuro-semantics in this way, we *meta-state* when we're getting rapport, when we're asking questions, when we're setting frames, when we making off-handed comments, when we're offering suggestions, when we embed a command, when we breathe. That's the marvel and wonder of meta-stating, you cannot *not* meta-state. It's really only a question of having sensory experience about it and mindfulness of the meanings and frames you're setting.

And as you undoubtedly know by now, the meanings you attribute to your experiences, your self, health, relationships, emotions, thoughts, history, etc., these meanings *create your reality.*

Language as the Meta-Representation System

Realizing that we are a neuro-linguistic and neuro-semantic class of life enables us to appreciate more fully *the crucial role of language* in our everyday conversations. What explains this is the fact that we code the majority of our meanings linguistically.

What we call "body" language plays a role, but not a primary role.

Yes, I know about the one-word utterance research that generated the 7%, 38%, and 55% numbers which others then mis-quoted and applied to generally to all human communications.

"One word utterances?" Yes. Dr. C.E. "Buzz" Johnson (1994) traced back the source of those statistics and discovered that they came from a 1967 study in the *Journal of Consulting Psychology* that centered around one word (get this!), "maybe."

> "Three female speakers were tape recorded saying that word while varying their tone of voices so as to communicate three different attitudes (i.e., like, neutral, and dislike) towards an imagined addressee. Then the tapes were listened to by 17 female subjects with instructions to imagine that the speaker is saying this word to another person and to judge by the tones what the speaker's attitude is towards the imaginary addressee.

So there was no direct feedback by anyone who was being addressed. ... Next black and white photographs were taken by three female models as they attempted to use facial expressions to communicate like, neutrality, and dislike towards another person. The photos were shown to the same 17 subjects with the instructions that they should be shown the pictues and at the same time hear a recording of the word 'maybe' spoke in different tones of voice." ... The conclusions from this experiment were that the facial components were strong than the vocal by the ratio of 3/2.

They integrated this study with another one and came up with the .07, .38, and .55 coefficients. That study was most expansive, they used three words to convey a positive attitude, "honey, thanks, and dear." They used three neutral words: maybe, really, oh. And three that were negative: don't, brute, and terrible.

Body language will just *not* do for conveying and transferring concepts, abstract understandings, or complex meanings. We can't easily communicate even a simple (!) idea like, "Supper will be ready at 5:00," with just facial expressions, tones and volumes, and movements. Only 7% of meaning is communicated verbally? I don't think so.

Watch any movie in a language foreign to and see how much *meaning* you pick up! Did you ever play charades with a group? So you were able to effectively communicate 93% of the meaning most efficiently, right?

It's *language* itself that encodes complex ideas and abstract understandings — beliefs, values, identifications, paradigms, etc.

Conversationally Meta-Stating Dragons & Princes

What you say to yourself *about* various facets of life will radically affect your emotions, behaviors, experiences, etc. It will determine and even create the conceptual world that you live in. And yet, so much of our internal self-languaging or self-talk occurs outside of our awareness.

This means that we humans have this unique skill of *going unconscious* so that we don't notice what and how we're talking to ourselves. That's why we often truly *do not know* how we create and maintain our Dragon States. We have come to *not* pay attention to the kinds of things we're saying to ourselves, the implications of those statements for our neurology, or the frames that they set. We only pay attention to the end result.

> "Why do I feel this way?"
> "What in the world has come over me?"
> "I don't know why I do those things. I know better than that!"
> "Why can't I get myself to do what I know?"

By *not* attending to our languaging, we lose awareness of the very mechanisms by which we make meaning of things and set frames that meta-state us into various neuro-semantic states.

Discovering Meaning

How then can we get at, discover, and alter the meanings that run, control, and induce us into various states and meta-states?

We do so primarily by going on a search for frames, meta-states, and meanings.

> "What does this mean to you?"
> "What significance do you give to that event, person, or word?"
> "How do you experience that?"
> "How do you know to think that way, to call it that?"
> "And what do you believe leads to that, causes that, or contributes to that?"

By repeatedly asking such meaning questions, we can begin to discover the world of meaning that a person lives within—the person's semantic reality.

But heed this caveat. When you ask meaning questions, people will typically *not* answer you by giving you their meaning. No. They will rather first give you *their primary feeling about the event or how they want to respond.* You can expect this. Why? Probably because our minds go to these two facets of our attention more often, and with greater ease, than it goes to the presuppositional meanings (i.e., our premises, understandings, world-view, model of the world, paradigms, and frames).

For example, we ask, "What does it mean to you that you lost that job?"

And the person says,

(1) "It means that my boss is a real jerk!"

In this case, we don't know the person's *meanings,* we only know the person's immediate judgment *about* the boss; that's not the meaning of what the job loss signifies to the person. So we may ask again. "And given that, what does it mean to you that you worked for a jerky boss

who fired you?"
(2) "It means I wish I could get back at him!"

Again, we don't have the person's meanings. This time we got a statement about an action that the guy's emotions urge him to take. So validate (or pace) him, and ask again.

"Undoubtedly you feel very angry at him and some revenge might taste sweet. You would like to respond that way. I still don't know precisely what it means to you that you have lost that job."
(3) "It means I failed at something important..."

Bingo! We finally got some real live *meaning!* Continue and you will move deeper into the person's depths.

"What does it mean if you have lost that job in terms of your 'self,' future, career?"
(4) "I wonder if there's something wrong with me."

In asking these meaning questions, we are exploring the person's over-riding paradigms, frames, or model of the world which informs him or her of the over-arching meanings, values, and significances. And it's these meaning frames that ultimately runs the person's belief systems about self, others, life, work, relationships, etc. If the response speaks *about* something beyond the skin (i.e., others, the boss, the world, history, etc.), this signals you that they have accessed and operate from a primary state. The first two responses in the example above illustrate this. But if the response speaks *about the person and his or her own states* (i.e., the person's thoughts, emotions, abstractions, etc.), then you have them describing a meta-state (e.g., the last two responses).

We can also invite people to try on new meanings. We can ask the person to go inside and give him or herself some new meaning about something. We can ask the person to stop, become quiet and see if the new meaning "takes." "And as you become quiet, listen for any part of your mind which might have an objection to the new meaning."

We can even do this with ourselves.

"I give myself permission to listen to the sound of her tonality when she gets stressed and upset and let it indicate that she's feeling insecurity, and meaning that she wants to make things better— and not meaning that she's attacking me."

When you say that, does it seem to "take" or do you sense any part of your mind raising any objections against it? Notice if you *hear* any objections, *see* any, or *feel* any.

Suppose you have built *an equation meaning* that goes, "Harsh voice and tonality involving tight throat muscles and greater than usual volume *means* rejection, hurt, verbal abuse, etc."

Now try on a different meaning.

> "Strained voice *means* the speaker feels stress, and therefore operates out of an unresourceful state. It does not say anything about myself; it refers to their state."

When we give ourselves new meanings, we give ourselves new programs or frames. And doing this provides us some new and different ways of functioning: thinking-emoting, valuing, perceiving, understanding, remembering, speaking, relating, etc. What if it doesn't "take?" What if we have internal parts which object?

We can then *use those very objections* to build into the permission a more enhancing meaning. Suppose a part objects, "This will mean only you have to change, not them." Then, "I give myself permission to think about it as their ineffective tonality so that I can then stay comfortable and centered as I ask them to take a deep breath and restate their concern. Actually, this gives me more power and options for bringing about change."

Meanings Do Not Exist as Externally "Real"

Think about the last time you might have seen, heard, felt, smelled, or tasted a hunk of "meaning" that you left laying around the house. Oh, yes, that's right, *meaning* does not exist outside of us. It's an inside job. It only occurs via the nervous system and brain of a meaning-maker.

In this sense, we could even go so far as to say, *"Nothing means anything"* and be right. In and of itself, *a priori*, nothing carries any inherent meaning. Meaning only emerges from the encounter of a thing or event with a meaning-maker. We link, associate, and then reference things, and that's how we create, discover, and invent meanings.

Then the magic occurs. Whatever meaning we give to something, it then *means that to us*. It then operates as a self-organizing frame that sets neurological processes into motion that seek to manifest or "make real" (realize) the meaning.

In this we have a means for "turning off" the old tapes that keep inducing Dragon states. We can simply begin by recognizing ourselves as *the Maker of Meaning* and that apart from our meaning-making, *events do not mean anything.*

"I give it meaning."

"The meanings I give to it creates my state."

Making this Map/Territory distinction enables us, and frees us, to search for the non-enhancing meanings by which we disempower ourselves. This explanation gives a richer sense of the terms that I've been using throughout this book, *neuro-linguistic states and neuro-semantic states.* Meaning does not occur at the empirical level nor in world-words, but at the meta-level of reasoning, interpreting, inferring, judging, believing, valuing, etc.

When it comes to our neuro-semantic states, the meanings we give and attribute to things also explains why we can or cannot access certain states. Our attributed meanings control the spells that we can and cannot cast.

For example, consider the meanings you have given to the state of "forgiveness." What does it mean to you to forgive someone who has hurt you? Many people give this idea meanings which then lock themselves out from ever experiencing it. They probably give it a meaning like: "It means letting evil triumph." "It means acquiescing." "It means not holding true to my values." "It means letting her get by with things so she doesn't learn anything from it which makes her more likely to try it again next time."

If we install those meanings in our heads, and then notice the emotions and behaviors that we then produce in our body, we can begin to get a sense of the driving influence of *meaning* in our lives. In this case, we will become a card-carrying member of the Resentful Association of Bitter Persons, Inc. (i.e., an unforgiving person, a "hurt" monger, an embittered soul). Then, all of these frames of mind would raise holy hell in objection if we asked permission to forgive.

The "meaning" anything holds determines or expresses its value to us. In this, we *value* our "meanings" and our *meanings* comprise our "values." These terms function as synonyms. Accordingly, we can say that, like meaning, nothing inherently has value. Nothing *"is"* "good" or "bad" in and of itself. These *value judgments* arise when a meaning-maker enters the scene and begins to evaluate and compare the thing against some standard. Only then can we say that something *is good or bad.* We think of something as "good" for us or "bad" for us. The "value" arises from how we compare the thing against some criteria that we have in our heads.

This explains, in part, why two or more people can experience the very same event in very different ways, give it very different meanings, value or dis-value it in different ways, and experience different states. If these high level meaning maps differ from the territory, then we are relatively free in how we *choose* to represent things and what meanings we give choose to give to things. By our meaning-making we can empower ourselves or dis-empower ourselves. There's no obligation or constraint that we have to represent things in limiting or negative ways. We can even represent a tragedy, even a devastating tragedy with many painful consequences in ways that will empower us rather than victimize us. We have *that* much freedom.

Building Layers of Meanings

Given that our self-reflexive consciousness supports our thinking and feeling almost whatever thoughts we want to think-and-feel *about* other states, we actually have the psychological power to mold and make our mental-emotional world as we so choose. We can simply move to a "meta" position and create the meta-states we desire and appoint them as our higher frames of mind. Conceptually, we can step back and up and create layers upon layers of meanings.

We can do all of these because of the *mechanism* that governs our power of reflexivity: symbols, language.

The mechanism of language arises from the magic of "arbitrary symbols." We can appoint anything to *stand for* and *represent* something else. And because we can, we can manipulate the structure, form, and content of our mental landscape.

This difference differentiates primary states of consciousness from meta-states. We access, alter, and manage our primary states via the sensory based representations that we use to "think" at that level. But to access, alter, and manage our meta-states we have to use *the meta-representational system of language itself.* This includes other symbolizations, non-linguistic symbols, e.g. mathematics, art, diagrams, etc. Again, this underscores the importance of language and the nature of language as a meta-phenomenon.

With the *word* "strawberry" we can reference and point to a sensory-based referent. The term stands apart from, outside of, and beyond the sensory-based reality (e.g., sights, sounds, smells, etc.) of strawberries.

Via our linguistic symbolic system of words, we can encode higher level concepts that we never seen, heard, tasted, felt, or smelled, or ever could. Give it a try. Taste "time." Smell "time." Feel "time." Hear "time." (If you hear a clock ticking, you hear the mechanisms of a clock, not "time.") "Time" does not exist as an empirical reality.

Try the same with "causation." Try it with any of the Kantian categories or universals: time, space, self, cause, destiny, purpose, meaning, etc. Immanuel Kant postulated that these categories or universals were *a priori* categories. Because we find these ideas universally in humans, he believed that they come built in at birth, *a prior*. In mid-twentieth century, Noam Chomsky, blew away Behaviorism and founded Transformational Grammar by showing that language acquisition and linguistic capacity has to exist *a priori*.

To negotiate such categories of mind, such high level abstractions, we are driven to use language. This explains why infants and young children do not even know that such "things" (conceptualizations) exist. Until they develop language, and especially high level abstract language, they do not and cannot fully enter into the human dimension. They will only move there after they progress from the stage of concrete thinking into the formal operations.

Dragon Meta-States

No wonder then we have to "take to us words" (and other symbol systems) *to code and recode* the more abstract understandings and beliefs. This highlights also the role that neuro-linguistics play in our experiences. As a symbol user, whenever we use ill-formed, non-referencing, toxic, and non-enhancing words, symbols, and language forms, we can and do induce ourselves into some very unresourceful states of consciousness. This should warn us against automatically assuming that all words are useful or productive symbols. *Some are not.* In fact, we have a whole host of dysfunctional words and language at our disposal for creating unnecessary Dragon States.

Alfred Korzybski (1933/ 1994) recognized *this dangerous potential for words* for inducing horrendous neuro-semantic states. In his classic work on neuro-linguistics, *Science and Sanity*, he used the Map-Territory distinction as an analogy for recognizing the true nature of words. As an architect, he said that words and language function, at best, *only as a map* of the territory. Our words do not *are not* the territory. Our words "are" not even real, but at best maps of the real.

Further, we can never say *everything* about the territory. We always leave things out. We always delete vital information. And because our maps operate self-reflexively, we can (and should) make maps about our maps. The usefulness of our maps ultimately depends on its relational and structural correlation to the territory.

Listening for the Dragon Spells
What semantic states do you typically induce with your words and languaging? Do you create an inner world of frames that brings out your best? Do you create frames that facilitates your resourcefulness? Do you find yourself better able to navigate life? All neuro-linguistics do not. Some induce Dragons.

In "taking to us words," always *Quality Control* your languaging. What language will enable me to conceptualize and format human value so that empowers people? What words can I use that will facilitate me operating with more optimism, hope, commitment, loyalty, trustworthiness, love, etc.?

Beware of the language that engenders the Self-Rejecting, Self-Contempting, Self-Blaming, Self-Disgusting, and Self-Discounting Dragons. Do you have any words that quickly casts a spell for those neuro-semantic states? Do you need to keep such language? Do you really want to directionalize your brain in that way? Suppose you used your Dragon Sword for ripping up those words and eliminating them from your vocabulary?

As a Dragon Master, you'll know how to hear the words you utter and question them.

"This traffic makes me so angry!"

Oh really? It *makes* you? You don't have a choice? Your anger isn't your own thinking-emoting response to the traffic?

Talk that way and guess what states you will induce? You'll call forth Dragons of Victimization, Powerlessness, Anger, etc.!

"She *makes me crazy* when she does that!"

"I can't stand the way he makes messes and won't clean them up..."

Linguistic awareness on this order alerts you to recognize Dragons in the making and the hypnotic trance inductions of ordinary language.

All languaging (whether in individual words, sentences, stories, parables, metaphors, gossip, etc.) **gives you the power to cast spells.**

As a symbolic system, the words you string together, the injunctions that you command, and the suggestions that you weave into your conversations always and inevitably operate hypnotically to put people into state, to generate meta-state structures, and to order mind around some spell. Make sure that yours are good ones.

In the following chapters you will get an opportunity to learn how to Tame and Slay specific Dragons and to cast new spells, spells for health and vitality, for fun and relationship, for wealth and prosperity, etc. There you will have specific opportunities to practice your and meta-stating skills for creating truly spell-binding words for casting the best spells possible.

Summary
- The *meaning making mechanism* emerges from our ability to represent experiences and grows as it reflects back onto itself, so that we can represent our representations.
- As a semantic class of life, we cannot *not* make meaning. We begin with associative meanings and then move on to the higher levels of contextual or frame meanings. These create the frame of references and frames of mind that we can then carry with us and use to order our world.
- Language predominantly governs the meta-levels of consciousness. As a meta-representational system, language moves us into a world of meaning that moves us far beyond the see-hear-feel world.
- As you now tune up your neuro-linguistic ears, you are beginning to hear *the casting of spells in your own talk and that of others*. This makes you a great Dragon Detector.
- So go forth. *"Beyond here there be Dragons."* Slay and Tame them at your command!

PART II

INTO THE FRAY

DRAGON SLAYING & TAMING

FOR FUN AND PROFIT

Having discovered the **Meta-States** model in the previous chapters, you now have all of the necessary tools for state management, for design engineering of the highest of states, and for Dragon Slaying and Taming at its best.

We now are ready to translate and implement these meta-stating skills as we practice the art of Dragon Slaying and Taming.

In the next chapters we will take on several common Dragon States that can make life a living hell. But no more. Not now that we know the Inside Story about them! Not now that we know how to jump logical levels in a single bound!

So, if you're ready, access your best Dragon Master State and let's do it. Let's face and master our Dragons, bring them under our dominion and Tame those that we can use for greater vitality and fun in life.

There's magic in "them thar hills" — magic to cast Neuro-Semantic Spell that will transform the very landscape and mind-scape of your existence.

Chapter 10

SLAYING THE SELF-CONTEMPT DRAGON & CASTING A SPELL FOR SELF-ESTEEMING

While some Dragons only need to be tamed and harnessed, there are some that just need to be slain. Killed. Knocked off. Put out of their misery. Destroyed. Defeated. That's all there is to it. We don't need them around at all.

The Self-Contempt Dragon is one such critter. He's a nasty one. This is a state of mind that dis-values, discounts, insults, and shows contempt. It's a neuro-semantic frame of disgust and disrespect that has lost the ability to appreciate, value, honor, and show respect. It needs kicked in the butt. I'm up for that, are you?

The Self-Contempting Dragon shows no respect for that high level concept that we call the *"self."* This negative semantic state operates under the delusions that if it tortures, torments, and violates everything holy and sacred about the "self" —that somehow contempting will make things better. It doesn't. I don't know anyone who's a better person, more lovable, more productive, more vigorous and energetic, healthier or saner who *contempts* his or her self. Do you?

Self-contempting only makes everyday life a living hell. It initiates some of the the most painful and distressful experiences known to human beings. People who operate by self-contempting, self-despising, self-hating, self-rejecting, self-sabotaging, self-abasing, self-negating, etc. only make their own minds less and less sane and increase the level of misery in the world.

I say, "Enough of that!"

"Self" — Highly Esteemed Or Thoroughly Despised?

We come now to address one of the most central facets and frames of our experience, our sense or mapping about ourselves as human beings, namely, *"self."* Having learned to distinguish between world-words and mind-words (description, empirical vs. evaluative), how would you classify "self?" Ah, that's right, it's a concept. It describes a non-sensory based term, hence, a mind-word. This means that our "sense of self" arises *from* (and exists as) a "concept." And as a concept, our "sense of self" exists solely as a mental abstraction, a generalization, the "thoughts" and representations that we put together and construct about our self.

Do animals and other sentient life have "selves?" Do they operate out of a self? Well, they certainly have some basic *sense* of being a living, sentient self. The more intelligent animals may even have a rudimentary self-image.

Yet what they do not have is a *self*-awareness of themselves as "selves." This *reflexivity*, in fact, distinguishes them from our "class of life." We experience ourselves as selves, as self-aware of our self-awareness. We can even get into recursive loops as we think about our self-reflexiveness and reflect on that awareness, etc. Nor do we stop there. We go on to load up our "self" with multiple definitions and concepts using even more mind-words (Figure 9:1).

This allows us to have many selves. The following offers a partial list of the many facets of our self which we represent, think about, develop various senses about, and which struggle in an uneasy alliance to find some kind of synthesis and integration.

Figure 10:1

A bodily self	A financial self
A social self	A health self
An intellectual self	A moral self
A relational self	A mechanical self
A musical self	A work, career self
A recreational self	A spiritual self
A sexual self	A male/female self

Etc.

Dragon Slaying   Chapter 10   *Slaying Self-Contempt*

We all have many thoughts, awarenesses, understandings, abstractions, etc., about all of these facets of our self. What comes to your mind when you think about your existential, ontological being-ness? Now don't blank out on me with those words, this isn't a book on hypnosis.

How do you define these facets of yourself? To which do you give the most importance? The least? Which selves do you really like? Which selves do you not like very much?

Okay, do this as a thought experiment. To discover how you think about yourself, write five to ten sentence completions on a sheet of paper for the following sentence stems:

"I am the kind of person who..."
"My father/mother says I am the kind of person who..."
"My mate/partner or lover says that I am..."
"The first five adjectives that come to mind when I think about describing myself are..."

The Self State: *Scene 1*

Charlie Brown tells Violet, "I've just been reading about the Decline and Fall of the Roman Empire."

Continuing he adds, "I've also read about the Decline of Hollywood, the Decline of Popular Music, the Decline of Family Life."

Then holding up and reading the title of other books, he continues, "The Decline of Imperialism, the Decline of Morality, and the Decline of Boxing."

In the final four he looks at her and as if to explain things, he says, "I've always been fascinated by failure!"

Now, if our self state grows and develops from our fascinations, what does this say about Charlie Brown?

The Self State: *Scene 2*

Charlie Brown looks out of the window from the school bus and thinks to himself, "So here I am being sent home from camp. Just think... wishy-washy ol' me being sent home because I'm a troublemaker... Ha! I can't believe it!"

Then with a smirk on his face, "This was the best camp experience I ever had. The girls talked about me. I got to go home early. And, best of all, I never had to clean out the grease trap!"

Did I miss it or did Charlie Brown just turn a problem, a rejection, a dismissal, into a reason to feel good about himself? This experience seemed to enable him to begin to tell a new story about himself. *The story we tell* ourselves about ourselves, about our history, our future, our style of relating, caring, etc., narrates a structure that controls the states and meta-states we get into. What stories do you use for self-definition? Where did you hear those stories? Do they serve you well? Would you like to construct a new story for yourself?

The Self State: *Scene 3*
Lucy tells Snoopy, "You know, there are times when you really bug me!"
Then she stretches out her arms and says, "But I must admit there are also times when I feel like giving you a hug..."
And so she hugs Snoopy.
Snoopy takes this information that posits two of his states as he comments about myself, "That's the way I am... bugable and hugable!"
It lies within our map making tendencies to use our experiences, especially our relational experiences with emotionally significant persons, for defining ourselves. But what if we have had far too many hurtful and unpleasant experiences? Does it make sense to give this much importance to our experiences?

The Self State: *Scene 4*
Sitting on a bench at lunch hour, Charlie Brown says, "It's stupid to just sit here and admire that little red-haired girl from a distance."
Sometimes we talk to ourselves in that kind of a way. I suppose we do it to try to work ourselves up to do something, to take some effective action on life.
Charlie Brown stands up, "It's stupid not to get up and go over and talk to her. It's really stupid. It just plain stupid."
In frame three, he questions himself: "So why don't I go over and talk to her?"
But finally sitting down, he draws this conclusion which undoubtedly functions as a Dragon state, "Because I'm stupid!"
Charlie Brown languages himself into a Dragon state. He first judges his behavior of sitting and admiring from a distance as "stupid." He then judges the behavior of not going over "stupid" — as "really stupid." Then he goes off into the next higher meta-state wherein he explains the cause-effect reason for his stupid behavior. It occurs because he

"is" a stupid person.

Perhaps this should serve as a warning against basing our self-definitions merely upon our experiences. If our "self" exists as a concept, then we have the power and choice about how to formulate that concept. And eventually, *what* and *how* we conceptualize about our self will then, in turn, affect our experiences.

The Self State: *Scene 5*

On the wall, with head resting on the palm of his hand, Charlie Brown frowns.

Lucy comments, "Discouraged again, eh, Charlie Brown? ... You know what your trouble is? The whole trouble with you is that **you're you!**"

Charlie turns to her, "Well, what in the world can I do about that?"

Lucy turns away, "I don't pretend to be able to give advice. I merely point out the trouble."

What do we do with our problematic Dragon States when they involve our definitions about who we "are," when the arise from our essential identity?

Self-Accepting and Self-Appreciating

A word about the term "self-esteeming." In an earlier work (*Meta-States*, 1995), I explained why I use "self-esteem" in the verb form, hence self-esteeming.

> "I have another reason for referring to this process as 'self-esteem*ing*.' By keeping the linguistic term in verb-form, it reminds us that we do not have to wait around helplessly like a victim, but *we can take effective action right now to start esteeming our self.* The term 'self-esteeming' reminds us that I stand responsible for giving myself 'self-esteem.'" (p. 133)

Take a look at some your self-generated self-definitions. Gauge them from 0 (for not at all) to 10 (for total):

"How *accepting* are your self-identifications?"
"How celebrative?"
"How much self-rejection, self-dislike, self-denigrating, or self-contempt do they contain?"

Meta-states of self-rejection, shame, disgrace, contempt, etc., represent some pretty horrible Dragon States. To frame oneself in that way means that you have turned your psychic energies against yourself and to thereby create internal conflict, negativism, self-sabotaging, etc.

Conversely, to meta-state yourself with acceptance, appreciation, and respect (or esteem), describes some truly powerful frames that indicate the alignment of one's psychic energies. To so meta-state yourself enables you to become even more of who and what you can become.

Esteeming your self as a human being with value, potential, importance, and lovability emerges from ideas about human beings as special and sacred beings. It grows out of beliefs and values about people. This means that your self-esteeming skills depend upon your ontology, upon your beliefs about being human. It springs directly from your beliefs, understandings, and paradigms about people and about unconditional worth or dignity.

What do you believe about these concepts? What ideas, references, and mental constructs have you grown up with, have people languaged you with, and have you concluded regarding the value and worth of persons? Unless you grew up in some greenhouse apart from the general American culture of the late Twentieth Century, or in the Western civilizations—you probably grew up with lots of ideas about *conditional* human worth. You grew up receiving lots of messages of the conditionality of your worth.

"You will be valued and esteemed **if**..."

"You will be honored **when**..."

Yet to posit human esteem as *conditional* means that we should not send self-validating, self-celebrating, self-worthing and self-esteeming messages to ourselves. First we have to "earn" the right to that, we have to "deserve" such honor. Until then, we really do not have the right to think of ourselves as a "Somebody."

I do hope that the nonsense of that mapping about human worth jumps out at you, that it feels like a slap in the face! Building a mental construct that our personal value, worth, dignity, potential, respect, etc., *depends* becoming worthy of it would mean that we cannot view a newborn baby as having any innate value or worth, We would have to view it as totally and completely worthless, having no value, no dignity. Yet who thinks that? We aren't so cruel as that. We know that even though newborns are completely useless in terms of being productive members, we unconditionally esteem them as having innate worth and dignity.

If we can do that, then what stops us from *unconditionally esteeming* ourselves? Apparently, most people already have the skill to do this. So what gets in our way?

The old programming of *thinking conditionally about human value.* That's the old frame that stops us. It's the toxic Dragon of conditionality then that we need to slay.

Okay, so how? Begin by exploring your own "conditional thoughts" about people, about worth, dignity, honor. Think of someone you highly esteem and then someone you think about contemptuously. What thoughts and beliefs drive each state? What stops you from highly esteeming the person you dislike? Do you let their *behaviors* get in the way? Their temperament? Their grumpy states?

Typically, we *confuse person with behavior.* That's what gets in our way from valuing the person. We can't see *the person;* we can only see their obnoxious behavior and we confuse that with their person. So more often than not we let something about the person's ways of thinking (i.e. valuing, believing, etc.) emoting, speaking, or behaving get in our way. Check it out.

Yet in so confusing person with behavior, *being* with *doing,* we forget that each of us is far more than any of these functions or responses. For me, this distinction also separates and sorts out two phenomena that we should never confuse, namely, *self-esteem and self-confidence.* The first (self-esteem) deals with the process of valuing ourselves as human beings, apart from our actions. The second (self-confidence) speaks about our feelings of confidence regarding the faith we have in our abilities (see Figure 9:4).

Distinguishing Our Differing Facets

Suppose we put *"person"* in the core circle of "Self" and consider that our essence as special and unique human beings. Viewing our *person* as the center core, then we would call that self by such terms as "soul, spirit, transcendent self," etc.

Then, beyond that, in the next circle around that core, we could put *our powers* or functions as persons. This would be the circle wherein we would name all of our personality powers: our four basic powers of thinking, emoting, speaking, and behaving. It is from these core functions that all of our other responses arise. These describe our powers for responding to the world and for navigating that world. And while these powers enter our definitions of ourselves, into our sense of ourselves, and yet, *we* are much more than just these powers.

From those central powers then emerges yet another circle of responses that make up yet another layer of our self-definition. In that circle, we find the peripheral selves that arise from the roles that we play and the relationships we experience—our social self, our career self, our relational self, our musical self, etc.

Figure 10:2

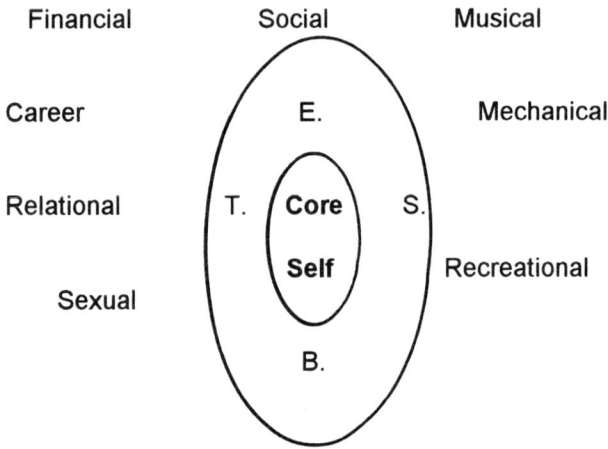

Making these distinctions in these varying levels, layers, and facets of our selves enables us to more effectively *esteem* our core existential self—and the core self of others. In so doing, we make the distinction between person and behavior. Thinking of our selves in this way assists us in *not* confusing unacceptable behaviors with a self. A self always exists as more than, and other than, his or her behaviors.

The following diagram (Figure 9:3) charts the difference between Self-Confidence and Self-Esteem as it graphs two lines over the time of our life. The first is *the lower roller-coaster line* which designates *self-confidence.* The confidence that we have in our abilities and skills is a conditional line. It moves up and down depending upon the development of our skill, our health, the circumstances of life, etc.

The second line, *the straight line* at the top that runs along at the 100% mark designates our self-worth. It registers, not so much our feelings, but our appraisal (esteem) of a human being. How much worth do we esteem a newborn baby? The self-esteem line puts the worth of an infant at 100%. Regarding that same child, in terms of personal confidence in ability to do anything, we have to mark him or her at almost 0%, hence the bottom line. After all, as newborn babies we all come into the world *incompetent* (we can't do much beyond crying, sucking, wetting our pants, etc.), *ignorant* (we don't know anything, consciousness mostly undeveloped), *inarticulate* (can't talk, can't put into words what we think-feel), *irresponsible* (can't assume personal responsibility for anything), helplessly *dependent*, etc. And yet... we highly, highly value the precious little things, do we not?

Figure 10:3

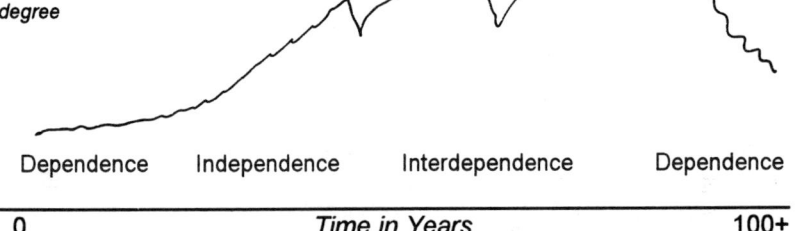

The bottom line graphs our growth from dependence into independence and interdependence through the lifespan as we become increasingly more competent, informed, intelligent, articulate, responsible, and independent. Accordingly, our confidence or faith in ourselves (that is, our skills and abilities) grow. We discover and develop new interests, skills, hobbies, etc. Of course, if you live long enough, or suffer some misfortune (i.e., illness, accidents, etc.), you may lose some or all of your confidences. The self-confidence line therefore, like a roller coaster, goes up and down, up and down. And toward the end of life, if we live long enough, can really take some steep plunges.

Self-confidence refers to your *confidence* to do, achieve, accomplish, perform, etc. It refers to the *"faith you have in your abilities"* and relates to you as a human **doing** in contrast to you as a human **being.** What confidences do you now have in your self?

The second column of self-confidence refers to facets of ourselves that come and go throughout life and facets that we can lose. This makes them temporary and transitory in nature. And whatever exists in such a temporary and transitory state can't serve as a very solid foundation, especially if we try to build self-esteem upon it. That would then make self-esteem also temporary and transitory.

Esteem-ing as a State

Now, given that the verb *"esteem"* refers to the process of making a mental appraisal about the value of something, and that ultimately, how we think about people and about our selves as human beings, lies at the heart of the meta-state of "self-esteem," then *esteeming* operates the central factor of this state.

To cultivate your self-esteem meta-stating or to improve your esteeming capacities, simply identify the ideas, concepts, and meta-level frames that support unconditional esteem of persons. Write out belief and value statements that compelling articulate supportive belief frames for seeing, recognizing, and acknowledging the innate value, dignity, and honor of persons. Once you have done that, then simply personalize your statements. Put them into first person using "I ..." and utter them about yourself.

Ready, set, go.

Okay. What thoughts did you come up with that allow you to go into a state of valuing people? What referents? What succinct and compelling language? Will those thoughts sustain your sense and feel of the innate uniqueness and sacredness of people? Will the ideas carry you through and maintain the state of valuing people even when they misbehave? What meanings empower this meta-state for you? What meanings or representations put you in a strong state of respect and appreciation for people?

Now run a checklist on your self-esteem-ing thoughts using the energizing criteria in the chapter on creating empowering meta-states. Make sure that you have built *powerful state-inducing thoughts* that will effectively enable you to access this meta-state. Let it now engulf you as a canopy of awareness as you move out into the world so that you use it as your way of "being in the world."

Did you grow up in a home where you received lots of esteeming messages about you as a person? Or did you receive lots of discounting, rejecting, and contempting messages? Did your parents or others take away permission from you to self-esteem? Many do. Some people fear it. "If you think positive thoughts about yourself, it will go to your head!" My attitude is, "Well, let's hope so!"

To check your own internal sense of permission, go inside and give yourself permission to highly value and appreciate yourself. Then stop and see what happens. Quiet yourself as you do this so that you can pay close attention to any internal responses that might emerge. Deep inside yourself say,

> "I give myself permission to esteem myself highly and unconditionally, to value myself as a person with potential and dignity."

How well does that settle inside? Does every fiber of your being seem to fully accept it and that utters a resounding, *"Yes!"*? If not, then continue this until you get that kind of celebrative response.

In doing this, also remember that when it comes to meta-states, *language drives our meta-states.* As a meta-level understanding, mere pictures, sounds, sensations (sensory-based representations) will probably not sufficiently encode this concept. This explains why you probably will not find any single image, movie, sound, music, etc., that will by itself induce you into a self-esteeming state. First, you need words. Later, you can use an image or sound to symbolize the idea of human dignity. As you find the particular language expressions that you find especially compelling for encoding this empowering idea, the language that absolutely grabs hold of your mind and sends your brain in the right direction, capture those words for your self-esteeming trance.

Figure 10:4

Self-esteem-ing	**Self-confidence** Self-Efficacy	**Self-Image**
Act of the mind/thought	Feeling of body	Overall self-definition

Based on Ideas of Self Person, Humanity, Ontology	Based on skills, abilities, experiences, learnings	Self-talk & self-images to represent Self
What one *"Is"* being	What one *"does"* one's doings	What one portrays to Self
Human Being	Human Doing	Human Representing
Declared/ Asserted Permanent/ Lasting Mental primarily	Earned/ Developed Temporary/ Transitory Emotional—Experiential Sense of Effectiveness	Created/ Represented Lasting as a thought Sense of essential Self Sense of identity

Once you have words that effectively describe some empowering meanings for self-esteeming, close your eyes. Float down ... deep inside yourself ... relaxing and finding a comfortable time and place in your memory ... when you appreciate a human being simply because he or she was and is a *human being* ... a mystery and wonder, sacred and special... and just allow your unconscious mind to pick a picture or diagram or word or something, it could be a color or sound, something that for you can now symbolize all of the rich meanings of your understandings about unconditional self-esteeming of human beingness...

Self-Confidence

Distinguishing between *being* and *doing* does not downplay the value or importance of self-confidence. Quite to the contrary. In fact, most of us take our first step to self-esteeming due to our confidences. As teenagers, we first learn to give ourselves permission to highly regard and respect ourselves because we develop some confidence in ourselves around some skill. And while this describes *conditional* self-esteeming (esteem conditioned upon a competence), it nevertheless supples us with some first experiences in self-esteeming. As we further develop, we eventually learn to esteem ourselves without conditions.

What do you do with effectiveness that you can allow induce the feelings of confidence? Begin there. Access the representations that cues your brain regarding "the ability to do" something. Notice how you represent abilities and skills. Pay attention to your internal voice which enables you to feel confidence that you can pull off the skill. Amplify and anchor those feelings.

Self-Responsibility

Self-responsibility refers to our *sense* of our response-ableness, that is, our power to make responses, and our *willingness* to accept and own our responses as our own. Low self-responsibility puts one into *"the world of reactivity."* High self-responsibility takes us into *"the world of proactivity."* Because most high self-esteeming necessitates proactivity (i.e., to value myself and others), the more we access our *power zone,* the more we can cultivate and develop our self-esteeming abilities.

Figure 10:5

World of Reactivity	World of Proactivity
S—>R World:	S-O-R world
Mood/Emotion driven	Consciousness Driven
Condition Driven	Value/Vision Driven
Things happen to me	I choose my responses to things

We all have four basic, inescapable, and undeniable *powers* which comprise our zone of power or "response"-ableness. This power zone consists of two private powers that work as one process (thinking-emoting) and two public powers (speaking and behaving). When you know fully how to center yourself in these powers and to own them, they establish the foundational powers by which you express your personality. By these powers, you also have the ability to take effective action in the world. This includes owning and taking effective action in esteeming yourself. You can mentally-and-emotionally esteem yourself; you can esteem yourself verbally and behaviorally.

At birth we all lived in the world of reactivity. Life then was all about reacting to stimuli. After a couple decades of development and growth, maturity enables us to enter the world of proactivity.

We inevitably undermine our self-esteeming abilities whenever we look outside ourselves for esteem from others, things, and experiences. Certainly, receiving esteem from others feels good. But that is not *self-esteem, it is other-*esteem. And when others esteem us, that can begin an induction into a state of feeling confirmed, validated, and valued. Use it to get the feeling, and then *do it yourself.* Use the good feelings that arise when another esteems you, but don't confuse the esteem from others for *self*-esteem. Confusing the two causes us to move through life seeking approval and validation from others instead of proactively esteeming ourselves.

Think of something that you esteem as of value and worth. Pick something small and simple, something that has innate value. Think about a newborn baby, the starry sky, a beautiful sunset. By picking something small and simple, you will be able to *get the sense and feel of valuing and attributing worth* in its most pristine and discrete sense. Step into that state fully. Amplify your representations so that you feel it twice as strong. Double that feeling again.

Then, apply all of these feelings to *yourself*... Imagine *feeling this* about who you are as a human being... And just stay with those feelings for a moment, letting them set the frame for how to think and perceive your own value, let them organize all of your other thoughts-and-feelings so that this sense of valuing becomes your frame of reference for being human... and imagine moving into the world with this glorious and sacred sense of worth.

Layers of Self in a Self-reflexive System

At the primary state level, we have thoughts-feelings *about* various objects, events, people, and ideas. Then, out of that primary experience we speak and behave as an actor. This represents *self as actor or experiencer*, $self_1$. As we do, we then develop thoughts-and-feelings about ourselves having that experience. This represents a meta-level of consciousness and so generates yet another facet of ourselves, *self as an observer of self*. $Self_2$ now has consciousness of $self_1$.

For a moment, recall an experienced that you had this week, pleasant or unpleasant. Notice that, at that time, you experienced various thoughts-and-feelings about something. As you observe that self in your memory, you have now adopted a meta-position to yourself. This now gives you a chance to see yourself in action.

How does your $self_2$ function with regard to your $self_1$?
What qualities do you bring to yourself at that higher level?
- Accepting or rejecting?
- Validating or discounting?
- Judging or perceiving?

Does your higher self treat your experiencing self with honor, dignity, kindness, appreciation?

If we want to become philosophical we can now ask, "Who observes the self that's performing at the primary level?" Well, of course, *you*. We can now ask some pseudo-questions about that. The real you? The true self? Is your observer self ($self_2$) more real than your actor $self_1$? Who now thinks-and-feels and observes *the observer self*?

Ah, the infinite regress of consciousness! We have to be careful here in our languaging or we'll created some false-to-fact loopings and recursive spirals.

These questions only arise when we fail to adequately recognize and map our *self-reflexive consciousness.* They also arise because we have not carefully distinguished the fact that we can use the same term (in this case, "self") at multiple levels and mean something different at each level. Korzybski gave a special term to this kind of term; he called it *multiordinality.*

Figure 10:6

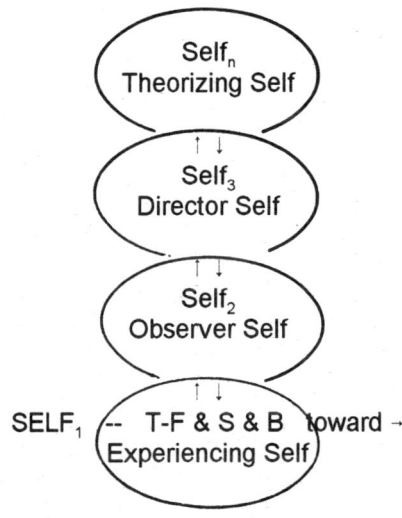

Because we have the ability to reflect on ourselves, we can always entertain thoughts-feelings *about* previous thoughts-feelings, states *about* states. Self-reflexivity allows us to keep on creating higher levels of self-awareness in an unending way. Every time we step back from ourselves to think or describe the previous level of awareness, we thereby generate yet a new level. So we construct all kinds of levels of self: $self_3$ *directs* $self_2$, who theorizes about $self_n$ who observes the experiencer self.

From the level of $self_2$ and above, if I catch myself contempting, despising, rejecting, hating, blaming, disgusting, etc., myself, *I can now decide to stop it.* I can catch this non-enhancing and non-ecological way of dealing with my reflexive awareness. Because we all face this challenge once we start thinking-feeling at meta-levels, we must choose to learn how to respond in a kind and gentle way at the meta-levels toward ourselves. If we don't, we will turn our psychic energies against ourselves, put ourselves at odds with our self, and suffer a living hell.

There's a simple way to think about all of this. Simply think about *operating each level.* When you do, then you know that at times "I'm operating at the level of awareness of the world" (my experiencing self), then there are times when "I operate at the level of awareness of myself" (self-awareness). "I can also operate at the level of choosing my thoughts and feelings" (director of self level). "I can operate at an executive level and make decisions about my life's directions and experiences" (executive level of consciousness).

Know that it is the one *you* who can and does operate at all of these different levels enriches our appreciation for the mystery and wonder of our self, does it not? In fact, the ability to step back and use your higher sense of self to observe, direct, and theorize about yourself with "eyes of appreciation," "eyes of acceptance," "eyes of value and dignity," allows you even greater skill and art in casting a spell for self-esteeming, does it not?

Sequencing Your Meta-State Strategy

There's nothing that challenges the strength and sustainability of your self-esteem frame than facing a situation of criticism, rejection, and/or failure. Yet esteeming ourselves highly in the context of insults, disrespect, manipulation, etc. are precisely *when* we most need this ability.

> How quickly can you *access a state of self-appreciation* **when** you feel disappointed about something you did or said?
> How much do you live out of a meta-state of self-esteem when things don't go well for you, when you face discouraging events, criticism, rejection, etc.?

Most of us can feel pretty good about ourselves when things are going well. When we have a good job, caring friends, money in the bank, status, reputation, a supportive family, etc., we have no problem thinking self-esteeming thoughts. But what happens when we lose our job, our spouse runs off with our best friend, we have to declare bankruptcy, our family disowns us, or we fall ill?

You have undoubtedly already begun to develop your own meta-state strategy for self-esteeming. To refresh or design you own personalized strategy, decide where you first want to send your brain as you consider the experience of recognizing, appreciating, and celebrating yourself as a human being.

I'll give you my strategy.

I first send my brain to a rich awareness of myself as a valuable human being who's dignity and value is a given. I say to myself such things as, "My worth is a given. I don't have to prove anything to anyone. I don't have to earn anything or even achieve anything in order to fully know-and-feel myself as a valid, worthwhile, valuable, and dignity-possessing human being. It's my inheritance as a member of the human race." (A_d).

The next step occurs almost simultaneously (hence a $A_d \rightarrow K_m$ synesthesia). I move my hands in front of me as if I'm miming out the boundary or territory of "my space." I think of it as my *Power Zone* wherein I get to exercise fully my powers of thinking-and-feeling, speaking, and behaving. In that zone, I think about my innate worth as my "circle of dignity and value."

This motor (kinesthetic-motor) response of miming a circle of dignity of sphere of world helps me to anchor this symbolic way to code my dignity statement. And, as I do that, I thereby access a visual constructed image (V^c) that I've colored bright blue, the blue in a bright blue Colorado sky. For me, that represents and symbolizes personal dignity, and so I live in that space.

With this **$A_d \rightarrow K_m \rightarrow V^c$ strategy** I am able to access my concepts and belief frames about *human selves* as having an innate sense of value. This meta-state allows me to then send my brain to my meta-thoughts about my own self in my many roles as I speak, act, move, and respond. I then say additional words to myself (A_d) which allow me to *comfortably accept my fallibility* (several more meta-state levels) while simultaneously giving myself permission to fully respond as I go for some of my desired outcomes regarding experiences and accomplishments that I want to achieve.

If there's a situation before me such as criticism, frustration, or the lack of success, I may then allow myself to more fully remember the feeling of confidence (K^+) in previous achievements and use that feeling to recall some visual memories (V^r). As this amplifies my sense of confidence (K^+), I then ask myself whether I think the criticism, insult, or lack of success is legitimate (A_d), and begin searching for other resources to use.

If I'm facing a dignity-denying experience wherein someone or some thing is calling my sense of worth in question or blaming me for some error, then I run another strategy. I access my sense of being *a gloriously fallible human being* with not only the right, but the inevitably of making mistakes on a daily basis. This involves refreshing the meta-state frame that "My Worth is a Given." I then remember and fully accept that all of my powers in my Power Zone are *fallible powers*. I don't have a single *infallible power* among them! (That keeps me from delusionally thinking I've got to play some "God game.")

I can then warmly and gracefully acknowledge that I'm a "response-able" person with legitimate and quite fallible powers. This allows me to accept and sometimes to even *appreciate* errors and mistakes as "errors" and "mistakes." I give it no other meaning than "feedback about what didn't work." No need to awfulize here. No need to use a mistake as "proof of being a lower-class human being." Legitimate criticism only identifies what didn't work and provides information about what to do improve upon.

Summary
- Today you can Slay the Dragon of Self-Contempt, Self-Blaming, and Self-Disgust if you want to. Get out of your comfort zone and do something radical: esteem your self of value and worth innately and unconditionally. It's just a thought.
- Have you turned your self-esteeming frame into your canopy of consciousness so that it becomes so much a part of your mental world that you just *live in that state* and have that sense of personal dignity "in your eyes," in your muscles, in the way you move through the world? Anything stopping you?

Chapter 11

SLAYING THE WHINY DRAGON THAT ACTS LIKE A VICTIM

AND CASTING A SPELL FOR RESILIENCE

Have you ever felt the *"Dragon of Feeling Like a Victim"* breathing down your neck with his hot breath?
Has it ever killed your dreams and hopes by whiny and whimpering away in some antic of your consciousness?
Are you ready to say, "Hell, No!" to that old Dragon?

You know the old *Victimizing Dragon* has been stomping around in your head when you constantly feel down, negative, stressed-out, impotent, and pessimistic. Dragons leave signs, and those are a few of the cues that you've got a meta-level state of Victimhood going on. You can also tell when people have experienced this Dragon by the songs they sing,
"If it weren't for bad luck, I'd have no luck at all!"
"My baby ran off with my best friend, then my dog bit me, then..."
People under the dominion of various *Victim Meta-States* mumble, whine, grumble, badmouth, fuss, and bitch. And they're really skilled at it. They can whine and fuss even when things are going along just fine. They can run the strategy when it's sunny and bright. What they do not demonstrate is a powerful resilient spirit of determination or guts. They don't have the spirit of, "Nothing will keep me down!"

The meta-state of *resilience,* as the ability to "jump back, recoil, sally, and withstand shock without permanent damage," shows a very different spirit from that generated by the Victim frame of mind. When you have a spirit of resilience, it empowers you to stay resourceful regardless of what happens. In the resilient state, we can even bring our own atmosphere with us so that rainy days, winter storms, and blistering heat doesn't stop us.

Resilience: *Scene 1*
Charlie Brown and Linus slump as they sit on the ground up against a fence. Linus speaks first, "Life is difficult, isn't it, Charlie Brown?"
"Yes, it is."
Then as they begin to philosophize on that fence, Charlie Brown says, "But I've developed a new philosophy." "I only dread one day at a time!"
Now that's a picture of non-resilience! There's no "eye of the tiger" motivation there. There's no bounce in the soul or fire in the heart to face whatever and to dream big bold dreams. There's no outrageous courage to resourcefully move out into the fray of life. There's just a little whimpering that comes from the Dragon who believes that life is hard.

The Spell of Resilience for Bouncing Back from Defeats
Resilience, as a meta-level frame of mind, fires us up about a bold dream and endows us with the ability to "bounce back" after misfortunes. Have you *constructed* this frame so that it serves as your program of thinking-and-feeling and responding after a set-back? Do you think of yourself as "a totally resilient person" yet? Would you like to make that part of your self-definition?
As we begin our exploration of this state, explore your own frame of mind about lying there in the dust after a set-back and about getting up and bouncing back with resilience.
> (1) *How quickly* do you spring back from set-backs? Does it take you a day, a month, three years, ten minutes?
> (2) *What* thoughts-and-feelings and physiology enable you to more easily access the state of resilience? What do you need to think, and how do you need to code that thinking in the representational systems so that it puts you into a state wherein you feel that *bounce* in your soul?
> (3) *How much* resilience do you feel you have as you move through life?

Harry Overstreet (1954) raised a crucially important question about resilience in the following statement.

> "A lack of resilience can best be understood as a lack of anything *to be resilient with* [a lack of resources]."

So, what do you have with which to respond resiliently? What states allow you to produce bouncing back behaviors and beliefs when things do not go the way you want them to?

Figure 11:1

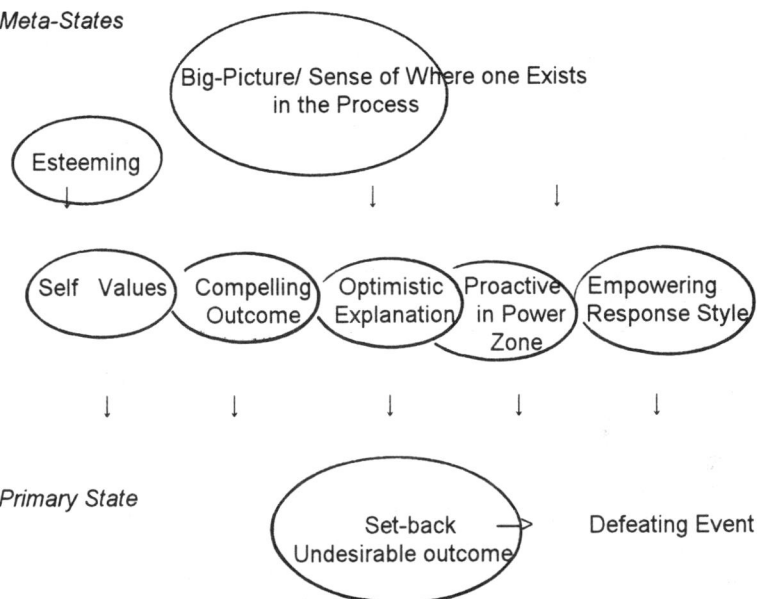

Rediscovering Resilience

Here's a thought experiment for you that will help you access the meta-state of resilience. Think about a time when you got knocked off your feet... but then, at some later time, you bounced back. You got up again. As you do this, pick out a time about which you feel proud of your resilience (ah, another meta-level frame!). You got thrown for a loop with some setback. Some obstacle blocked you and it seemed to knock the wind out of you. You felt laid low in the dust of life. But you picked yourself up, dusted yourself off, and headed right back into the fray. Go to that event in your memory.

Once you find that experience (or create it in your imagination, that is, imagine what that would be like), I want you to explore it in more depth.

> First, see what you saw then, hear what you heard, and completely feel what you felt.
>
> Notice the *qualities* ("submodalities") that characterize your pictures, sounds, and sensations of that event? Notice in detail the features of your representations that helped you in bouncing back. What things did you say to yourself? What ideas, beliefs, values, proverbs, sayings, etc. did you use?
>
> List all of the resources which supported you in bouncing back. What enabled you to get your fire renewed and your hope rekindled? How long did it take before you accepted the setback, took some action to avoid depressing, called a time-out on self-pity or simply refused to give in to such?

In a world where things can go wrong, and do frequently go wrong, where hurtful behaviors occur, and where we can suffer from mental and emotional shocks, *we really do need resilience.* For one thing, we cannot live vigorously or fully if we avoid danger and risks. And resilience describe the process whereby we can *constantly right whatever goes wrong.* This process of recuperation and ongoing renewal and self-healing provides us the confidence to take risks. After all, a healthy personality has recuperative ability and it is resilience that gives us this *ongoing ability to recover our health.*

The primary state within which resilience arises involves *a set-back, defeat, upset, or some other undesirable outcome.* This describes the context from which we bounce back. The thoughts-and-feelings that comprise this primary state involve those that recognize certain events, situations, and responses as "a set-back" or defeat to our goals, objectives, etc. When we experience such a defeat or upset, we feel it on the emotional level as a disappointment, upset, frustration or some other negative emotion.

From that state, we could obviously go into many other meta-states about it. If we used a *"pessimistic explanatory style"* in response to some "bad" thing occurring, we would use such circumstances to think-feel defeated, destroyed ("I'm ruined!") and use it to engage in self-contempting, etc. We could anger and rage over it, we could feel embitter and resentful about it and set out to get revenge from someone or something, we could hate it, headache ourselves over it, whiny and moan, etc. We have a lot of choices ... if we want to "go negative" and to generate a Whiny, Bitchy, Hateful, Resentful Victim-like Dragon. We could Awfulize. We could pound our fist against the fabric of Reality and Demand that God or Somebody up there stop tormenting us and just let us have our way!

Or, we could opt for the resilience strategy.

Building the Induction for Resilience

As a generic overview of the structure and strategy of resilience, *Figure 10:1,* tracks some of the general steps and stages in the process of being up a set of higher frames of mind to put *resilience* into the very canopy of your consciousness. You can now customize it for yourself by adding in whatever other specific states (of beliefs, values, understandings, decisions, etc.) that will facilitate your experience of resilience. I offer what follows as some potential beginning places.

Self-Esteeming

Unless you already have *self-esteeming* as a permanent fixture in the higher levels of your mind, be sure to access and bring *esteeming your self* to bear on your primary state of setbacks and defeats. "Bounceback power" in life easily emerges when you know in your bones that *nothing, but nothing can call your dignity and worth into question.* So be sure to get that one well-ingrained into your muscle memory.

If you do not stay centered in your value as a person, you are likely to fall victim to the *Self-Contempting Dragon* and "pee" all over yourself with the *three Ps* of Seligman's "Learned Helplessness" (1975) model. You do know about those three Ps, do you not?

        Personal — It's about *me!*
        Permanent — It's going to last *forever!*
        Pervasive — It affects *everything!*

Think that way, appraise the meaning of distress events with those frames, and you'll create some real Dragon States. But I'm getting ahead of myself. I'll come back to that in a couple pages.

Defeating, frustrating, and upsetting events will powerfully tempt and seduce you to call your value and dignity as a person into question, if you don't have self-esteeming well installed in your mind. Do you want to do that? Then get back to the previous chapter and make sure you have that one set as an empowering frame. When you can "fly into a *self-esteeming"* state at the snap of a figure, then you can feel confident that you will avoid taking any "bad" event *personally* and then falling into the pit of thinking of your self as contemptful.

The meta-state of *self-esteeming,* in fact, will inoculate you from letting a defeating experience "define" you or question your worth, value, dignity, future, potentiality, confidence, etc. Whenever we "identify with" a setback, we create a major problem for ourselves. We load up that event with negative meanings about ourselves and this casts the spell for the Self-Contempting Dragon.

But once we know that the event does **not** have to define us, then we can bounce-back quicker and more efficiently. If we get our "identity" tied up in the setback, it will take a much longer time because then we have to disentangle our identity from the event and sometimes people spend years attempting to do that. So *dis-identify* from the beginning.

People who suffer the ravages of divorce frequently do this to themselves. They start to define themselves by their experience.

"I am a divorcee."
"I'm an alcoholic."
"I'm a thief."

Any time we take a behavior and use it to define us or have "the last word about ourselves," we engage in the unsanity of *identification.* That makes a major mistake. You *are* so much more than any self-definition you can invent. And you *are* so much more than anything you think, feel, or experience. You "are" not your behavior. Your behavior simply manifests some of the ways you can and have acted in given circumstances upon given occasions when you experienced some state. Don't over-invest your conceptual definitions of being-ness in behaviors or events.

Centering Yourself in Your Values and Visions

Here's another set of resourceful states to access and center yourself in. When you've experienced a setback, then immediately re-focus on your highest values and visions. Keep them before you in a clear and unmistakable way.

Suppose the setback or defeat puts you down in the dirt flat on your face. At that moment some of the most important questions that we can ask concern the status of your visions and values.

Has the setback affected, destroyed, or dampened your vision?

Do you still have a clear vision of some of your desired goals and outcomes?
Has the upset fragmented your hopes and dreams?

To the extent that you lose your visions, dreams, desired outcomes, values, etc., to that extent you will find bouncing back extremely difficult. To be visionless and without a sense of the importance of yourself, your life, your energies, etc., is to give in to the disorganizing effect of having no direction or purpose.

What does this mean? It means that the intensity, focus, purity, and clarity of our values and visions crucially affect our power to bounce back. These are the very things that put fire into our heart and steel into our backbone. This means that we empower ourselves by esteeming our values and visions and staying centered. This gives us staying power and the spirit of resilience.

- *What* values and visions have you commissioned to run your life?
- What meanings and purposes could you commission to become your guiding principles?
- What holds significance to you?
- What new passions would you like to develop and identify with?
- *What* grand vision pulls you out of bed every morning?
- Do you have a big enough of a "Why" you're doing what you're doing?

A Compelling Outcome State

Once you highly esteem your self and the importance of having a great big why that you've encoded as your values and visions, then you're ready to do something about it. You're ready to commission these values as your designated *outcome state.*

How clear do you feel, right now, about your values and visions in life?

If something pulled the rug out from under you tomorrow, do you have *a compelling vision* of your future regarding the kind of person you want to become, the kind of experiences you want to have, and the kind of achievements you want to accomplish?

An old proverb says, "Where there is no vision, the people perish." If you get knocked down, and you have weak values and vision, you may have no vision with enough power to pull you up. You would then become a prime target for the Whiny Victimization Dragon to get you. Is that what you want?

I'm glad you said, "Hell, no!" Okay, then go to work and make your values and visions so compelling that you can't wait to get up in the morning. Do you have outcomes that compelling right now? Visualize the contributions you'll make, the differences you effect, and the achievements you accomplish.

> What do you need to do to develop an absolutely compelling set of outcomes?
>
> What vision compels you so much that you can feel it pulling on you and pushing you into your future?

Truly resilient people know how to *use their meaning-making powers* to formulate and design an attractive future. Now that you know about setting higher frames of mind by meta-stating yourself with ideas and feelings, just begin to pick a set of *vital* meanings that you want to install as part of your higher mind. Choose the meanings that you can use to revitalize yourself. Make this your test: Do you have vital enough meanings to pull you out of bed in the morning in wide-eyed anticipation of the day?

Vital meanings can invigorate out outcomes and make them highly compelling, compelling enough to put *bounce* into our souls. When that happens, we are able to bounce-back after set-backs.

Viktor Frankl demonstrated a marvelous resilience in a German concentration camp and later lived to tell his story in his book, *"Man's Search For Meaning"* (1953). He refused to let the pain, defeat, humiliation, and insult of that experience poison his spirit. There he discovered, what he called "the ultimate human freedom," the freedom to always choose his response. No matter what they do to me, he said, "I refuse to hate them." By so centering himself in his values, he created a vision of his future (of life beyond the death camp), a vision that empowered him with a reason to live.

With a strong compelling outcome state pulling on him, he could ask himself the kind of questions that allowed him to focus effectively:

> What one effective action can I take right now, in this place, that will assist me—even in the smallest way—to move in that direction?"

If you read his story, you will discover a lot of the little everyday things that he did that enabled him to maintain his sanity and his dignity.

In the concentration camp he discovered humor, civilization, humanity, compassion, etc. I think you will find his story an amazing tribute to the spirit of resilience. Now, what is the situation that you need to face and deal with?

Now most of us don't need to develop *that much* resilience. We don't need to bounce back from a four year stint in a concentration camp. But we do have other setbacks and traumas that we need to bounce back from. Name yours.

> Now imagine, as a thought experiment, what life would look like and feel like if you made a complete bounce back...

When I recall those times and events that have knocked the props out from under me, when I landed flat on my face in the mud, the resilience factor that always got me up and going again inevitably involved **a renewed vision.** Whether that vision reappeared immediately or whether it took several months to rebuild, I didn't experience the power to bounce until I renewed my dreams about the kind of person I wanted to become, the kind of experiences I wanted to have, and the kind of achievements I wanted to create and contribute.

When I did, then I felt renewed. That's how it works.

If our goals and objectives fuel our bounce-back power, then we should *Quality Control* our desired outcomes and make sure we have well-formed and compelling outcomes pulling on us. Do they provide a big and compelling enough vision to keep pulling on you in the face of obstacles, set-backs, upsets, etc.? If not, how do you need to energize your thoughts to make them truly *dynamic ideas?* Do that and the Floundering and Wallowing in the Dirt Dragon won't get you.

An Optimistic Explanatory Style

An optimistic explanatory style refers to the style we use when we *explain* the source, nature, and meaning of something. How do you explain things when "bad" events happen to you? *Whatever* you do mentally with regard to your explanations determines the states and/or Dragons that you will create for yourself.

> Adversity alone does not "make" us victims or victors, depressed, or joyous. Such creation lies in our *explanation* of adversity.

This makes our *explanatory style* crucially important. To our glory we always seek to understand things, search for causes, the nature of things, the significance they hold, etc. Problems arise with this when we *jump to unenhancing conclusions.* Problems arise when we rashly create irrational, unrealistic, distorted, dis-empowering, or just plain stupid explanations. To the extent these explanations become *our style of thinking,* our frame of reference— to that extent they also become our perceptual grid for seeing the world and so operate as ourMeta-Program.

Because the nature of our human consciousness inevitably and inescapably seeks to understand things in terms of cause, reason, source, meaning, destiny, etc., we are forever searching for explanations. Hence:

Searching Exploratory Questions	Domain of Understanding
Why did this happen?	Purpose / Design
	Good / Bad
Why did this happen to me?	Bad, Inadequate / Test
What is the source of this?	Personal / External
	Interactional, Other Factors
How long will this last?	Permanent / Temporary
How significant is this?	Pervasive / Contextual
How shall I judge this?	Horrible / Curable
What significance does this hold?	

The Pessimistic Explanatory Style

This style attaches pessimistic meanings to the occurrence of "bad" things. This frame of reference interprets events as:
- *Permanent* in time (hence unchangeable, insoluble, insurmountable)
- *Pervasive* in space (hence effecting everything and undermining every facet of life) and
- *Personal* in source (hence positing the problem with the self).

Using this frame of mind (or meta-state) we see ourselves as inadequate, deficient, lacking, selfish, mean, criminal, etc., which, in turn, then creates disempowerment and non-resilience. It calls forth several fire-breathing Dragons: Depression, Passivity, Reactive Suicidal Thinking, Despair, Victimization, etc.

The Optimistic Explanatory Style
Conversely, this style creates a very different focus. With it we attach neural or even positive and bright meanings when "bad" things happen. It's not that we get off on "bad" things, it's that we see it setbacks in a very different light. We interpret such events as
- *Temporary* in time,
- *Specific* in space, referencing a particular person, situation, moment, etc. and
- *External* in source.

We frame the problem as having more to do with the environment, our behavior, some response, etc., and not as an ontological problem about ourselves or the world. This style thereby prevents us from over-generalizing and coloring dark the future, life, ourselves, or another. By making such distinctions, we perceive what happened as occurring at a specific time, in a specific situation, involving specific people, etc. As it thus indexes the "evil," it contains it. This prevents it from spilling over onto everything else.

> How do you language yourself when adversity comes your way? What do you say about the difficulty? About yourself? About your potential? About life? About God? About people?

The more you know and recognize your own non-resilient thinking and believing about such things, the more you can do something about them. Non-resilient thinking and believing create and induce non-resilient states, and thereby cast a spell for a Dragon. Awareness of this enables us to put the spotlight on the Dragon and to use our Dragon Slaying and Taming Meta-Model sword to rip through the web of lies and unresourcefulness.

What old lines do you have to fight and slay in order to live resiliently? "Life sucks." "Why do bad things always happen to me?" "Life is so hard." Name the dragon-food that feeds your non-resilience dragon.

I think about the series of "Rocky" Movies as providing some powerful metaphors about resilience, about getting an "eye of a tiger" motivation to keep bouncing back. The Stallone Movies of "Rocky" portray part of his resilience by the gentle way he had of verbally responding when provocative, insulting, and frustrating things occurred. Years ago, I even prescribed *"Rocky I and II"* as models for anger control.

In *"Rocky II,"* Rocky's damaged eye prevented him from getting back to the ring. It forced him out to look for some new kind of career. But then, as one attempt after another didn't work out, he finally got Mick to hire him to clean up after the other boxers, and to carry the spit buckets. When a boxer bumped into Rocky Balboa, Rocky said, "Opps."

"Is that the toughest word you can say?" the guy insultingly shot back at him?

No response.

Rocky assertively fogged the guys despising attitude and his antagonistic "come on" to return with some of his own "tough talk" (i.e. to use crude, degrading, cussing language).

Talking "tough" with strong, evocative, insulting, degrading, etc., words may give a person an immediate relief, but *it inevitably creates a pseudo-sense of empowerment*! Damning people, events, drivers, inanimate objects, etc., only gets our nervous system boiling and fuming. If it provides any secondary benefits like intimidating someone so that they cower before your gruff style, it does so at the cost of your own centeredness, stability, and empowerment. The signals that your brain gets from such "tough" talk only gives you hysterical semantic-reactions.

In view of that, what *re-languaging* can we create or invent that would enable us to use *the optimistic explanatory style* to induce us into a more resilient state? What statements can you come up with that would help you *put the best possible interpretation on things*? Or what statements would enable you to frame problems as solvable?

Coming up with such statements will essentially provide you *the language of resilience.* Then, with that neuro-linguistic power (the power of your talk, of your languaging) you will be able to reprogram your neuro-linguistics and set the kind of frames that will keep you resilient and powerful. I've done this for myself. Here's some of the re-languaging that I use in my strategy:

"Putting the best possible interpretation on the events of my life keeps me positively focused and oriented."

"I will keep focused on my desired outcome and my dreams

even when setbacks occur. I refuse to lose my Vision!"
"I accept and welcome difficulties in my life. Just because I find something difficult gives me no reason to resent it or hate it. Excellence usually rises from such challenges."
"Staying solution focused and outcome-focused will always keep me in the running, attract creative people and ideas, and make for resilience."
"I refuse to allow myself to wallow in self-pity or to wimp out."
"I have learned, and will continue to learn, how to use setbacks to my advantage, as stepping stones to some greater opportunity."
"I will ask myself, 'How can I use this defeat positively?' 'What can I learn from it?'"

Proactive Response-ableness

Knowing that we have the *ability to respond* (response-able) a particularly resource state of mind and emotion. By recognizing my inherent powers and then owning, accepting, and claiming them, we can step into our own personal *"power zone."* This *zone* comprises that area wherein we have the *ability* (or power) to make a wide range of responses. It makes up our ability to choose our responses as we take control of our thinking, emoting, speaking, and behaving responses. Recognizing and defining ourselves as a response-empowered persons enable us to become *proactive,* rather than whiny victims. Traumatic experiences may tempt us to re-define ourselves as helpless, unable to do anything about our situation, victims, etc., but that only feeds and engenders Dragons.

This kind of thinking-feeling inoculates us from adopting a victim identity. Viktor Frankl used it in the concentration camp. It induces the state of proactive responsiveness that has this attitude:

"I can always do something, always take some effective action. Things have not become so hopeless that I have no choices left about how to respond."

Take a moment to write out an induction for yourself, one that would evoke a strong proactive state. The following gives you a taste of what I wrote for myself:

"I accept with celebration as I recognize myself as totally responsible for my happiness and my misery. I hold no one else accountable for my emotions. I therefore take proactive action each and every day in my life."

What do you need to say to yourself that will slay or tame any Dragon Victim thoughts in yourself? What symbol will you either invent or discover to represent this concept?

Empowering Response Style

Given that we each have a power zone and can own and claim it, we can now also use it to induce ourselves into another resourceful state that supports staying resilient. We can also bring to bear on our setbacks a state wherein we *respond effectively.*

What comprises an empowering response style? What describes a style of response that puts or keeps *"bounce" in our soul* so that we don't stay down? The following provides a short but crucial list of responses that enable us to bounce-back from defeats. To improve your ability to respond in an empowered way to adversity, conflict, difficulty, set-backs, upsets, etc., which of these responses would make a significant difference in your ability to master things?

1) A good relationship to failing. The ability to use as "feedback" positively.
2) Healthy nurturing relationships.
3) Kind toughness: the ego strength to look reality in the face without blinking, fainting or whining!
4) Flexibility: the ability to adapt, adjust, change.
5) Reality receptivity: good "uptime" skills which refers to the ability to go into sensory awareness of reality.
6) Living in the present "now" and not stuck in past or future.
7) Self-disciplined: able to give self instructions and follow through.
8) An accepting style: accept what exists as existing.
9) Forgiveness: the ability to release, forgive, keep your own spirit sweet.
10) Conflict Resolution skills so that we're not put off by differences or conflict, but can deal with conflict constructively and effectively.

A Meta-Awareness of the Big Picture

Resilient people seem to have another thing going for them. They seem to operate from a larger level perspective that allows them to know what's going on and where they are in the process. This seems essential in staying resilient. We must maintain *an ongoing sense of where we stand in respect to our long-term vision and my day-by-day position in moving toward that goal.* This further enables us to keep perceptive especially during set-backs and defeats. Then we won't give up our visions. Otherwise, we could lose track, get caught up in the details or the pain of disagrace. The ability to step back from things and to transcend the current ups-and-downs of problems and challenges, enables us to keep focused, up, and renewed. This also prevents us from getting caught up in short-term thinking about things.

To develop a sense of the big picture, we need to step back so that we can keep track of all of the frames of mind, meta-states, resources, etc. that we can use. It means being able to keep track of ourselves in the process and to know that there will be ups-and-downs in the recovery process. Without this meta-awareness, we could otherwise easily get caught up in the problems of the set-back and give it too much importance. We might even become confused and seduced into questioning our ability to survive or our worth. A meta-awareness of where we stand in the process enables us to stay aware of our long-term goals. Then we can think more strategically.

Take a moment to identify your big picture. Language this big picture in compelling words that attract you toward it. Keeping perspective includes awareness of the terrible price you would pay if you don't stay resilient. What would happen if you fail to develop resilience? What consequences would you suffer in terms of health, relationships, career, etc.? What ideas do you entertain that weaken your resolve? That makes you feel like a victim?

Summary

- Slap the face of the old Whiny Self-Pity Dragon with a firm fist of Resilience. Let it know that you mean business. Let that Dragon know that you won't tolerate its nasty whiny little minded attitude. Tell it where to go.
- Now that you know that you can exchange feeling defeated (non-resilience) for feeling un-defeatable, step right up into that state of mind. Build and install the pieces and components that you need for an outrageous and ferocious state of resilience.

Chapter 12

SLAYING THE DRAGONS OF REACTIVITY & DEFENSIVENESS

AND CASTING A SPELL FOR PROACTIVITY

- Do you ever get into *reactive* states and just go off on something?
- How *reactive* are you in your thinking, feeling, judging, speaking, etc. in everyday life?
- How often do you go into defensive states?
- Do you become reactionary when you feel defensive?
- Can you easily take an insult or hurt?
- How skilled are you in taking things personal?

If you want to see a Neuro-Semantic Dragon, just catch someone in a state of *reactivity or defensiveness*. Talk about two Dragon States that afflict the human soul and tear up relationships! And yet these states are so natural.

Reactivity and defensiveness describe a very vital part of our neurological equipment. Arising from the General Arousal Syndrome or Fight/Flight Syndrome, these states describe basic operation of our neurology. Whenever we face (or think we face) a threat or danger, this general functioning of the human nervous system enables us to cope. The *arousal* system activates our lower or more primitive brain so that it gains ascendency and takes over. And it's a great energy system.

Fight/Flight responses occur whenever we use our neuro-linguistics skills to "think" about things. And when semantically we represent something as *threatening* or *overloading* of our resources, boom! we immediately pop into Fight or Fight responses. The Dragons then arise and sometimes, they are just the resource we need.

That we all can easily go into these survival states of reactivity and defensiveness tells about some of our basic wiring. To go there, all you have to do is entertain a simple signal to your brain. Just signal your higher cortex, **"Danger!"** And that will do it. Suddenly blood is withdrawn from your cortex and stomach and sent to your larger muscle groups and you're off an running ... or fighting ... or both.

Send any message of "danger" to your brain be it physical danger, psychological danger, financial danger, self-esteem danger, relational danger, etc., and your brain knows what to do. It shifts control to the thalamus and at that point it doesn't know any better than to *activate all of your fight/flight responses.* And so it does. It lets loose a dose of adrenalin for **total activation of all defenses.** When that happens, your autonomic nervous system withdraws blood from your brain and stomach because you don't need or have time to engage in finer discernments or for digesting your meal. You need quick and immediate energy in your larger muscle groups. It's time to *survive*, not eat or think!

Do you know the physiological signs that indicate these *survival states?* Most of us do. The heart pounds faster, the lungs pump harder, the skin sweats, eyes dilate, and we feel our stomach doing somersaults. And more often than not, three hours later we say things like, "Now I know what I should have said to him!" Muscles tighten in fight/flight; we think in black-and-white patterns, etc. These are some of the more obvious signs of the general arousal syndrome.

At such moments we become highly reactive and defensive. We feel the Fight/Flight emotions in terms of fear and anger. And, most of us have a preferred emotion and hence direction of response. Some prefer anger and aggression; others preferred fear and avoidance or freezing. If we prefer to **go at** *the stressors* and dangers, we develop a more aggressive style. If we prefer to **go away from** *the stressors,* we adopt a more passive style. Yet they both arise from the same source— we feel threatened and insecure. So we engage in these responses to regain more of a sense of security and control. Ah, yes, these Dragons do operate to achieve some *positive intentions.*

As fight and flight, passive and aggressive responses describe different emotional responses to insecurity, we experience them, at the level of conscious awareness, in terms of the twin emotions: *anger and fear.* Yet both anger and fear arise from the same underlying sense of danger, threat, and insecurity.

This explains why we so naturally and easily go into states of reactivity and defensiveness. Anger-fear drives those with the aggressive style into the fight mode; they try to emotionally cope with their stressors by "going at" them. Fear-anger drives those with the passive style into the flight mode as they try to emotionally cope with their stressors by avoiding them, "going away from" them, escaping them, etc. (I have written about these in *Speak Up, Speak Clear, Speak Kind* (1987) and in *Fight/Flight Responses in Human Responding and Communicating.*)

We really should not classify people as strictly "passives" or "aggressors." That over-simplifies things in a way that creates more confusion than clarity. The Fight/Flight arousal syndrome in our bodies operates in a much more complex way than that. Actually we either experience the reactive and defensive state as **anger-fear** or as **fear-anger.** This means that for the aggressive group beneath their awareness of anger we'll find fears—fears that they often deny, repress, and refuse to know. This means that for the passive group, beneath their awareness of fear we'll find angers—angers that they don't want to know about, own, or register.

All of this depends upon our preferred direction. The aggressive style moves one to go at things, to confront, make demand, intimidate etc. And they do so until they run out of that kind of "coping." At that point the person then typically flips. They flip to the other side of the anger-fear continuum, that is, to the fear (or move away from) side. We then see those persons responding in an aggressive-passive way.

The passive style moves one away from things, and so these people avoid, deny, placate, and please, etc. And they do so until they run out of their way of "coping." At that point, they flip. They will then flip to the anger (or go at) side and begin to respond in passive-aggressive ways. The only difference between these two styles involves the timing or sequencing. One person first moves "away from," and later in a "go at it" way; the other does the sequence in reverse.

We activate and "fly into the reactive/defensive states" by sending our brain one of two messages—we send *either a threat/danger message or an overload message.* This means that a message of

"Threat!" can and will send us into these states. It also means that we can fly into reactivity by sending a message of *"Overload! Too Much! Enough!"* Linguistically we encode that message by saying things like: "I've got this to do, and that, and that!" "I can't get all this done. It's too much! I feel overloaded." When the brain hears all of that, it reads it as a call for the emergency state, of "Immediately Rush Adrenal!" and so it responds.

Untrained, undeveloped, and unschooled, our nervous system enables us to access these Reactivity and Defensiveness states all too quickly and easily. It can even become automatic to various triggers. When that happens, we experience what we commonly call *"Buttons."* All of us come equipped with this neurological equipment so that we can develop this skill. Watch a frustrated infant! And we have this to our benefit. For *when we face a true physical danger*, we need that kind of survival and emergency energy. Then we can fight or flee!

Only later does *consciousness* comes. This explains why we come into the world equipped to be reactive and defensive. These comprise our first and basic coping mechanisms. And for awhile, we have no other mechanism for coping. Consciousness does not develop to a sufficient degree for quite some time. Even at six years of age, or nine, or even fifty(!), we can see children still living in highly reactive and defensive ways.

"But mom, I had to hit her—she stuck her tongue out at me!"

"But officer, he had it coming to him. He insulted my mother!"

At this stage, there's just not enough consciousness to manage the state of affairs. Later, however, if we train, order, discipline, and develop consciousness, and learn how to *live consciously* do we find that we can actually access states of reason, intelligence, wisdom, patience, self-management, understanding, empathy, etc. *in the midst of emotional stress and distress.* That takes some doing. Then we can learn assertive responses in the place of passive/aggressive responses.

Dragon Checking

So, *how much of a Dragon* do you find Reactivity and Defensiveness in your life?

Given the inherent value of these states in the right occasions, we will not want to Slay these Dragons. No. We will only want to Tame them and transform them so that they can do us service when we need to call upon them.

Further, as we learn to fully activate and use the mechanism that drives the higher states of proactivity and un-insultability, namely, mindfulness or *awareness or consciousness,* we will then be able to control the messages that we send our brain. Then we will not falsely signal the brain "Danger" or "Overload" when there are no actual *physical* dangers present. And as you have probably already guessed, as we *secure ourselves* in the knowledge of our own worth, value, etc., we create a psychological sense of security. Our brain instead receives messages of calm confidence:

> "I can handle this. I can use my powers of thinking, feeling, languaging, etc. This only represents a mental or psychological stress."

When we can do that, we can then access a presence-of-mind state so that we can use clarity of understanding, intelligence of thinking and discovering, etc. for coping rather than the Fight/Flight response. .

Figure 12:1
Meta-States Resources / Higher Frames of Mind

> Clear and Compelling Outcome
> Consequential Thinking: Able to think Long-Term
> Knowledge about Steps & Stages for coping
> Presence of Mind — Sense of Choice
> Self-Definition as Proactive person
> Ready Access to Calming Oneself
> Ownership of One's Power Zone
> Self-Esteeming: Centered; Non-Personalizing

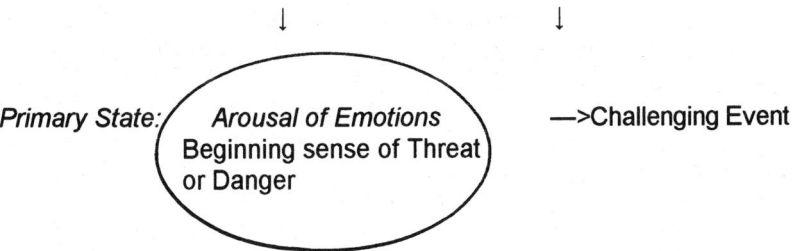

Primary State: Arousal of Emotions   —>Challenging Event
                Beginning sense of Threat
                or Danger

The State of Proactivity

Proactivity refers to the thinking-feeling, valuing, choosing, etc., *prior* to taking action so that we think *about* our thinking-and-feeling, our speaking, and behaving before and during our responses to stress. Fight/Flight which drives reactive defensiveness eliminates thinking and so puts us immediately into action. It initiates the internal actions which we feel in the activation of our body and nervous system and which then shows up as we act out those feelings. To access proactivity, we have to act on the mental and emotional level *prior* to when the fight/flight syndrome kicks in. We have to train ourselves for calm thoughtfulness (see *Instant Relaxation*, 1998).

This description enables us to recognize proactivity as higher and more than a primary state of mere activity, responsiveness, impulsiveness, and motivation. Proactivity means using consciousness itself in order to think-and-feel *about* our primary state wherein we feel threat, overload, stress, etc. Proactivity means that we first think *about* our situation and *about* what actions we can take that would allow us to respond effectively.

What does this mean? It means that in order to cast a spell for proactivity, we have to develop empowering thoughts-feelings *about* stress, problems, "threats," etc. We have to feed our mind some lines that will allow us to *reframe* the meaning of these activities so that we can program ourselves to *not* respond reactively to threats that are not physical. Getting to a calmly proactive minds necessitates some new frames-of-references, new awarenesses.

Since *stress* itself (e.g., the amount of energy you expend in coping with life) drives reactive defensiveness, begin by *taking your stress pulse* at the top of every hour for a week. Do this until you begin to develop a more conscious awareness of your internal "sense of stress" and the things inside and outside yourself which tend to send that stress level up and down.

This will greatly assist you in becoming conscious about your thoughts-and-feelings regarding your states of stress, energy expenditure, overload, etc.

"What stress do I feel?"
"What possible threats have I read into the events of today?"
"Do I need to take a few minutes to relax, calm myself, breathe deeply, etc.?"
"How should I evaluate this threat: a true threat or just a

perceived threat?" (Perceived threats will feel just as real and dangerous as a real threat.)

Calmly Stressed

The primary state that we will want to bring *calmness, security, centeredness, self-esteeming*, etc. to so that proactivity emerges is none other than states of threat, feeling upset, disappointment, stress overload, etc. To elicit greater awareness and understanding of your Dragons, use the following questions:

- What are your automatic thoughts-feelings which you bring to such experiences? (These will probably name your Dragons.)
- When do the Dragons of reactivity and defensiveness typically emerge in your life?
- What do you most typically react to? When? To whom?

If we most naturally respond to distressful events with *reactivity, passivity, and victimization,* then as we develop greater awareness about these responses, we can live more consciously. And that, in turn, will give rise to the higher meta-state of proactively.

Take a moment to identify some of the times and places when you experience these Dragons. Doing this will actually develop your proactivity. Why? Because to answer these questions you have to become more conscious about yourself, your states, your life situation, etc.

First, we must develop thoughts-and-feelings of taking a proactive stance regarding our thinking, responding, etc. Then we proactively become more aware about the dangers, threats, and overloads that we commonly experience. Doing that then allows us to develop some empowering responses to commonly occurring problems and conflicts. In proactivity also, we simply accept and assume *total response-ability* for ourselves and our responses. The heart of this state acknowledges:

> "I am solely responsible for my own responses. I acknowledge and own my thoughts and mental responses as my own. I accept my emotional and somatic responses as mine."

To the extent that we think in this way in times of stress and difficulty, to that extent we have accessed the higher frame of mind that we call *proactivity*. To the extent that we do not think that way, we make room for the Dragons of Reactivity and Defensiveness to arise.

Thought Experiment

Take a moment now to think about a time in your life when you were thinking and feeling in a way that you'd label as *proactive*. Close your eyes and allow your unconscious mind to begin to search through your memory banks for an instance in your history where you could have responded in reactively or defensively, but you did not. You chose not to. Instead you responded by thinking and talking out some problem— you responded proactively.

When did you take some proactive action? With whom? In what context of life? As your let your unconscious mind find an instance, give yourself some credit. The instance did not have to meet every criteria of proactivity. Go find a time regarding something small and simple. Perhaps when you dealt with a child. When you find that instance, allow yourself to experience that memory again, fully and completely. What did you see at that time? What did you hear? What did you say to yourself? And what did you feel in your body?

How did you experience that state of proactivity? How would you describe that state from the inside, phenomenologically? What linguistic structures of awareness did you use as beliefs or understandings that supported you in pulling it off? What thoughts enable you to make that choice? Notice as you identify some of these resources, how you accessed them?

When I ask these kind of questions in workshops, I get the following kind of answers:

> I just felt calm enough to do it.
> I knew I would have to listen, so I thought I might as well pay attention.
> I knew I had a choice about what to do.
> I decided I wouldn't waste my energy on this.
> I knew it really wasn't about me... so I didn't take it personally.
> It felt like the problem was at a distance.
> I knew I wouldn't value responding that way.
> I felt the name-calling was so absurd, there was no need to react to it.

Resources for Proactivity
Sense of Choice, Sene of Power

My preference is to first access an awareness about my sense of choice and personal power. This allows me to then use that mindfulness of my ability to respond as I choose.

> "I have the power to make a wide variety of responses to this or any other situation."

By acknowledging and accepting our *power zone,* we build up more of a sense of control and personal security. Consequently, this initiates a non-victim kind of thinking,

> "I can *choose how to take a trauma*, how to think about it, what attitude to adopt, behaviors to engage in, etc. I have a choice!"

Access a state of proactivity necessitates that we keep our *mind and heart active and vigorous* as we own our consciousness of choices. This leaves us with a sense that "I always have choice about my choices." "I can always choose what and how to represent things internally to myself. No one can control my thoughts; no one can force me to think in a certain way."

The moment of proactivity occurs inside **the gap** which we can pry open between a given between Stimulus and the resulting Response. Viktor Frankl, William Glasser, and Steven Covey describe this gap as "the freedom gap." Within the space of thought that occurs between a stimulus and our response, we have a psychic space or moment to think, represent information, reason, imagine, remember, fantasize, and engage other cognitive "world-making" functions which, in turn, determine the response we generate.

Figure 12:2

Stimulus → *The Gap of Consciousness* → **Response**

The gap wherein consciousness occurs not only gives us freedom of choice, but because consciousness inevitably reflects back on itself (self-reflexive consciousness), it expands our choices. We can now develop the ability to experience what psychologists call *an internal "locus* [or circle] *of control."* This increases our sense of *self-efficacy* in contrast to *"learned helplessness."* We inevitably live reactively when we think and posit our problems as existing "out there." This erroneous thought dis-empowers as it posits our circle of control beyond our responses.

To exercise your proactivity, identify lots of little things that you can do, then commit yourself to doing them. This will cultivate your sense of self-management. "I can management myself and my responses." Refuse to merely suffer the blows of fate. Don't discount something because you deem it a "small thing." Exercise your power zone by discerning between *your circle of response and your circle of concern.*

To empower yourself, focus on things in your power circle; to disempower yourself—focus on things beyond that arena. When we do that, we *give our power away!* Proactive people focus on things inside their "power" arena. They orient themselves to taking charge of their own thinking-and-feeling, and their speaking and behaving. They release everything beyond that zone.

With these understandings in mind, take a moment right now to write an induction for yourself, an induction that will induce you into a sense of your own powers and choices state. I'll share mine:

> "No matter what happens, I cannot and will not hold any person or event *responsible* **for** my choices. I claim, own and acknowledge my behaviors, choices, emotions, thoughts, etc., as mine. They belong to me. I produce these responses, useful or not, enhancing or limiting, empowering or disempowering. They come out of my mind and emotions. They express my thinking, valuing, understanding."

All I have to do is read that state if I want to refresh this frame and be re-induced into an internally active stance. And when that happens, it inoculates me against feelings of being a victim.

Figure 12:3

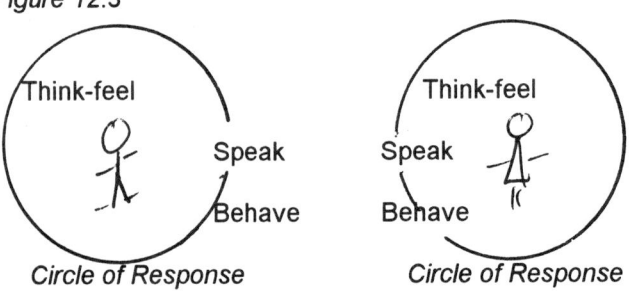

Circle of Response   Circle of Response

Another facet that helps to build this state involves practicing *talking the language of proactivity* to replace the language of reactivity, passivity, and victimization. Own all of our thoughts-feelings, values and wants as our own. Avoid speaking for others, reduce "you" statements, eliminate all statements of blame, accusation, excuses, etc.

Compelling Desired Outcomes

As we discover the secrets about thinking-and-feeling proactive, one secret involves learning to cultivate "consequential thinking" so that when we act, we do so while thinking about the long-term effects of our actions. Thinking consequentially, and "with the end in mind" enables us to operate from a larger perspective. It enables us to form and use desired outcomes, plans, visions, etc. as part of our navigational system. So as with resilience, when we bring a strong compelling desired-outcome to bear upon difficulties, setbacks, and problems, we also train ourselves for proactivity.

To form and design *well-formed* outcomes, use the following list from the NLP model to check-list your outcomes in order to do smart goal-setting:

1. State it in the Positive. Describe what you want. By all means avoid writing goals that describe what you do **not** want. "I don't want to be judgmental." Command negations typically evoke the very ideas that it seeks to negate. "Don't think about getting all flustered and acting stupid when he calls you names."

2. State what you can do. If you write something like, "I want others to not contradict my plans." you have not written anything that *you* can take charge of and accomplish, and because of that, the very goal will *dis-empower you.* State things that you can *initiate* and *maintain*, things within your response-able power zone.

3. Contextualize. State the context within which you want your goal. Specify the specific environment and situation. "In the context of working with my co-worker Joe who has such a negative and grumpy attitude, I want to be able to maintain my own peace of mind and internal focus. I want to only respond from carefully thought out strategies and not react out of frustration."

4. State in Sensory Based words. Describe specifically and precisely what you will see, hear, and feel. Whenever you use an abstract or vague word, specify the behaviors that someone could video-tape. Not, "I want to be charismatic in relating to people." Write, "I want to smile, warmly greet people with a handshake and use their name..."

5. State in Bite-size steps and stages. Chunk the outcomes down to the kind of size that becomes do-able. Otherwise the goal could become overwhelming. Not, "I will write a book." "I will write four pages every day."

6. Load your description with Resources. What resources will you need in order to make your dream a reality? More confidence in your ability to speak in public? Write that as a sub-goal to thereby load up the desired outcome with this resource.

7. Check for ecology. Does this goal fit in with my other goals and values? Does it fit with my relationships, health, and overall functioning? Does any facet of my mind object to this desired outcome?

8. Specify evidence for fulfillment. How will you know, in addition, to the previous criteria, when you have reached your goal? Make sure you have specific evidence for this.

As you use these criteria to *Quality Control* your goals, your desired outcomes will become well-formed as healthy mental maps. This will empower your ability to directionalize your brain into developing the kind of proactive responses that you choose.

Readiness To Implement

When you're proactive, you have a readiness and responsiveness for *taking effective action* to implement what you know. Proactivity arises as we bring *a doing state* to bear upon our knowledge. In implementing what we know, we typically translate our big ideas into bite-size details of specific responses that allows us to translate our understanding into real life. As we meta-detail things into bite-size bits, they become "do-able."

It usually helps to visually imagine the scenario of taking effective action and playing it out vividly and graphically on the screen of the mind. We can then learn to use mistakes as feedback for learning. And that's the proactive approach to mistakes, that is, to welcome them and quickly use them for enriched learning and development. The proactive do not waste the value of errors or mistakes.

To develop a proactive focus, we ask ourselves *solution-oriented questions.* This also directionalizes our thinking-and-feeling.

- What can I do as a highly constructive response to this situation?
- What ways of thinking, speaking, behaving would empower me to cope best?

- What resourceful states do I need to access with greater skill and speed?
- What one thing can I do today that would put me "on track" with my desired outcome?
- What feedback can I gather from this setback that will improve my next attempt?

Further, the proactive person takes care of things while they are still *small and manageable,* rather than waiting until they become large and unmanageable. This avoids the stress of letting things build up and get bigger and at the same time helps in reducing "threat" or "overload" messages.

A State of Self-Reflexive Awareness

In proactivity, we transcend our primary state to take a meta-view about the idea regarding our *ability to respond* as existentially "free" persons. This then leads to yet another abstraction, an empowering belief whereby we posit our "locus of control" within. This self-reflexivity provides us not only basic awareness of our thoughts-feelings and actions, but also awareness of our awareness.

Proactive people *live consciously.* They make themselves a friend to reality so that they think-or-feel no aversion to it so and engage in no defense or escape mechanisms in relation to it. They cultivate awareness. They accept and appreciate awareness. This enables them to engage in constructive consequential thinking as they build and plan their tomorrows today. Doing this positively uses our consciousness.

"Self" Definition as a Proactive Person

We can also *bring* another state *to bear* on our state of difficulties. We can bring a defining ourselves as *proactive* state. Doing this necessitates that we build and install a self-definition of proactivity and then habituate it in our thinking processes. What language would help you build, code, and access a proactive self-definition? To what extent do you already think-feel yourself as a proactive person and can fly into the proactive state? To what extent can you access those thoughts-emotions when things occur to which you normally would respond reactively? To do that describes a high level ability of moving into the proactive meta-state. Here's part of my self-definition as a proactive person:

"The ultimate freedom consists of my freedom of choice,

therefore I will maintain an active and thoughtful coping style. I will stay alert as I move through life and maintain my locus of control within myself. I can and will make use of any opportunity for purposeful action and will take the initiative whenever possible. I will proactively ask empowering questions to shift my focus to thinking in a solutions oriented way.

Summary
- Welcome and accept your Fight/Flight responses so that you can begin the taming process over reactivity and defensiveness. These Dragons need no longer be feared when you know how to ride them.
- Taming Reactivity first involves understanding and welcoming our neurological wiring for dealing with physical dangers. From there, we can begin to tame the Dragon by developing clear cues about true physical danger and non-physical threats.
- Casting a spell for becoming *Proactive* further tames the Dragons as we take the initiative in taking charge in our lives.

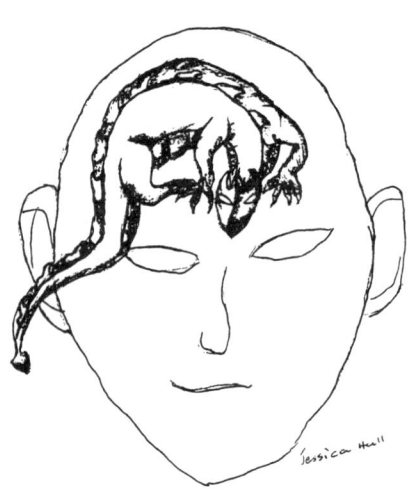

Chapter 13

SLAYING THE DRAGONS OF CRITICISM & INSULT

AND CASTING A SPELL FOR UN-INSULT-ABILITY

The ultimate expression of proactivity shows up in none other than the state of *un-insultability*. Of course! To refuse to take insult or to feel put down in the face of criticism prevents us from giving in to the Dragons of Reactivity and Defensiveness. This spell gives us the ability to keep our mind and composure in the face of potential threats and dangers and to hold our ground with dignity.

Because of that, we just have to take a brief look at the incredible state of being un-insultable.

The State of What?
Un-insultability.
Living at a level *above and beyond* the peevish state of taking offense easily and taking things personal. Living in, and from, this un-insultable state empowers us to then look "criticism" right in the face and to handle it with the grace, charm, and power of a Knight. It gives us the ability to stay positively effective in the midst of interpersonal conflict and stress. It allows us to handle communication confrontations and even people in bad moods with graceful resourcefulness.

When you attain the ability to resist taking *insult* even when people legitimately attempt to *insult* you, you live in a very different dimension than most humans. It means that people can't "push your buttons" anymore, that they can't "play your keyboard" and wrap you around their little finger, and manipulate the hell out of you. It means that you just don't give them that opportunity because try as they may to rattle you, you just don't take insult. Nothing they can say or do can get you into a semantically reactive state.

Interested now?

Would you like to custom design an *Un-insultability* state for yourself and install it in the higher levels of your mind? Would you like that kind of a defense system against Dragons?   Then read on.

The Dragons of Insult and Feeling Criticized
Let's see if we can flush out some Dragons and name them.
- How do you think-and-feel about criticism?
- What first comes into your mind when you hear someone offering you a criticism?
- Does it mean "negative information, personal attack, blaming, putting me down?"
- How easily do you take offense?
- What do you think-and-feel about the person who offers the criticism?
- Do you inevitably feel a sense of displeasure toward that person?

We grow up "taking insult," and treating the words, tones, and gestures of others as "real," and somehow as having the power to "abuse" us. Yet in Neuro-Semantics, we know that what actually leads a person to experience *abuse* is *the belief itself,* the believe that "words can 'abuse' a person." Words alone do not abuse. Yet we may use them to beat ourselves up. *We* can *abuse* ourselves with words. We can use the words we hear from others, believe them, take them to heart, and confuse such word maps with the territory.

To *not* buy into the non-sense of "hurtful words," we have to rise up in our minds to a meta-state about that criticism which keeps it harmless. Namely, we have to think of it as just information, just feedback from that person's map, a critique according to another person's value system.   You may have some other ways to render words innocent and harmless.   You may have access to such a high level resourceful state that you just don't need to get off on taking it in a negative way, with displeasure, dismay, discouragement, depression, etc. Suppose you were centered enough and clear enough about your value and fallibility that you took negative critiques with contentment, delight, appreciation, sympathy, etc.? Wouldn't that be a trip?

Un-insultability: *Scene 1*

While Snoopy perches on his dog house, Lucy approaches and says, "You know what really annoys me about you?"

Then in Lucy fashion, without pausing to catch her breath, she says, "The way you live without responsibility."

Then staring at him with a frown, she says, "That really annoys me!"

Snoopy doesn't say a thing. But later, as he reflects on it, he thinks, "We all have our hang-ups!"

Un-insultable! The insult just didn't disturb him. He felt perfectly at home with the critique or perfectly adjusted to the fact that there's a Lucy in his life!

Un-insultability: *Scene 2*

Nancy shouts at the top of her lungs at Lucy Brown, "...and I don't care if I ever see you again! Do you hear me?"

Linus approaches and having heard some of what Nancy was shouting, commented to Charlie Brown, "She really hurt your feelings, didn't she, Charlie Brown? I hope she didn't take all the life out of you."

With a downcast face, Charlie Brown said, "No, not completely..." "But you can number me among the walked wounded!"

Zing! He took the insult and he let it do a job on him.

Un-insultability

I use the unformidable term *un-insultability* to describe *a higher state than our ordinary states*. It consists of many layered components of awareness that allow this gestalt to arise. At the primary level, we have the experience of receiving some insult, criticism, put-down, indignity, etc. At this primary level, we recognize that someone has communicated information to us about something in a critical and negative way.

Do we inevitably feel a sense of displeasure or dismay? Not necessarily. As we move into a positive meta-state of thinking-and-feeling about that criticism— a whole world of opportunity lies before us in terms of *how we could respond*. We could respond in the kind of thinking that would produce no displeasure, no dismay, no discouragement, and no depression. And if we did, we could then experience contentment, delight, appreciation, understanding, pleasure, etc.

As a meta-state, the layered pieces of consciousness *on top of* the criticism will inevitably temper, modulate, modify, and transform that primary state. All meta-states so operate. With that in mind, we now only need to explore, develop, and install the kind of meta-level ideas, beliefs, values, understandings, expectations, identifications, etc. that will allow us to so respond. When we engineer this un-insultability state, we will then have the ability to respond without "taking offense." At that point, criticism will do us no damage. Now wouldn't you like that? Think of the things you could then allow yourself to explore, try, or experiment with.

The Primary State of a Critique

Most of us *try to make things better by criticizing.* I have given that one a very good try over the years! The sequence is really pretty simple and it goes like:

    (1) I feel bad.
    (2) I evaluate something that does not meet my expectations, standards, or desires, and so
    (3) I open my mouth to let loose my critique concerning what I think ought to change. I begin, "You know, the problem with you is..." Or, "You ought to..." Or, "Why don't you...?"

Now given my very positive, even holy, intentions, you'd think people would listen to me, recognize my motivations, and forthright just change to make things better. Wouldn't you think that? You wouldn't?

Well, I have to admit that it has almost never worked. And yet, given that most people are so skilled in critiquing, and can dish it out so quickly, frequently, and sharply, it does seem —well, at least conceptually—that they should have the ability to take it well and use it for learning and growth.

Right? Wrong!

Most people actually seem particularly sensitive to being criticized. In fact, very few people seem to really know how to *make good use of the criticisms they receive.* (Amazing, what an under-developed skill!) Most who receive criticism never think of responding to it with good feelings or of putting the best twist on the criticism. Most of us *take* insult all too easily. Have you noted your own patterns regarding this at work, from loved ones, about things you really care about, about things you don't feel invested in? Have you identified some Dragons that need taming a bit?

Check out where your brain goes when you hear criticism. What sentences do you automatically use on yourself then? What words induce you into an unresourceful state?

    __ "This is insulting!"
    __ "I don't want to hear this."
    __ "I don't want them to say these things."
    __ "These words mean I am inadequate."
    __ "They don't have any right to talk this way to me!"
    __ "This feels like an attack of my self-esteem!"
    __ "Horrors! This means I'm going to have to change."

To begin to generate and to fine-tune a higher state of *un-insultability*, take a moment to think about a time when you did indeed listen to criticism that someone gave you and to which you did not feel bad. Pull out two instances from your memory banks. In the first, a peer or a work acquaintance offered you a criticism. In the second, remember a time when someone with whom you have close emotional ties. You heard this critique about yourself and somehow you appreciated it, you evaluated it as useful feedback for yourself, and you used it to alter your behavior. (If you just can't identify some historical referents, then create two scenarios of what it would be like if you could. Pretend away!)

With those references, now explore the following:

- What beliefs, emotions, values, etc. had to be present in your mind and heart for you to do that?
- What resources did you utilize so that you heard it and took it as information and feedback?

Having worked on this for a number of years, and conducted trainings in this and in *Defusing Hotheads*, I now have a well-installed belief about criticism that helps me stay more open to it.

> *People never offer me totally non-sense criticisms; they always offer critiques to me that contain enough truth and validity that I can learn from.*

I don't know about you, but no one has ever criticized me for having green skin. No one has ever criticized me for coming from Mars. The

criticisms that I receive strike much closer to home:
> "You come on too strong," "You didn't fully listen," "You raised your voice and it sounded like yelling," etc.

Such criticisms, in fact, usually "hurt" precisely because they do strike pretty close to home and make me aware of some of my imperfections, fallibilities, and weaknesses. Here are two more supporting beliefs that I've developed:

> *I am fully fallible and make lots of mistakes— mistakes of comprehension and understanding, emotional mistakes, mistakes of the tongue, misbehaviors, etc. It's easy for people to see my errors and flaws, the problem isn't that they do, it's that, thank God, they don't know the half of it!*

> ***If*** *I don't get defensive or closed-minded, every criticism offers me insights and feedback which I can use for self improvement and greater effectiveness.*

I no longer care whether a criticizer cares about me or not, whether he or she intends or not to hurt my feelings, I figure I can always learn from criticisms and use them to personally develop, and so I choose.

Figure 13:1

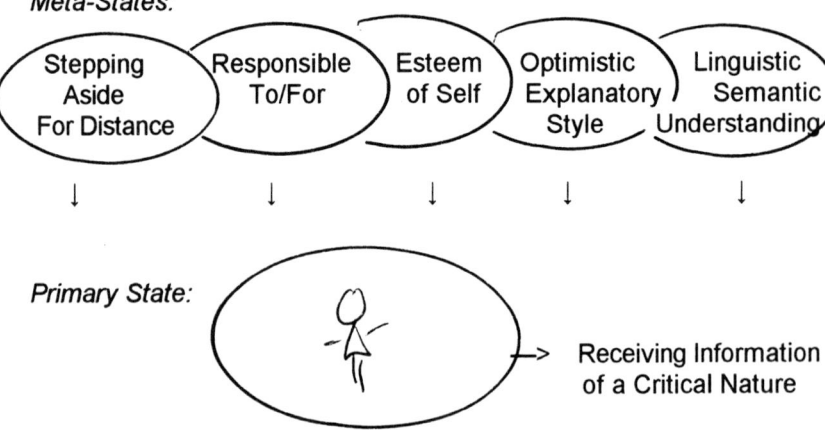

When we operate from the meta-state of un-insultability, the emotional black-hole of criticism is eliminated. This frees us so that we can treat it as simply—a just a piece of information. From this un-insultable state, we can take such communications positively and use them constructively. As we further develop this resourceful state, we can eventually develop the skills to hear out even harsh and cruel criticism *without getting defensive*. Then we don't have to get hooked into it and engage in self-dis-esteeming.

Stepping Aside for some Distance

In un-insultability, you will almost always find that the person has *an internal sense of distance* from the criticism. The person can step back from the criticism to think about it clearly and objectively without taking offense or getting defensive. The person doesn't feel like the criticism rips out his or her heart. They treat it as information, and not as a personal attack.

To step back from the experiencing state, just imagine observing or witnessing yourself receiving the criticism as if watching a movie of *that you* in that experience. Stepping back to observe the content of the criticism allows us the room or internal space so that we can think clearly and comfortably about *what* the person is saying, the context, etc. Practice stepping back and imagining a movie of the event. Not only will you be able to think more clearly, but because it gives you a sense of "psychological distance," you won't feel as involved personally. It process actually helps to prevent you from *getting caught-up in the content* of the criticism.

Now if you fear information (a phobic response), then you must have set some frame whereby you give words and ideas lots of *unresourceful symbolic meanings.* To hear without personalizing, re-own your *power zone,* draw the *"responsibility to/for" line* between your thinking and feeling responses and those of the speaker.

> "What anyone says to me *is not mine!* I do not have to *immediately* believe it! I can *just perceive* it."

This way of perceiving will then set up some useful boundaries that will allow you to become centered in your values, principles, relationships, identifications, and visions. It will facilitate your own self-integrity.

If *stepping back and dissociating* from a criticism help us to process criticism comfortably and with presence of mind, how do we learn do do that?

1) You may put your internal movies at a greater distance than normal. Sit back, as it were, in the twentieth row of the theater. That should give you some distance. Or the 120th row if necessary. Stop representing the person "in your face."

2) You may listen to the criticism as if originating from a source two blocks away. Hear the voice come from that distance. Note the effect it has on your emotions.

3) Or you may imagine yourself behind a wall of plexiglass that protects you from the other's words and ideas. You can stand behind the plexiglass in the projection both of your mental theater and put your hands on the window to fee safe.

4) You could turn your pictures into black-and-white snapshots. Freeze frame the movie and drain all the color out of the images.

5) Focus in on the you who was criticized in a particular place and on a particular day. Step back so that you watch that younger you— if it that you was just a day younger.

6) If someone unloads a whole truckload of mental and verbal garbage containing junky thoughts, offensive, nonsense words and ideas, then see that person dumping it on their side of the responsibility line. After all, it belongs to them. Decide to not buy into it, receive it, or want it. Imagine it coming out of their mind and mouth into their space, not yours. Use this to empower yourself to stay calm, collected, and sane. Tell yourself the truth that their ideas, words, and responses belong to them, not you. This prevents you from taking responsibility *for* their statements, feelings, wants, etc.

7) Develop lots of higher level reasons and reframes for handling criticism. Use these as *Mind-Lines* for changing your mind about how you think of criticism.

> "When a fool is annoyed, he quickly lets it be known. *Smart people will ignore an insult*" (Proverbs 12:16 TEV).

The more reasons you have for your un-insultable stance, the easier you will access a non-defensive position. To feel insulted, you have to *take* insult. Stop it! Frederick Douglas said,

> "A gentleman will *not* insult me, and no man not a gentleman *can* insult me."

8) *Actually surprise the critic by thanking him or her!* "I appreciate you for bringing this to my attention. It offers me feedback of possible benefit." Adopt the supporting idea or belief: "Criticism doesn't exist,

only information." Thanking a critic provides an unexpected response and usually interrupts the pattern. Look for positives in the information. Listen with *a quiet and receptive mind*. You can always thank your critic for his or her concern and straightforwardness.

As you treat it as "information," if the critic speaks in vague statements, gather more information.

> "Would you tell me more? Just how do you think I exist as a turkey? How did my behavior seem clumsy? How specifically do I remind you of a turkey?"

Evaluate the criticism for usefulness. All of these responses communicates a very powerful message. In essence it says:

> "I have nothing to fear from information. If you say something that I find completely off-the-wall, I have nothing to fear. I will simply consider it erroneous. My self-image does not rest so tenuously upon your words. If your words accurately portrays something, I will take interest in that. I want to improve and will use that information to do so."

Decide that you won't let criticism stop you. After you take time to consider the advice, gather more information, evaluate and re-evaluate, then cast your sails to the winds, and *go for it.* Stay true to your own values and visions.

Discern the Line Between Responsibility To & For

The *Responsibility To/For Line* provides a method for stepping aside from criticism and other unpleasant experiences wrought by others and at the same time owning our own power zone.

The idea behind this simple model is clear and straight-forward. Namely, we all stand totally and solely responsible **for** ourselves. We can legitimately hold no one other than ourselves responsible *for* the responses that we make from inside the circle of our Power Zone. Our responses to the world are *ours*. Accordingly, the little word **"for"** carries a lot of wallop! It defines our arena of *accountability*.

"For," however, totally differs from the other tiny word, *"to."* **"To"** speaks to and describes the space between our circle and the circles of all others. Between *my* circle and the circle of all other selves we have *"to"* which encodes the area of our public responses of speaking and acting, the very things which we give **to** others. *"To"* therefore defines and describes *relationship*.

So, we are responsible **for** all of our responses, our private mental and emotional responses as well as for our public speaking and behaving responses. By our public responses, however, we create and sustain relationships. We enter into arrangements whereby we promise to act from a responsive position as we talk and act in certain ways *to* another person. For example, I assume responsibility *for* my languaging and actions in *relationship to* you.

By distinguishing between responsibility *for* and responsibility *to* we are enabled to tell the difference between those things for which we stand accountable and those responses that create relationship to others. And as this model sorts out these things, it empowers us to recognize that criticism always comes *from others.* That's why we don't have to take it personally. It's not ours!

So suppose someone screams at you. At that moment you can realize,

"Hey, whatever comes *at* me must not belong to me. I did not produce it. It belongs to another."

Then from that non-personalizing state of mind, you can say in all honesty and forthrightness:

"Apparently you have some very strong and negative emotions you want to express. I want to hear what you have to say. But given your volume, I can only hear bits and pieces of it, would you repeat what you just said in a calmer way? I promise to listen carefully."

Un-insultable!

This languaging defuses the situation, stops the push-shove interaction, and creates a negotiation for improving communication. Such responses give us time to decide on *how* we want to respond. Often it's the element of the speed and the surprise of the criticism that sucks us into push-shove matches. We get caught "off guard" when someone launches a loaded missile at us. That's why we first respond with shock. "I can't believe he said that!" We reel back from the mental jolt. As the dust and static settles and we regain a little composure, we can use that moment for gathering information to pace our critic.

"So you think I'm a dirty-rat; what specifically gives you this impression?"

This enables us to mentally sort out responsibilities and empowers us to stay emotionally and verbally clear and centered.

Suppose someone goes so far as to scream obscenities at us. We can now think about their words with a humanizing perspective and actually listen empathically to the person.

"Interesting words. *His* words, of course, not mine. He has the right to say such. He must really feel insecure and grumpy to talk this way."

Un-insultable.

"I really want to hear what you've got to say. It sounds like you feel very angry at me, and I will hear out your anger. Yet when you cuss at me like this, I have a hard time hearing you. If I promise to listen to you would you promise to stop the obscenities?"

Un-insultable.

In this process, stubbornly refuse the give in to the pleasure of counter-attacking. Responding in kind defensively counter-attacks. Just curiously explore.

"It sounds like you have some things about which you really want to set me straight. Does that represent your position? Do you feel that this comprises your best choice to accomplish this? What do you hope to accomplish by this? How do you expect me to respond to you as you so express yourself? I want to hear you out, would you express yourself so that I could feel you offer this within a context of care and respect?"

In so speaking, you begin to negotiate the relationship you have **to** that person. This keeps the responsibility to/for distinction clear. *Hold a critic responsible* by asking him what he wants.

"If I do this wrong, what do you suggest I ought to do? Will you help me to do it right?"

This last question flushes out those critics who merely unload their negatives, who have no intention of identifying a better way. Also, listen for exaggeration and catastrophizing words ("all, nothing, always, everybody, all the time").

Highly Esteem Yourself

We really misuse criticism when we let it question our value, worth, dignity, visions, principles, etc. We misuse it if we let it demotivate us, break our spirit, and hold us back from living life fully. So decide now that you will stubbornly refuse to put your self-esteem on the line. Instead, access a meta-state of unconditionally self-esteeming. Create a transcendent state that empowers you to think-and-feel personally empowered. Consider your esteem, value, and dignity as a given.

Optimistic Explanatory Style
Where does your mind go in inventing explanations about *why* your critic criticizes? What motives, intentions, and agenda drive him or her to criticize? Evaluate your *explanatory style* to determine if you have a positive or negative frame set to assist you in your way of explaining things. Do you respect the critic's dignity or show disrespect? Do you use a humanizing perspective or a demonizing one? What effect does your explanatory style have upon you in terms of what state it induces in you?

Danger lurks for us at this point. It's important that we do not confuse the critic's *behavior* with his or her *person.* In fact, make sure that you highly esteem your critic *in spite of the words or actions* given you. Refuse to let their hurtful words run your negative emotions. As you assume their good will and positive intentions, then you can hear your critic out, avoid reading his/her mind or motives, and invite them to disclose their intentions.

"This seems pretty important to you. How does it hold so much meaning to you?"

"What do you hope to achieve by this criticism that you consider positive?"

Discern the Inside "Reality" of Language and Meaning
Ultimately, when people offer us criticisms, *they only and merely say words* to us, words which we dislike and do not prefer. But how do you think about such words? How do you code "critical words" in your mind? How much "reality" do you attribute to and invest in words? The more "reality" you invest in words, the more impactful the criticism will feel to you—and the more power you give away.

Actually, words are not objectively "real." They do not have the same kind of reality that we experience in their referents. Remind yourself of the *unreality* of words. The word "cat" cannot scratch you as can a real cat. The word "menu" cannot fill your stomach in the same way that actual food can. The word "sunset" cannot delight your eyes as can a sunset. The word "sun" cannot tan your skin. *Words only function as symbols.* They do not share the reality of their referents.

We experience *"word phobia"* when we have given too much power to words. We thereby create programs for ourselves that generate semantic reactions to symbols! Do you have any words that can "get" you—rattle your cage? Then you have forgotten the true nature of words as *symbols*, as maps about some territory. You have *identified*.

So, just because someone calls you an "idiot," that doesn't make it so. Give them permission to use and misuse symbols. Give yourself permission that they can make their thinking and speaking responses, it all occurs in their power zone. This will help you to give up the impossible task of trying to control *their* thoughts. Talk about a way to waste perfectly good time and energy! Doing that will then allow you to move into negotiating with them about the speech that they give you if you have, or want, a relationship with them.

Today I now know that even when others use my "name in vain," it's really none of my business. Who am I to think I need to put out an edict that forbids people from taking my name in vain?

Which belief puts you into a better state— to construe a person's critical words as "negative, hurtful, unfair, stupid, criticism" or to frame it as "feedback" and information regarding their thinking? Beware of over-evaluating and over-loading their words with too many negative meanings. That will send you down the path to confusing map-symbols with territory.

As we use *the feedback frame,* we can more fully recognize that all words exist only as words. They are maps, not the territory. If criticism only consists of words, as symbols of another's discernment, evaluation, critique, etc., then we have nothing to fear, and much to learn. These words (especially if you find them unpleasant, untrue, unacceptable, etc.) only functions as *feedback* about *that* person, the world he or she lives in, and the symbolic meanings, state, thinking, limitations, etc. that govern that person's experiences. Saying them does not necessarily make them real, accurate, or useful. As we use the feedback frame, we become more empowered for attentive listening and staying calmly centered.

And with that, we also become skilled in accepting "reproof" while maintaining a good spirit. Many of the old Hebrew Proverbs speaks about this. Guess this has been an age-old problem:

"A wise man listens to advice" (Prov. 12:15).
"A scoffer will not listen to rebuke" (Prov. 13:1).
"A rebuke goes deeper into a man of understanding than a hundred blows into a fool" (Prov. 17:10).

"Whoever loves disciplines loves knowledge, but he who hates reproof is stupid" (12:1).

This strategy also enables us to utter a strong, but kind, *"No!"* to criticism that does not fit for us. If someone offers a criticism you think inappropriate, say, "Thanks, but it does not fit." Listen to criticism and explore it *without buying it wholesale*. Just listening to a criticism and exploring it *does not mean you accept it*. You can evaluate it to determine whether it represents something true or false, accurate or erroneous, useful or irrelevant. Hearing it only comprises step one. Later you can dismiss it safely knowing that you have purged it of everything useful. If you dismiss it outright before thoughtful consideration you may miss something valuable.

Summary
- We can indeed tame the Dragons of Reactivity and Defensiveness and do so to such an extent that we can become *Un-Insultable*.
- Un-insultability doesn't mean that we become cold and uncaring, it rather means that we become so centered and focused, that we don't respond to insults by personalizing or confusing them with a physical blow.
- Insults are just words. Just symbols. And when you know that, you know that they cannot hurt you.

Chapter 14

SLAYING IRRITABLE NASTY LITTLE RESENTFUL & GRUDGE HOLDING DRAGONS

AND CASTING SPELLS FOR MAGNANIMITY & FORGIVENESS

If you want to reduce your life and live on a much lower level, give yourself to thinking in *"little-minded"* ways about yourself, others, and the world. Do that for a month and you'll end up feeling resentful and bitter. The world will turn dark. You'll begin carrying grudging and then, lo and behold, the Grumpy Dragon will have total control over you!

This will undermine your happiness, success, and empowerment. It will give you training in how to fly off the handle, speak and act with intolerance, be boorish, grumpy, and irritable. Then, with a Dragon like that, you'll be able to make anything seem sour. You'll be able to badmouth on cue!

But, if none of that sounds particularly appealing, then we'll just have to face those Dragons, tame them, and set out to cast spells for some very different neuro-semantic states, states like *magnanimity, being big hearted, forgiving, compassionate, etc.*

Grumpiness: *Scene 1*
In a most playful mood, Snoopy says, "I wish I were a piranha fish." Then scooting along the grass pretending, he says, "If I were a piranha, I'd be in south America in some jungle stream, and I'd lie in wait until a victim came near, and then I'd..."

".... GRAB HIS LEG!!!" as he jumps for Linus' leg in the frame, startling Linus.

Later, back at the house, Lucy looked at Linus' leg and asked him, "What happened to your sock?"

"Well," he said, enjoying the playfulness of the experience, "I was crossing this jungle stream in South America, see, and..."

Nice playfulness.

Later, Lucy informed Linus that she had to go to the store and he playfully warned her about the piranha in the neighborhood.

So when she opened the door to leave the house, she said in a voice loud enough for Snoopy to hear, "I hear there's a piranha swimming around in the neighborhood."

Then louder, "By golly, that piranha better not try to chomp me!"

And then raising her voice to the level of a yell, "Any piranha tries to chomp me, I'll POUND him!!!"

As she down the sidewalk and by Snoopy, she has a very grumpy frown on her face.

Snoopy looks away, "There's nobody around here but us beagles!"

No playfulness here. And no magnanimity either. Lucy just doesn't live in those states.

Grumpiness: *Scene 2*

Schultz drew one cartoon showing Charlie Brown and Linus playing marbles, when Lucy came upon the scene and tried to play with them. But she can't flip the marble into the circle. "Fooey!" she says.

Linus thinks, "'Fooey' is right!" And then he tells Charlie Brown, "She's hopeless, Charlie Brown. Why do we have to let **her** play?"

Charlie Brown has a plan. So he whispers in Linus' ear, "Don't worry about it. She'll get discouraged right away and go home."

And sure enough, as Lucy keeps failing to flip the marble, she gets up and leaves, saying "Rats!"

Charlie Brown comments, "See? She's discouraged already. Now she won't bother us any more."

So the guys got back to their playing. Shortly thereafter Linus looked up and exclaimed, "Oh, no!" at what he saw. Lucy had returned with a basketball which she "whams" into their circle of marbles sending everything flying.

Reeling from the blow, Linus speaks sarcastically, "See? She's discouraged already. Now she won't bother us any more."

Ah, the appearance of the Dragon! Lucy's frustration boiled over until she felt so grumpy, so irritable, and so angry, that her "Let all hell loose on the marbles" Dragon asserted itself. What brought this about? Lucy's feeling of powerlessness in playing marbles. She let her state of frustration feed back onto itself until she couldn't stand it any longer. But she didn't just go home; she went home and returned with a vengeful spirit designed to "blow away" the game that had so defeated her!

Grumpiness: *Scene 3*

On the wall, Charlie Brown mutters with his head in his hand, "Sometimes I get so lonesome I could cry."

Lucy went into her fix-it mode, "What you need Charlie Brown are some friends."

Then, out of character, Charlie Brown raised his voice and yelled at her sarcastically, "Of course, I need friends!! If I had some friends, I wouldn't be lonesome!!"

In the next frame Charlie Brown leans his head against his hands and Lucy just looks on at him. Stunned.

Then she leaves, and as she does, she comments, "No wonder you don't have any friends... you're too crabby!"

How shall we describe the state that Charlie Brown got into? It seemed to have started with feeling lonely, then perhaps he added a touch of self-pity to it as a dash of helpless in his feelings of being disconnected. Then, when Lucy gave him that piece of advice that was merely stating the obvious, Charlie Brown experienced "the last straw." He couldn't stand it any longer. So he exploded with some anger. His was the Dragon of built-up anger that he had turned on himself until he couldn't take it anymore.

Grumpiness: *Scene 4*

With head down and shoulders slumping, Charlie Brown says, "Another ball game lost! Good grief! I get tired of losing. Everything I do, I lose!"

What a state he has put himself into. He's playing the Failure and Victim Game, the Poor Me Game. And he's feeling most disappointed. Lucy tries to encourage him, "Look at it this way, Charlie Brown. We learn more from losing than we do from winning."

That did it. Over the limit of his threshold, he now yells, "That makes me the smartest person in the world!!"

Irritability—the Dragon of feeling, speaking, and behaving in an irritable, fussy, and grumpy way.

Framing the Mind with Magnanimity

Magnanimity refers to a most noble and resourceful state. It refers to "a loftiness of spirit that enables one to bear trouble calmly, a disdain of meanness and revenge." This term arises from two smaller words, *magnus* for "great" and *animus* for "spirit." Hence, a big spirited-ness, a *big-mindedness,* a lofty and courageous spirit, a nobility of feeling/generosity of mind.

A new translation of an old biblical text uses this term when it says, "Let your magnanimity be manifest to all" (Phil. 4:5 NEB). Yet if you compare that to other translations, you will find the synonyms for this state:

>forbearance, moderation, considerateness, gentleness, sweet reasonableness.

This gives us some other perspectives about *magnanimity.* This is "a reasonableness of mind that holds complete control over the passions." Magnanimity describes the valuable and empowering state where it enables us to truly transcend the frustrating events of life, wherein we win a victory over our own spirit in such a way that we can deal with ourselves, others, and life in a big-hearted and noble way. That sounds like a winner.

So, as we start to learn how to cast a spell for this state, begin by re-accessing a time when you found yourself in a state of *sweet reasonableness* when you faced a situation wherein you *could have* reacted with an irritable, fussy, resentful, and bitter attitude toward some frustration in your life, *and yet you did not*. Instead, you responded with a sweet reasonableness, a big-hearted consideration and gentleness which, in turn, enabled you to effectively handle the frustration. Now my guess is that at such a time, you felt pretty centered, you had good boundaries, and you operated from a clear sense of your own values.

Take a moment right now as you just allow your unconscious mind to search back into your memory files so that you find an instance of this resource. Fully experience it by seeing what you saw then, hearing what you heard, and feeling what you felt.

After you have done that, now identify *what enabled you* to respond with sweet reasonableness, with a big-hearted response? What resources did you access? What thoughts and beliefs supported you in that resourceful state? What images, sounds, any music, words, self-talk, etc.?

What *big-level thoughts*, ideas, understandings, and/or beliefs did you have at that time that allowed you to respond with big-hearted emotions? You can count on finding some *large* (magna) *thoughts* at the center of this experience. Ultimately, these large-minded or large-spirited perceptions drive this state. They enable you to *transcend* your normal thinking. This stands in contrast to small-minded and narrow-minded thinking-and-feeling.

Additionally, these transcendent thoughts may take the form of some guiding proverb, parable, or story. In slaying the Dragon of Defensiveness and casting a spell for un-insultability, I sometimes mention proverbial statements like:

"If I meet a jerk, how will having two jerks in the room make things better?"

"If people talk behind your back— it means that you are out two or three steps ahead of them!"

Overall, magnanimity thinking will move us out of the gutter level where we engage in reactive thinking in little-minded, grumpy, revengeful, hateful, and irritable ways. It empowers us to transcend such littleness of soul.

Contexts That Call for Magnanimity

The primary states that most of all call for the magnanimous response involve situations where we experience things *not go the way we want them to go.* We find the stimuli unpleasant, undesirable, and irritating because in some way it blocks us and hinders some important goal. Then to this state of affairs not going well, we bring several other states to bear upon it which in the end will generate the gestalt of magnanimity.

How do you currently meta-state yourself about things not going your way? *When* you feel frustrated about things not going well, what frame of mind do you get into?

Figure 14:1
Structuring Magnanimity

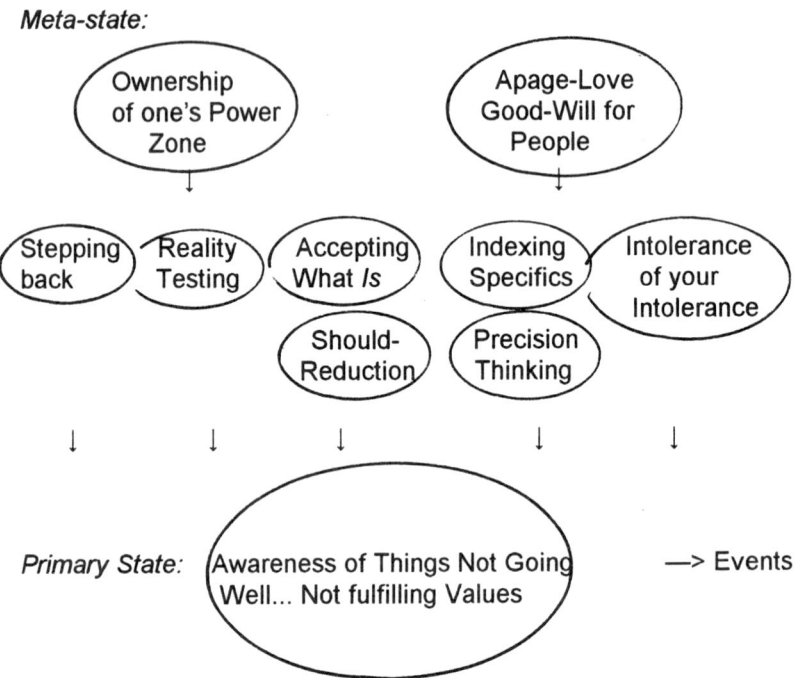

Do you depress your self and your goals when you feel frustrated or irritated? Do you whine: "Nothing ever works out for me!" Do you anger at your frustration? Do you despise your annoyance? What meta-state do you create in response to this primary experience? Do you accept your annoyance? Do you appreciate it? Enjoy it? Get curious about how you can use it for a learning? Obviously these describe a more noble way to take the frustration.

With magnanimity, because we do not take the irritation personal, we don't react in a negative or grumpy way. Rather, we take it in a big-hearted way: patiently, tolerantly, forbearingly, compassionately, nobly, etc. If we let the circumstances gall us, if we become angry, frustrated, intolerant, demanding, etc., we may enter into a dragon state. If we then become angry at our frustration—we can really crank it up. This lowers our frustration-tolerance level thereby making us more fragile.

Stepping Back & Reality Testing States

By stepping back, emotionally. from the irritation, frustration, and problem, we can dissociate from the negative emotions and begin to gain and sustain a noble perspective. This helps us to avoid personalize things. What enables you to step back from an irritation? How does that facilitate you developing a bigger picture? By contrast, when we process things associatedly as if "in" the irritation, then we will more likely develop a tunnel vision. The irritation becomes "everything in our world!" As we then become caught up in the details, this prevents us from responding magnanimously.

Staying calm and collected, we have to learn to represent the irritation and the frustration as if dissociate. By taking a spectator's view of the difficulty, we can encode our "thoughts" as a movie that we then put up on the screen of our mind. As we step back from those memories and just observe it, we encode the memory in a much more useful way. Physically, sit back in your chair or, if standing, lean back. Using this physiology to dissociate further. Then, let your dissociation drive your primary state so that it begins to modify the painful memory sufficiently, thereby allowing you to think about it comfortably. Send your brain whatever messages it needs in order to get the message:

"Then, not now or here," "Distance, not in it," "Not personal," "Safe," etc.

From a spectator or dissociated perspective, you now can treat you mental material as an editor treats a film.

- How do you want to edit this so that you can handle it cognitively and stay okay?
- So that you can transcend the little irritating emotions it could evoke?
- Would it help if you took all the color out of it?
- Or, if you made it a series of snapshots rather than a movie picture?

Then you can do some "reality thinking" about your thoughts. You can index the what, when, where, how, which, etc. You can adjust your expectations to make them realistic. What can you truly expect in this or that situation, with this or that person?

Use the following exercise to custom-make your own *"adjustment to reality."* I recommend that you get a blank sheet of paper. Then, at the top of the paper, write the words: *"I can expect____ to..."* Then, identify the person, event, situation, etc., to which you need to develop a better adjustment.

What do you find difficult to accept?
What do you tell yourself that you "can't stand?"

Once you have the targeted "reality" that tends to "get" you, then you can step back and make some reality statements about it. Identify the actions, behaviors, relational patterns, talk, etc. that seem fully "in character" with that person or system.

Expectations that do not accord with the reality of a person, system, event, situation, etc., cause us to become mal-aligned and ill-adjusted. We call these "unrealistic expectations." What can you truly expect— anticipate in terms of the way something or someone functions? Frequently, we let our desires, wants, and hopes filter out reality. Yet that only sets us up for unnecessary disappointment.

Accepting Reality

What do you accept even though you may not like it? Think of something small and simple that fits this criterion. It may be something as simple as that it sometimes rains, that the traffic will be backup at five o'clock, or that there are taxes to be paid. As you now access that *acceptance*, re-experience it fully, stepping back into it and seeing, hearing, and feeling it. When you have fully access that small and simple acceptance, stay with it. Notice what this state feels like, how you represent it, what words you say to yourself, and how your body experiences this *acceptance*.

Now, keeping the *feel* of that state so that you can use your anchor of *acceptance,* allow yourself to feel this same thing toward some irritation or frustration that you would like to accept. As you bring acceptance to bear upon some upsetting or personal slight of someone, just accept it as something that exists... and notice how your primary experience changes.

In meta-stating the irritation with acceptance, we are using a referent experience for acceptance as the framework. When I talk about the state of acceptance, I notice that my physiology which reflects acceptance involves moving my arms outward in front of me as if embracing something, welcoming it in. What did you notice about your physiology for acceptance? What did you notice in terms of your muscle tension/ relaxation, arm position, breathing, facial expressions, etc.?

With non-acceptance, we get ourselves upset more often and more intensely than necessary. And because non-acceptance leads to tunnel vision, intolerance, and dogmatism, it causes us to become stuck. No wonder *acceptance* provides us a resource for our everyday irritations.

What resourceful state do we want to bring to the primary irritation of feeling grumpy and out-of-sorts because things are not going the way we want to them? *Warm acceptance.* Acceptance does not mean a cold or sterile resignation. Do a contrastive analysis between these resignation and acceptance. Think about something you warmly and positively accept, then think about something to which you have "resigned yourself." What differs in how you represent these two experiences?

Let's now apply acceptance consciously and purposefully to our irritation. As a sentence completion exercise, write the following sentence on a sheet of paper. Then fill in 5 to 10 states that finish them:

"The frustration / irritation I need to accept is... (X)"
"As I fully accept X, I notice...'
"I accept X because..."

Another part of acceptance involves *reducing* our *"shoulds."* The opposite to accepting is demanding and "should-ing:" "It shouldn't be this way!" "You should do X." *Should*-ing cranks up not only our non-acceptance, but also intolerance, rigidity, irritability, etc. *Should-Reduction* enables us to become more accepting. Find your "shoulds" and reduce them. Albert Ellis proposes that we argue against our shoulds philosophically.

Why *should* life be fair?
Why *should* you get your way?
Why *should* s/he see things your way?

To "should" statements like, "Things should be fair for me at work!" "She should pay more attention to me." "I should get my way!" he would ask, "Why should things be fair?" "What order or structure of the universe demands this condition?"

How do we answer these questions? No answer exists. The world exists as it exists in spite of our "shoulds." Certainly, we would prefer to get our way, more attention from others, and more fairness. But preference, desire, pleasantness, etc. does not create a "should" obligation or demand on others.

Reducing our "shoulds" enables us to distinguish desires (wants, likes, preferences, etc.) from demands. It would certainly be desirable and pleasant to experience these conditions. It would make life more enjoyable. But when we move into *demandingness, we* put us into an "ordering the universe to serve our needs" state. And that creates a Dragon state indeed.

Figure 14:2

The Desire Continuum

Wish	Desire, Want, Passion	Need, Demand
A faint hope	A healthy passion	Obsessive-Compulsive
No Effective Actions	Excitement, Motivation	Needy, Dependent

Reducing our "shoulds" further enables us to discover our true wants. If we begin with a Desire Continuum as in Figure 14:2, then in the middle of it, we have *"want, desire, passion, etc."* Here we experience healthy drives and desires. At the far left we have *"wish"*—a weak version of wanting. It's so weak, in fact, that we wish and wish and wish without ever taking effective action.

> "I wish I would win the lottery." "I wish I had more physical fitness." "I wish I had more friends." "I wish I had more confidence."

To the far right of the continuum, we have *"want, should, ought."* Here, as we cross over the line from want to demand, we send messages to our brain of "need!" and necessity. On this side of the line, we become obsessive-compulsive so that our wants become over-exaggerated in their importance.

When we **under-do** any basic healthy human *want* so that it functions as a faint little wish, we deprive ourselves of passion, excitement, and motivation. When we **over-do** any healthy human *want* we turn it into a "need"—a demand, should, and order. This leads to an unbalanced and un-centered life where we treat work, relationships, approval, status, etc. as absolute needs. This develops a compulsive personality. We do have a few true needs, the Maslow Survival needs" include air, water, food, etc. Maslow erroneously labeled love and affection, security, belonging, self-esteem, self-actualization, etc., as "needs" when they rather function as "wants."

Indexing Reality

Not only do we need to accept reality, we also need to gain as much clarity as possible about the constraints, structures, and dynamics of what occurs in external reality. We can do this by "indexing." *The indexing questions* empower us to develop much more precise maps about the external world (not perfect maps, but maps that allow us to negotiate the territory).

Indexing— We index
- the content or subject using *what?*
- the time using *when?*
- the place using *where?*
- the persons using *who?*
- the process using *how?*
- the reasons and motivations using *(why?*

Indexing information using these formats or categories and in these terms enables us to gain mental clarity and focus.

By way of contrast, sometimes when we experience some irritation or frustration, we end up over-generalizing that experience. Then we start in with catastrophizing or awfulizing. "Because I got rejected by two females, therefore all women will reject me." This over-generalizing process makes accepting and adjusting well to a rejection much more, and unnecessarily, difficult.

By indexing a difficulty or a series of difficulties, we gain the clarity and precision that then allows us to create more appropriate mappings in terms of understandings and beliefs.

> Who specifically said no to you? When? Under what circumstances? To what proposal of yours? How did you present yourself? Etc. What other contributing factors played a part of this?

In so indexing, we can *keep perspective* of the big picture so that we are not allowed to become caught up in painful details which we could then so easily blow out of proportion and use to awfulize.

Without indexing we easily distort our pictures of reality and our memories of hurts. Without indexing, we lack precision which encourages the pain, irritation, upsetness, etc., to grow. Consequently, we code the experience as painful, unacceptable, "bad," etc. And this puts us at an ill-adjustment with the reality of fallible and unpleasant things that do occur.

Bring with an indexing state of mind and bring this *search for precision and accuracy* upon your frustrations and irritations. This will enable you to *contain* whatever "evil" circumstances that you have suffered so that you can stay resourceful and *not* misread it. If we suffered a painful experience, as a "B" rated movie, we can frame it as an experienced we once went through. Doing that allows us to *contain* it in the time-space continuum in which it occurred so that it doesn't become "the movie of my life." Then, once contained, we can ask a multitude of intelligent solution-oriented questions that enable us to build a powerful map for navigating life from this day forward:

What can I learn from that?
"What learnings do I **not** need to make from that?
How can I use this to my profit?

This way of thinking and responding then enables us to transcend to larger-level understandings and empowering beliefs so that we can think-and-feel and respond much more graciously, with much more sweet reasonableness.

Proactivity As a State

You will more likely respond in a big-hearted and noble-spirited way if you have a deep sense inside that you have lots of "response" power — lots of choices about how to handle frustrations or irritations. The more you operate from *a multiple-choice list* of choices, the more magnanimous will be your response. You could still respond in a reactive, hateful, vengeful, narrow-minded, and peevish way, but you probably will not, especially when you have better choices.

In developing the "response" power that arises from our *power zone,* we develop an enlarged sense of ourselves. We experience a sense of *self-efficacy*:

"I have lots of choices! I don't need to blame or accuse—I can develop greater power in taking effective action and flexibility in how I handle set-backs. I can trust my thinking-and-emoting power in building up an effective map."

Take a moment and think about a time when you felt proactive. Once you re-access that state fully and completely, let your imagination bring that state to bear on some everyday irritation. Stay with those thoughts-and-feelings for a moment. Let the imagined transformations work in your unconscious mind and neurology. Wouldn't that assist you in developing more magnanimity?

Love as a Valuing State
Another way to access a noble big-heartedness is to access a thinking-and-feeling state of caring and loving. *"Agape"* is the Greek word which refers to this kind of noble love. It literally means a "benevolent good-will." This describes an obvious expression of big-heartedness—the resourceful state wherein we see value in people. In the first century, Paul said that "Agape-love is slow to lose patience, it looks for a way of being constructive...it never fails"

As benevolence and as good will, the attitude of agape-love enables us to think-feel respectfully of others rather than demonizing them as some incarnation of "evil" because they hurt us or act in an ugly way. The love of agape enables us to see beyond a person's behavior to their person.

Putting It All Together
Now give all of these pieces that make up this gestalt experience, it becomes clear why we may find it difficult to just *"fly into magnanimity"* as we fly into primary states (i.e., fear, anger, joy, calm, etc.). The consciousness of this transcendent state contains many layered pieces of thinking-and-feeling that we have apply to some slight or hurt. We have to put them together and rehearse the pieces until they become streamlined so that the over-all sense of larged-mindedness begins to drive our perspective, attitude, emotions, and behaviors. Then we can experience a "reasonableness of mind that holds control over our passions" and a "loftiness of spirit that enables us to bear trouble calmly."

Now add one more piece. Access the state of *intolerance.* Yes, intolerance! Part of the current problem that many people have lies in the fact that they "tolerate their intolerance" far too much. Consider what it feels like if you become truly and completely *intolerant about your intolerance.* Stay with that in your imagination for a moment as you map out how to feel completely *intolerant* about the intolerance about putting up with some slight or hurt in the first place. Now use this higher frame as a meta-state to support the entire gestalt for magnanimity.

Forgiveness

As magnanimity deals with and addresses hurts, so does *forgiveness*. Do these states differ then? Yes. While both address behaviors that wound relationship, the difference lies in *the **size** of the hurt*.

Magnanimity describes states wherein we think-and-feel so big-hearted that we can actually overlook the slights and wounds. Our enlarged sense of safety and security allows us to dismiss the hurt.

Forgiveness, however, takes a different approach because the hurt it addresses creates *so much suffering* that we experience the wound as *unacceptable*. In those cases, we cannot overlook, forbear, or ignore the behavior. We have to deal with it in another way—the way of forgiveness.

The hurt and suffering we need to forgive describes a major violation, insult, and betrayal. While we can overlook many insults, acts of selfishness, thoughtlessness, and slights, the things that we need to forgive address larger wounds, it involves things that harm the very fabric of the relationship or human dignity. This allows us to differentiate between magnanimity and forgiveness as resources.

When both little hurts or major violations occur, we easily "take it personal." Yet doing so induces a not-so-resourceful Dragon State. We access a Dragon state of feeling insulted, put-down, violated, etc., that arouses the Dragons of rage, hate, revenge, etc. In magnanimity, we learn to overlook it, dismiss it, take into consideration where the person comes from, etc.

In forgiveness, we don't overlook or tolerate, we rather separate sinner from sin so we can *rage against the hurt,* the ugly behavior while simultaneously maintaining respect and compassion for the person. In forgiveness we move to the place where we will "cease to resent an offender," to "pardon that offender," and to "give up our resentment." We will also "give up our claim for requital," so revenge and bitterness doesn't "rust out our pipes!" This gives us the capacity (whether we choose to use it or not) of "giving" to that offender as we previously ("fore") gave to them. It returns our powers to us.

What's the value of this highly resourceful state? It enables us to effectively interact with *fallible* human beings who will always and only can think, emote, speak and behave fallibly. Our interactions with them will inescapably involve responding in fallible and hurtful ways at times. Forgiveness enables us to not become stuck in the hurt. It enables us to recover and to move on. It allows us to keep our heart and spirit clean and sweet.

As you consider how to build up this higher level state, access a memory of forgiveness. Have you ever forgiven someone? Think about that time—a time when you received what you considered a major hurt. But then, later, over a period of time, you released that person from the hurtful behavior, so that you no longer held it against them. You have forgiven them for that hurt. After you have fully and completely accessed that resource, identify *what* resources enabled you to pull that off. What ideas, beliefs, understandings, feelings, etc. resources did you bring to bear on your state? What beliefs and values did you apply? How did you language yourself, the hurt, and the person?

Self-Esteeming
Put yourself into a state where you fully esteem your *self* as a person of innate value, worth, dignity, etc. Use the previous meta-stating process of self-esteeming. This will prevent you from making the mistake of thinking that the hurt robs you of your God-given dignity. We don't want to make that semantic mistake. We won't give our resource of self-worth away just because we experienced some hurt. Self-esteeming allows us to stay centered so we do not take it personal and we do not make the experience a self-defining event.

Distinguishing Person & Behavior
"People" are more than their behavior. Recognizing others as more than their actions, prevents us making mistaking and identifying a person with his or her *behaviors* (i.e., thoughts, emotions, languaging, etc.). People are more than their psychological functions.

Access then a state wherein you clearly made this distinction. You clearly distinguished between a human being and the particular ways that person expressed him or herself at a given time in a given context. If you have difficulty with this one, then think about your one-year old self, your five-year old self, and your thirteen year old self. Put an image upon the screen of your mind about these former selves and notice fully and completely the repertoire of behaviors and languaging that you had at those times and situations. Are you more than the sum of all your parts? Do you exist above and beyond any particular behaviors you may have produced on a given day? Or do you think,

"I am my behaviors"?

The mental surgery of distinguishing *person and behavior* crucially determines whether we will be able to experience the resource of forgiveness or not. This applies to self-forgiveness as well as forgiveness of others. Because this distinction plays such a crucial role in forgiveness, take a moment to think about some statement you could invent to assist you in performing this particular mental surgery.

The Rage State About Hurt

Making the discernment between person and behavior moves us to a place where we can effectively use your powers to rage against a hurtful and unacceptable behavior. So go ahead and allow yourself to get "as mad as hell" at the wounding behavior that you will not, and should not, tolerate for one minute! You can now fully recognize just how *intolerable* you feel about that behavior. In your value system, you say that you will not accept such behavior. Good.

In this, we do *not* want to access magnanimity. We do *not* want to accept, tolerate, or forbear with regard to the behavior. No! Instead we want to here identify our ethical boundaries and rage against insulting, degrading, violating behaviors that should never occur. Focus here on the **behavior**, of course, and not the person. So as you feel a total repulsion toward it, anger and rage *at the behavior*.

Esteem and Appreciate of the Person

As the person/behavior discernment allows us to rage against the behavior it also enables us to simultaneously feel compassion, love, appreciation, and respect *toward the person*.

This shows the complexity of this resource and the multi-layered consciousness involved in this higher state of mind. With this we can now see *the person* in a completely realistic way, that is, as a fallible, insecure, limited, ignorant about many things, etc., and a *person* (i.e., a human being). You can see the person as someone who *needs* our sympathy, empathy, pity, and support. We can also recognize that when we sin against someone and violate them by doing something unacceptable— we have not only hurt and wounded them, but we have also violated ourselves.

This understanding enables us to take a stand against such "sins" (i.e., moral violations) while simultaneously loving and appreciating the person. We now recognize "sin" as hurtful and ugly behaviors which violates everybody, perpetrator and victim. Does this languaging enable you to put this concept into a compelling, motivating, and memorable form? If not, be sure to phrase it for yourself so that you have a map that can enable you to move to forgiveness as a higher frame of mind. Do it for yourself—to keep your own spirit clean and sweet. Otherwise, the Dragons of Resentment and Bitterness will consume you with hatefulness.

Expressing compassion and grace to the person who hurt us enables us to break the all too easy confusion about identifying people with behaviors. It also leads us to the resource of firmness, strength, good boundaries, assertiveness, etc., *while still maintaining a loving attitude*. In so doing we don't have to become hard, cold, and unfeeling to protect ourselves from hurt. This saves us from getting caught up in bitterness, hatefulness, cynicism, etc. We can say, "Forgive them, they don't know what they truly do."

A "Decision to Release"

Forgiveness begins with a cognitive awareness of the person and behavior distinction and then leads to accessing two radically different emotions (i.e., rage and compassion). All of this then leads us to another cognitive awareness, awareness of our *conative power of decision*.

Conation speaks about our power of choice and will. We intentionally decide to *let go* of our complaint, our grief, our internal hurt, and not hold such against the person any more. Intentionally making this empowering decision, we are freed and released from the need of holding the hurt against the person. This allows us to become un-stuck in our own minds and emotions about the hurt. By so deciding, we cut off the possibility of holding on to our grievance.

Reality Testing the Context of the Hurt

Over the years of doing psychotherapy, I have noticed how very, very seldom that hurts and relational wounds occur in a vacuum wherein one party completely out of the blue decides to grievously wound the other. They almost always arise in the context of inter-actions between intimates (i.e., friends, spouses, family members) and that means that, at some level, *even we who suffered the wound almost always played some contributing part in the hurtful experience*. We neglected the other, ignored the other, provoked the other, etc. Personally, I cannot think of a single major hurt that I have received *as an adult* from another person that came so much "out-of-the-blue" that I didn't play some part in the process. (If we receive abuse, violation, abandonment *as children*—that obviously describes a trauma received before we entered response-able adult life and with access to our power zone.)

Thinking systemically about our part in a hurtful experience assists us in thinking realistically, taking responsibility for our part in the system, recognizing our own limitations and fallibilities, and identifying the things that we can work on and improve. Given this, take a moment to ask yourself,

> "What part did I play in that hurtful experience?"
> "As I put my memories upon the screen of my life and sit back in the projection booth and observe, how could I edit my behaviors and responses that would have changed the way the movie played out?"

If appropriate, offer the person a new beginning. Forgiveness does **not** create a new relationship, it only makes it possible. It does not compel it. Since relating to another person functions as a *conditional* set of interactions, of give-and-take, if the person has not and does not see how he or she participated in the wound—to re-enter relationship only courts more wounds of the same order ("casting pearls before swine").

Re-negotiate the relationship so that *the relatings* (i.e., the set of interactions exchanged verbally and behaviorally) with the other meet each person's wants. Promise to fill up each person's "emotional bank account," and to meet the behavioral criteria of respect, compassion, love, etc. Each person will need to relate from an attitude of personal response-ableness, accountability, and consciousness. Then we can create an "action plan" so that we do not reproduce the hurt again.

Summary
- We have the choice of two royal states for accessing some tremendous resources if we want to become unstuck from the places of the past: *Magnanimity and Forgiveness.*
- These two resources describe two very different phenomenaa. In magnanimity, we feel so big-hearted, noble, gracious, compassionate, tolerant, expansive, loving, etc. that we just release the person from whatever slights or hurts offered.
- Forgiveness is an entirely different story. The complexity of forgiveness involves feeling first anger-rage, upsetness, hurt, suffering, etc. and then more weakly (but ever growing stronger) compassion, love, grace, etc. At the emotional level, *forgiveness does not feel very transcending or even gracious.* It feels more like a decision; "I will not hold this against you in spite of how much pain it caused me." As a meta-feeling, we experience it primarily as a judgment that we make according to our higher values and beliefs.
- Both magnanimity and forgiveness are tremendous resources for relationships. They also function as marvelous resources for *keeping a sweet, gracious, and compassionate mental and emotional state.* Without such, we can easily fall victim to some pretty nasty Dragons: to Angry sullen Dragons, to Bitter and Resentful, to Dragons of Revenge and Dragons of Being a Victim.

Chapter 15

SLAYING THE DRAGONS OF INNER CONFLICT & DISQUIETUDE

AND CASTING A SPELL FOR SERENE INNER PEACE

When the winds of misfortune and difficulties blow our way, when the storms of life whip into our experiences and we suffer the rough weather, the strong winds, the agitated upheavals, we often come face to face with numerous Dragons. We encounter the Dragons of frustration, agitation, upsetness, confusion, chaos, distress, etc. Mind and emotions become conflicted as we lose our way, become insecure and confused, and feel helpless to positively affect things.

How do you respond to such difficulties?

Begin with a primary state of a mental-and-emotional storm, one wherein nothing seems secure or nailed down... When you imagine that, what meta-state frame of mind do you automatically go to or enter into?

Depending on how you think-and-feel about your primary feelings of agitation, frustration, distress, stress, confusion, etc., there's a multitude of Dragons that you may generate. You may get into inner conflict with yourself about...

    your values (confusion),
    your decisions (indecision),
    your understandings (erroneous ideas), or

your emotions (disquietude).

And when you get into those states, it then becomes easy to arouse the Dragons of dis-ease, reactivity, irritability, grumpiness, etc. If your thoughts--and-feelings about yourself turn negative, it then becomes typical for you to turn your psychic energies against yourself and to thereby call forth the Dragons of self-contempt and depreciation.

When we apply the resourceful states of peace and serenity to times of ease, peace, non-conflict, etc., we enter into a gentle and quiet sense of contentment and even happiness. We then begin to feel peaceful about our peaceful existence. This type of peace, however, could take the form of non-vigilant softness.

Yet if we apply this quality of "peace" to the times when we really need it, that is, in times of trouble, distress, problems, pains, and unsettling events, then what? What overall gestalt state emerges from that mixture?

In a way I suppose this expresses a seeming paradox about *inner peace and serenity*. We need this higher state primarily when we experience primary states of trouble, distress, problems, and frustrations. We need it most of all when things are not going well for us. **Inner** peace occurs *inside our thinking and emoting states* and empowers us to use calmness to create a larger level experience, an unperturbability and quietude of mind when all hell breaks lose outside.

Self-Distressing Skills: *Scene 1*

As Charlie Brown passes Snoopy one day, he off-handedly waved and said, "Hi, fuzzy-face!"

Snoopy found that startling, "Fuzzy-face?"

In the second frame, Snoopy continued to think about himself in terms of that jarring and unsettling phrase, *"Fuzzy-face?!"*

Then, looking sad and forlorn, Snoopy sighs, "I must be getting old and sensitive. A few years ago something like that never would have bothered me!"

And yet Snoopy felt bothered. He has no peace about this as the following scenes indicate.

Scene 2:

Night has come. Snoopy lies in his dog-house with his eyes wide open. He can't sleep. In frames two and three we see him going out to a hill, alone, and sitting them in the dark. Finally, we have a peek into

his consciousness as he sighs, *"Fuzzy-face!"*
    Snoopy drives his lack of peace about this with his brooding about those words. Have you ever done that one?

Scene 3:
    Walking along with his face down and body slumping, Snoopy thinks, "'Fuzzy-face'! He called me 'fuzzy-face.' It's wrong to be upset by such a little thing. I'll have to get hold of myself."
    Snoopy here meta-states himself with an awareness of the upset he's creating by his brooding. He does this by thinking about how "wrong" it is to feel so upset. In that, he meta-states himself with judgment about his distress.
    In frame three, Snoopy gets a hold of himself by forcing a grin. But it didn't last. Slumping down again, he sighs, "'Fuzzy-face'! Good grief."

Scene 4:
    Snoopy notices Charlie Brown walking down the road. "Here comes Charlie Brown," he says to himself, "If he calls me 'fuzzy-face' again, I don't know what I'll do!"
    And sure enough, when Charlie Brown comes by, he waves and says, "Hi, fuzzy-face!!" and then moves on with a little smirk on his face as if enjoying teasing him with the phrase, "fuzzy-face."
    Snoopy broods about it in the last frame, "I was right. I didn't know what to do!"
    By now Snoopy has really let this particular phrase get under his skin and irritate and bother him. As a piece of linguistic-semantic awareness, he has given it a lot of power to rattle him.

Scene 5:
    The next day, Charlie Brown comes by again and waves, "Well, hi there 'ol fuzzy-face!"
    Then he stops to rub it in some more. "How's ol' fuzzy-face today? You look kind of depressed." Then lifting his face up to his, he says, "Has something touched your fuzzy ol' heart?"
    Walking away with a smirk, Snoopy thinks, "I can't stand it!"
    Snoopy is here using the very linguistics that promote and perpetuate a state of inner dis-ease, *"I can't stand it!"* When we say the "I can't stand..." words, we essentially program ourselves for a semantic

reaction to some button.

Scene 6:
   Snoopy now deepens his semantic program or strategy for calling forth a Dragon of Disturbance. He sniffs as he broods, "Fuzzy-face! He walked by and he said, 'Hi, fuzzy face!"
   Slumping away, he says to himself, "I can't remember when anything has upset me so."
   Then stopping, he begins to reframe himself, "Still... I don't know why it should. After all, what does he expect me to be, *clean-shaven?"*

Scene 7:
   Nancy grabs a hold of Snoopy and hugs him and goes "Mmmmm!" And then, looking him straight in the eye, says, "I like you, Snoopy. I like you because you have such a warm, fuzzy face!"
   Charlie Brown sees this and comes up to Snoopy after Nancy leaves. Snoopy then turns and gives him a Brooklyn salute raspberry as he sticks his tongue out at Charlie Brown. The experience of having his *Fuzzy-Face* validated by Nancy has completely allowed him to reframe the meaning of that phrase. Thus dissolving the Dragon of Mental Disturbance completely.
   Our *peace of mind* has to do with how well our ideas and concepts relate to our experiences. Physically, when some part of our body suffers a wound, hurt, infection, etc., we say that we have a distress or disease of the body. Mental *diseases* refer to the ease or rather lack of ease we have with the *meanings* and interpretations we give to things. Mentally-and-emotionally we come to dis-ease when we have a poor relationship to various ideas.

Real vs. Pseudo Peace: *Scene 1*
   With Linus sucking his thumb and holding his blanket, Lucy approaches with Charlie Brown and says, "You talk about peace of mind. Well, look at Linus. He thinks he has peace of mind, but is that **real** peace of mind?"
   Then bopping him on the head with her fist, she shouts, "I say, **NO!**" Then walking on, she tells Charlie Brown, "Let me tell you what **real** peace of mind is..."

Scene 2:
On the wall, Charlie Brown asked Linus about his experience with his states of mind. "Do you ever hear something in your head that won't go away? You know like a tune or a certain phrase?"

Such can certainly disturb our peace of mind as when you toss and turn on your pillow, playing over and over the same dialogue. In the background Lucy shouts, "Where's that stupid brother of mine?!"

Linus answers Charlie Brown, "All the time."

Scene 3:
Calvin smiles and says, "Here I am, happy and content."

Then suddenly a thought pops into his mind. "...but not euphoric."

Then self-reflexively he comments, "So now I'm no longer content. I'm unhappy. My day is ruined."

Finally walking away he comments, "I need to stop thinking while I'm ahead."

Calvin thinks that he could solve the problem of the meta-state of discontent that he created as he continued to think if he only stopped thinking sooner. Yet we cannot *not* stop our reflexive meta-thinking. We need only to learn productive and enhancing meta-thinking.

Responding With "Peace"

What we need at such times consists of *a state of calm* (freedom from agitation in face of danger or provocation), *tranquility* (a more settled and deeper quietude of composure), and *serenity* (a lofty and unclouded peace). At the meta-state level, we need self-integration, wholeness, and balance.

This state of *serenity*, and the thoughts-feelings of *serene* arise from a powerful metaphor. It literally means, "clear and free of storms or unpleasant change, shining bright and steady." Coming from the Latin (*serenus*) and showing up in the Old Higher German word *(serawen)*, it refers to "becoming dry." The word then came to refer to the ability or power to face life's distresses and storms with presence of mind, clarity, stability, tranquility, wisdom, compassion, optimism, confidence, etc.

That sounds like a pretty powerful resource indeed! This meta-state functions similarly to the states of proactivity and defenselessness as it operates from the same kind of positive optimism that drives un-insultability. So we speak about this inner peace of serenity as *that internal unruffledness of mind-emotion which allows us to stay centered, stable, sane, balanced, etc.*

To begin to cast a spell for that kind of mental and emotional stability, think back to a time when you felt totally and completely at peace with yourself, your body, and your world. And allow yourself for a few moments to become bathed in that peace again—mind and body, delighting yourself in those sights, sounds, and sensations that induce you into a deep and magical sense of peace. What moment of tranquility can you recall and *use it now* to access an experience of peace? Use your representational power to fully and completely see, hear, and feel again... in your body... the experience.

Because as you take a deep breath and relax, really relax, your unconscious mind can pick out a good memory of a peaceful place where you found yourself not only feeling comfortable, but also contented in a happy and pleasant way. And you can allow yourself to *"snapshot"* this experience so that you can keep the things you see and hear and feel and recall them anytime you want to *feel this sense of peace.* And notice what happens when you give your unconscious mind permission to *double your sense of peace*— notice what happens to the images, the sounds, the words, and the feelings in your body.

And now you can begin to bring this resource of peace with all the peaceful feelings to bear on a time and place in your life that you might experience tomorrow, or the next day, or sometime next week where you anticipate some distress, or storm, or agitation, but now you can *feel peace about that disturbance.* Where would you really like to take this deep sense of peacefulness and apply it in your everyday life? With whom? In what set of interactions? Or perhaps in some instance in how you relate to yourself. Suppose you bring this peace to bear upon your thoughts-and-feelings when you make a mistake ... or receive criticism ... or get cut off in traffic. Because you can, and will, bring it to bear on some primary state of stress, knowing that when you do— you modulate that primary state in new and surprising ways.

Because in applying this resource of peace toward a lower state of "storm" enables you to build a meta-state of inner peace thereby empowering you to feel inwardly calm even when outward agitation occurs. Now you no longer have to feel dependent upon the weather of some person, place, or situation since you can take your inner weather of stability, calmness, and peacefulness wherever you go. And you can imagine how you can take a deep breath... and hold it... until you release it... and relax fully whenever you notice something stressful, challenging, problematic.

Spend a moment before you come back here to be with those thoughts-and-feelings of inner peace, fully and completely, integrating them into yourself, letting your unconscious mind store this resource so that you can access it as you choose.

Now what you have just experienced involves two things. First, you *accessed* a state of calm peacefulness and then secondly, you began using that resource to meta-state yourself with it by applying it to a state of agitation. *Access and apply*— that's the secret of meta-stating, of calling forth a new experience, of casting a spell that sets a whole new frame of reference for your thinking and feeling. The more thoroughly you do this, the more you *apply* your thoughts-and-feelings of calmness and mental collectedness and *apply* it to some distress. Setting a frame that "future paces" how to run your brain in this way *installs the resources of calmness, relaxation, peacefulness, etc.* into your very neurology, as a map for navigating the experience.

Having done that, now notice what happens when you bring the internal kinesthetic feelings of your state of peace to bear on the primary state of agitation, distress, and "storm." How does that change, alter, transform, and/or modify the primary experience? Notice how it becomes translated at the linguistic level.

Frequently, when you meta-state yourself, you will not keep the kinesthetic feelings which you originally experienced in the primary state. By moving up to a higher logical level and applying the resource, the primary feelings *go through a translation*, they become textured in a new and different way. They become languaged so that even "the feeling itself" becomes a new and different kind of subjective phenomenon. It may create a meta-level phenomena like a belief, a concept, an understanding, etc. We now create *feelings of the mind*, that is, "emotions," and "It feels like..." terms.

Now we experience (at the meta-level) the calmness and peace as *peaceful thoughts, beliefs, and concepts*. The kinesthetic sensations of peacefulness become structured and stabilized as they take the form of peaceful abstractions. This creates the "emotions" of the "mind" such as serenity which, in turn, guide and guard our heart in the midst of external storms.

To turn your experience of peacefulness into a higher level meta-state, take a moment to write some answers to the following questions.

Stop. Get a sheet of paper. Begin writing.
- *What* do you need to say to yourself *about* the distress, the storm, the problem, the agitation, yourself, your future, etc., to allow yourself to maintain a sense of inner peace and undisturbability? (Make a list of the supporting resources.)
- *What* specific statements enable you to think-and-feel calm, serene, and composed about your external storm?

"Inner peace," or serenity, arises as and exists as a linguistic-semantic phenomenon. It's a gestalt state that entirely depends on *how* we define, interpret, and appraise things. In that sense, it emerges due to whatever lies within "the eye of the beholder." What lies in your eye? What do you "see?" This explains how and why some people can maintain an inner calm, sanity, collectedness, togetherness, centeredness, etc., in some contexts that push the buttons of others. The higher level ideas that set the frame for their way of being in the world give them a map for handling things.

This means that until we find and/or create the words by which we can avoid thinking-feeling disturbance and think-feel from a state of *un-disturbability,* we will find it most difficult to access a meta-state of inner peace.

What languaging enables you to operate out of calmness, collectedness, contentment, presence of mind which therefore gives you ready access to wisdom, compassion, and general resourcefulness?

Resources for Inner Peace

Now if peace refers to "a state of tranquility or quiet," "a freedom from disturbance, a sense of security, order, harmony, concord between parties, no oppressive thoughts-emotions," then *what resources* in terms of beliefs, perceptions, values, etc. do you need to bring to bear on your primary states of disturbance and agitation? To take your "peace" representation one step further. Now think about a time when you experienced lots of disturbances (i.e., demands, frustrations, upset plans, disappointed expectations, criticisms, etc.), things that normally disturbed your peace of mind, yet in a given instance, you maintained composure.

As you quiet yourself and begin to search through your memory banks, look first for something small and simple. If you just can't find a time of inner peace, then let your creative imagination begin to imagine what it will feel like if you could have such an experience. Once you have so accessed a memory, or created a fantasy, in your mind, explore the resource question again.

> What belief, feeling, understanding, behaviors, etc. resources allow and enable this experience?
> What do you need to keep composure?
> To keep un-disturbability?

Identifying these resources will enable you to find the component pieces so you can build your own strategy and meta-state yourself.

You'll need the ability to *"not personalize."* Personalizing causes us to lose our peace. When we bring in the disturbance out there, we cause ourselves to become disturbed.

What resource enables you to not personalize? Keeping busy, keeping focused? *To stay focused on your values and visions.* When you become distracted from your values and visions—you become agitated and inwardly disturbed. *Clarity* of awareness (focus) helps us to keep perspective. *Self-esteeming* keeps our inner peace—the storms out there no longer define "us." Non-personalizing! This enables us to distinguish between external storm and internal stability of identity and purpose.

Patience gives us yet another resource. The ability to "suffer-long" (long-suffering) and to for-bear the storm which occurs as we realize, "This too will pass." When we suck the storm into our souls—we usually develop a tunnel-vision about things. We then get impatiently caught up in the details of the stressors. By contrast, when we have inner peace, we maintain *a larger and longer perspective* about things. We engage in long-term thinking.

Acceptance, in the sense of recognizing what exists as what "is" without necessarily liking it, provides another powerful resource. The internal state of hating and rejecting reality robs one of peace.

Align with someone who has gone through a disturbance. We call this modeling. It has the effect of *universalizing* the storm thereby preventing us from thinking of our experience as "unique in human experience!" Crying "Why me Lord?" cheats us of inner peace. Reclassify the storm as a common human experience.

Inner Peace, not Outer Peace

We need clarity that *inner* peace refers to, the peace on the inside—in our mind-emotions, rather than the peace on the outside. If we assume that we have access to inner-peace because we have a sense of peace in life that we derive because we experience "things going just fine!" (times of success, prosperity, ease, etc.), we may confuse *outer* peace with *inner* peace. Now without doubt, we all like and enjoy and long for *outer* peace. We like to sing *Oklahoma*.

"Oh what a beautiful morning! Oh what a beautiful day! Everything's coming up roses! Everything is going my way!"

Yet such outer peace *depends* on external events, people, situations, etc., going our way. *Inner* peace can occur *in spite of* external storms. It results as a high level complex state of consciousness where we take our internal weather of calmness and stability wherever we go. Instead of waiting for the external weather of circumstances to change—we bring a bright, sunny, stable, and warm disposition to the storms of life. This "living from within" means we have our "locus of control" inside us, rather than outside.

The Hebrews had a word that describes this kind of inner strength and wholeness. *"Shalom"* speaks about the richness and depth of an inner peace of mind and perspective. *Shalom* focuses on the positive facets of peace. It describes not so much the absence of conflict, hostility, disturbances, etc., (*freedom from...*), but the positive qualities of completeness, soundness, security, harmony, tranquility, wholeness, goodness (*freedom to...*). This means that "inner peace" describes our sense of transcendence over the distressful storms.

The Shalom Meta-Stating Process

While we need acceptance and lots of it for reality before we can move to that healthy form of acceptance, we must first attain a clear consciousness of external and even internal reality. This means that our willingness and skill in living consciously without deception, delusion, denial, or without using any other mechanism to defend self against reality precedes acceptance. We can't accept what we remain unaware of, ignorant to, or unconscious of. *Accepting difficulties*, troubles, problems, set-backs, life's ups-and-downs, distresses, frustrations, etc., recognizes that such things occur.

To become more conscious take a moment and write down a number of the unpleasant realities that exist in your life that you need to *accept*.

What agitating, disturbing, and problematic facets of reality in yourself, others, in your work environment, home environment, social environment, etc. exists that you need to truly take cognizance of, acknowledge, and then mentally-emotionally *accept*? Since we often get side-swiped in life by events that we "didn't expect," we first need to do some "expectation adjustment."

To find these current non-acceptances in your life, write five to ten sentence completion statements in response to:
    (1) "Things I can't stand include..."
    (2) "Things that rattle my cage include..."
    (3) "Things that really get to me and to which I feel upset include..."

Conversely you can take the following statement and apply it to any person, event, or situation with which you deal: **"I can expect X to..."** For the X, identify the facet of your world that seems to robs you of inner peace. Then write five to ten sentence completions to that statement.

For example,
> "I can expect dad not to call, not to say 'I love you,' not to demonstrate himself as an emotionally available person."

Or,
> "I can expect my coworker to act like a snob, to use condescending words, to act like I do not exist..."

Doing this makes us more conscious of the realities with which we deal so that we can begin to adjust ourselves to the facts, constraints, dynamics, etc. of those realities. Then we don't have to waste our psychic energy fighting those realities, hating them, despising them, and wishing they would just go away. We can now use our energy on coming up with good strategic responses to them.

Making these realities explicit enables us to *realign our expectations* so they more accurately fit our experiences. In this way we experience "a cessation of hostilities" within and stop fighting what exists as real in our world.

Acceptance

For many people, increasing awareness of what *is* induces a state of pained awareness. In knowing, they judge and evaluate and do so in a negative way. As a result, the more they know, they more they don't like what they find. This increases their awareness of the pains, problems, distresses, upsets, etc. of life. It makes them less and less in a place to embrace and welcome the world as they find it. So for them, awareness undermines acceptance..

Conversely, if we learn how to open our eyes and ears and come into sensory awareness without a mind full of evaluations, but in a state of simple *acceptance* of what *is*, then acceptance becomes a near magical resource and frame of mind.

It becomes even more magical when we bring *a state of warm acceptance* to bear on our primary states, especially those wherein we face trouble, distress, and frustration. By doing so, we can magically modulate that experience and texture it with a new feel and response pattern.

Now *acceptance* does not mean that we like, desire, want, condone, or even approve of what we have. It only means that we look it in the face, notice what it *is,* and then welcome it. We accept what *is* as that which does indeed exist. We recognize, acknowledge, and welcome reality in all its forms (i.e., social, political, inter-personal, external, etc.). In acceptance we do not judge reality as good or bad; we only perceive it for what it is and how it operates. By acceptance we can search for, perceive, find, and then look reality in the face without blinking, pretending, denying, angering, etc.. Our attitude becomes one of, "*Whatever is, is."* Such acceptance does not mean that we fall into a cold and sterile resignation. "Well, that's the way it is." Resigning and giving up does not describe the resource with which we want to color our states. Rather, we want a mental and emotional state of dispassionate welcoming so that we can then access what we can do about making things better.

> What do you find really easy to accept?
> What do you warmly welcome into your presence?
> How do you represent this?
> What qualities do you encode your sights, sounds, sensations, and words as you accept this thing?
> When you contrast that with something that you do not accept, how do the qualities of the representations differ?

Now think about some of the supporting beliefs that empower your ability to accept something. What beliefs assist you in moving toward a more conscious and explicit state of acceptance? I like using the following:

"I have nothing to fear from reality."

"I can boldly make myself a friend to reality; that will help me to effectively adapt and adjust to reality."

"Adjustment to any reality (physics, inter-personal relations, language, culture, etc.) comes after I first accept such realities."

What other beliefs support you in accessing a stronger state of acceptance?

As a perceptual orientation, acceptance recognizes two things as simultaneously true and valid:

(1) I did not create the universe and so I don't need to nor can I play god over the world. I do not have all-knowing, all powerful, or ever-present powers! I have a great many limitations in my powers of mind, emotion, speech, and behavior.

(2) While I did not create the objective world, I do play a key role in forming, molding, and effecting my subjective world. I do have some powers which impact and effect my realities.

This synthesis describes a balancing perspective which acceptance brings that reminds me that (1) I do not have all power or control and yet (2) I have some powers of creation and influence.

With such conscious acceptance, we can then move on to the state of serenity. *Serenity* emerges from the wisdom that develops as we learn to discern *what* we can do something about and *what* we cannot. Inner peace begins when we can recognize and distinguish *(1) our circle of response and power* from *our circle of concern.* The first circle describes an arena wherein we can take action to deal with the troubles, problems, and challenges. This arena of power enlivens our courage. The second circle describes an arena where we send out our heart, but in which we have no influence or power to effect anything. In this arena of non-power, we just accept it without fighting.

When we get into the converse, a state of *non-acceptance,* we experience a negative state wherein our thinking-and-feeling involves a rejecting of our difficulties and troubles. With that frame of mind, we then move through life hating and rejecting what we find. This also leads to tormenting oneself with lots of *why* questions.

"Why do bad things happen?"

"Why does everything always go wrong for me?"

"Why can't anything work out for me?"

In rejecting reality for what it *is*, the state of non-acceptance organizes us to see *what we want* to see *so much,* that these desires become our perceptual filters. Eventually, we can't see anything apart from those filters. In this way, non-acceptance puts us at odds with reality. It then leads to the use of defense mechanisms (i.e., denial, blame, self-rejection, etc.) which means that we begin defending ourselves from knowing reality. It makes us an enemy to reality. Yet in taking this stance, we only empower undesired things to have more power over us. It reduces our consciousness, rather than expands it.

Acceptance: *Scene 1*
   Peppermint Patty looked at Snoopy and said to Charlie Brown, "I don't understand. I thought the new law said that dogs have to be kept tied."
   Charlie Brown said, "There are some things that are stronger than rope, you know."
   Then looking at Snoopy and folding his arms across his chest, he said, "I have Snoopy tied up with a feeling of obligation."
   Of course, to feel bound up with chord of obligation robs one of the inner peace that comes from self-awareness. Here Snoopy had given his power away.

Acceptance: *Scene 2*
   Rather than catching a ball, the ball bangs Lucy in the head. That provoked Charlie Brown to yell at her, "Lucy, You're the worst player in the history of the game!"
   She responded, "You can't prove that! You should never say things that you can't prove!"
   So Charlie Brown tempers his statement, "In all probability, you are the worst layer in the history of the game!"
   Lucy mildly said, "I can accept that."

Acceptance: *Scene 3*
   Linus looks at the sign on Lucy's Psychiatry help booth, "When you say, 'The doctor is in' are you referring to his place in society?"
   Continuing he says more to a Lucy who grows increasingly frustrated. "Do you mean that doctors are 'in' the way certain pastimes are regarded by sophisticates as being 'in' while others are 'out'? Do you..."
   In frame three she slugs him. "Pow!"
   Reeling on the ground, Linus mutters, "I thought all doctors were patient, kind, and understanding?"

Guess that expectation misguided him. Lucy lost her peace. Some annoyance created a storm that got inside her and rattled her. If she had maintained her inner peace, it would have showed up in these words of Linus: patient, kind and understanding.

Meta-Esteeming & Confidencing

Having already described self-esteeming, this obviously describes one resource we can use to apply to a mental and/or emotional storm that will empower us to stay stable and calm. When you experience a storm of troubles, where does your mind go about *you*? Do you say anything about *you* when that occurs? What do you think-feel about yourself? We obviously lose inner peace if we *personalize* things. This shows how some questions are not very useful:

"Why did this happen?"
"What does this say about me as a person?"
"What does this say/predict in terms of my future?"

Although such self-referent questions tend to easily arise, we do not have to frame things in those terms. As self-reflective persons we can recursively move from the undesired events to an empowered sense of our self, one that supports us.

Self-esteeming becomes an important skill in running our own brain in that it can enable us to keep our self stable during storms. To do this, think *about* yourself with esteem, value, and dignity. Use your self-esteeming skills to build an inner sense of balance and centeredness. Develop a centered self so you have no need to defend yourself against reality. Don't code it as a threat to yourself. As a human *being* or person, you transcend being just a human *doing.*

We can also engage in *self-confidencing.* We can bring this state to bring to bear our sense of self in terms of what we do, our skills, abilities, and achievements. This generates our sense of what we call *self-efficacy.* Developing self-confidencing empowers us so that we can tackle the tasks and challenges before us.

By developing greater confidence in your confidence of using your consciousness to navigate your way through life we build *"self-efficacy"* (e.g, power, effectiveness). This gives us more of a sense of trust in being able to use our consciousness to gather information, check and test reality, update and correct our information, and use that data to move forward with effective actions.

Self-efficacy results from both of these "self" states. We feel, "I can handle things!" "I need not fear; I have resources for coping and mastering the challenges that come my way."

Meta-Stating Self with Being Calm & Collected
As we bring these resourceful states to bear on the primary state of trouble, namely, conscious awareness, acceptance, self-esteeming and self-confidencing, then we create for ourselves a mental calmness *about* troubles. And, to think-feel calm about troubles generates mental alertness and with that, the ability to *look reality full in the face* without going into a panic, fearfulness, insecurity, worrisomeness, or angry-rage. And doing that gives us a stabilizing referent.

A *stabilizing referent* refers to our internal sense of focus, vision, and clarity. The question becomes, "What can I think or represent that will serve as a stabilizer?" "What belief/meaning can I find or create that will give me an anchor in life?" The philosopher Neibhur made the now succinct statement that many have popularized.

> *"It is not **what** happens to a person that most determines the person, but **how** s/he responds to that happening."*

What happens to us (i.e., the event/s) does not comprise the most important factor regarding what we experience or how. The *meaning* we attribute to the event plays a more crucial role to our lived experience.
"What does it mean to me when I experience 'storms?'"
"What meanings do I attribute to this?"
"Do these meanings function as enhancing or unenhancing?"
"What immediate thought occurs to you? Do you grumble some "Oh no!"?
Examples of some empowering meanings that may stabilize your soul and equip you to more effectively cope include the following. These examples show *a mind stayed on a stabilizing referent.* Perhaps,
"Ah, a challenge for my skills!"
"A challenge for keeping my mind focused on God."
What stabilizing referent works for you? Search out your value system and belief systems to identify and create some. By contrast,

when we "let our hearts be troubled" we become *mentally ruffled*. We lose our cool, become agitated, access states of fear, anger, panic, confusion, etc. We worry about our worry, fret about our fretting, become agitated about our agitations!

Earlier, in describing "inner peace" as a linguistic-semantic "reality," I was describing a stabilizing belief or representation. Inward peace of mind necessitates having a rich and solid linguistic-semantic reality to occupy us. It presupposes thinking calming, securing, and stabilizing thoughts.

The pattern that you will want to create, design, and experience involves "a peace that passes all understanding" (Philippians 4:7). It transcends the common-sense "understanding" since the storm outside does **not** explain the peace inside. The peace inside must arise from, and continue in spite of, the external storm. We build that peace by building **stabilizing referents** that make that possible. In the context of *Philippians*, this refers to those of the apostle: joy in God, forbearance to all men, thanksgiving, and then a criteria list for thinking itself. "Whatever is true, whatever is honorable, whatever is just, whatever is pure, whatever is lovely, whatever is gracious, if there is any excellence, if there is anything worthy of praise, *think about these things*." (Phil. 4:8).

As we access this calmness, we can access and model it neurologically as well. So take a deep breath in a relaxed way. As you do, manage your posture, body movements, the tension and relaxation of your muscles, etc. so that it assists you to stay calm and cool.

The "peace that passes all understanding" sees the distresses, frustrations and troubles without exaggerating or personalizing them. Albert Ellis talked about this in terms of rational thinking/living. This means that inner peace will empower us to index troubles and contain them in larger frames-of-references. Thus, *long-term thinking* will enable us to view the immediate challenges and upsets more appropriately. To think that way you might want to use the proverb so popular a few years back:

> "The first principle for serenity: Don't sweat the small stuff. The second principle: It's all small stuff!"

Would that work as a stabilizing belief for you? Develop higher logical level beliefs about long-term processes and goals. These will empower you to stay centered, collected, sane, and whole. It will enable you not to give over-much importance to immediate distresses.

"This too will pass."
If you don't do this you might end up like Snoopy. Snoopy's dog house lies up against the back wall of the house where a monstrously large icicle has formed right over the front door of his dog house. Inside Snoopy thinks, "It's silly to be trapped in a doghouse by an icicle!" In the next scene: "I think I'll just make a run for it! I think I'll just zoom out of here!"

Scene 3: "I think I'll just leap up and zoom right out!" But he doesn't. Why not? Fear has paralyzed him. He feels stuck-- unable to move.

Scene 4: "I think I'll just lie here for the rest of my life." Stuck! Stuck in terror, definitely, not inner peace.

Summary
- *Peace of mind* is as close as your ability to make a meta-move and set a higher frame of reference (or many of them) that allow you to design engineer a higher meta-state for serenity.
- Once you get all of your references in place, simply step into them and experience them fully. Allow and even commission those higher frames (or meta-states) to become part of your basic existential standing and orientation.
- Doing this legitimizes your self as you esteem yourself, develop your powers (self-confidencing), and create a realistic adjustment to reality (acceptance). All you need to do then is practice taking a calm and serene attitude to the world of things and people.
- Do that and you will increase your acceptance of ambivalence, of the unknown, of the unknow-able, of the complex, and of the infinite. You can then give up the impossible fantasy of seeking inner peace through "being perfect," "knowing all," "being all powerful," etc.

Chapter 16

SLAYING AND/OR TAMING ALL DRAGONS!

All Other Dragons Put on Notice

Have you enjoyed using your frame-setting skills (meta-stating) and language indexing skills (meta-modeling) to identify, tame, and slay Dragons? By now I would think it's obvious that we could go on and on with this process of describing specific Dragons which plague our lives, Dragons who scorch us with hot firey air, that frighten and torment, and specifically offer suggestions for transforming those Dragons.

Yet I trust that by now *you get the idea.* You know the process and you can carry on with Dragon Taming and Transforming perfectly well by yourself.

Secrets of the Dragons
After all, know you know some of the key *Dragon Secrets,* do you not? Certainly you know that all of our internal psychic Dragons *do not exist—they do not exist apart from our constructing them.* And while we created a great many of them as children, some of us have continued to create them as adults. How? We create them via the way we think-and-emote, the way we build up our concepts and semantic reality, the way we use the symbolic system of language, and the way we "run our own brains," the way we frame things, the way we interpret things (our explanatory styles), and by the way we meta-state ourselves and others.

You also know how to de-construct them. If they have *no more existence than what we give them*—then guess what? We can deconstruct them altogether and/or tame them so that they begin to serve us well and make life more playful, enjoyable, loving, effective, and outrageous. We have the power to do that; you have the power to do that.

Our self-reflexive consciousness endows us with the power to *go meta* to whatever thoughts-feelings, experiences, speech, behavior, or responses that we have so that we can then constructively evaluate our neuro-semantic evaluations. And this provides an absolutely fabulous way to tame and transform Dragons:

> Do they serve us well?
> Do they generate conceptualizations that make life more vital and significant?
> Do they enrich, ennoble, and enhance our experiences?

We also have the power of choice (a meta-state) via our self-reflexive consciousness. This power of choice enables us to live consciously and to run our own brains and our meta-minds in terms of deciding upon the Quality and Direction of our states.

The Self-Sabotaging Dragons

The Dragon Question par excellence is this:

> *Do you any other programs left within you whereby you turn your psychic powers against yourself?*

Anything that stops you or interferes with you taking effective action and beginning to create highly desired outcomes that you want, or that sabotages that success operates as a Dragon to you. Now we can ask this question in terms of self-expectancy:

> *What can you expect of yourself* with regard to becoming successful, or thinking of yourself as effective, happy, pleasant, contented, fit, healthy, etc.?

When you pick a resourceful state or experience that you'd like to achieve, and then ask *the self-expectancy* question about it, you can flush out Dragons lurking in that arena of life. In this way, the self-expectancy questions empowers you to expose them. As a Dragon Detector, it works wonders.

You can also use *the permission process* for flushing out Dragons. It's this simple. Go inside and say to yourself,

> *"I give myself permission to X..."*
> (i.e., fully and absolutely to succeed in a wild and wonderful way, to feel delightful happiness in my everyday life, to express myself in loving and affection ways, to speak up, speak kind, and speak clear, to exercise regularly, etc.).

Then notice what happens.

Does it settle well? Does it *feel right?* Does it activate any other frame of mind? Does it provoke some internal objection? If so, just notice it calmly and with curiosity knowing that the objection may or may not be accurate, may or may not be useful, may or may not be a current objection. Notice and record the objection knowing that it provides you valuable information for making the permission more fitting.

Now rewrite the *permission* utilizing whatever you find of value in the objection. Re-write it so that the permission frees you and unshackles you from all of the old taboos that have imprisoned you. In re-writing take your time to find *just the right words.* As a symbolic class of life, we often have to language ourselves with a permission that has *just the right words* to re-order our internal model of the world.

As you undoubtedly already know, or suspect, many Dragons arise in our lives because *someone has tabooed us* and sometimes because we have tabooed ourselves. The Dragon has been called forth in our neuro-linguistics because someone has forbidden, inhibited, and tabooed us in some way against some basic experience, emotion, idea, or understanding. For example, someone might have shamed us from assertiveness, joy, creativity, fallibility, etc.

> "You shouldn't think so much about yourself; it'll go to your head and nobody will like you!"
>
> "Kids should be seen, not heard!"
>
> "What's wrong with you that you spilled that milk; can't you use your head?

Someone might have guilt-ed us for experiencing such states. Out of their own fears, their own mis-understandings, their own taboos, or whatever, they might have emotionally blackmailed us by depressing, head-aching, self-degrading themselves!

> "Your curiosity will be the death of me!"
>
> "Can't you shut up; your chattering gives me a head-ache!"
>
> "I wish I never had you—you're such a bad boy!"

The Dragons would then arise as we would lose permission inside of our own minds-and-emotions to live, love, risk, experiment, learn, grow, adventure, hug, embrace, cry, rejoice, apologize, make mistakes, have fun, etc. And, to the extent that *we gave them permission to take away permission* from us, the Dragons began to run amok in our lives. Eventually, they became habitual—habitual ways of using our neuro-linguistics and so we created the Dragon States and made them part of our internal world.

What can we do about all of this now?

As we have noted, *lots of things.* For beginners, we can *give ourselves permission.* This sets a frame and so meta-states ourselves with *permission to be human, to be real, to be fallible, and to experience life.* From there, we can begin to find and update our old "programs" that no longer provide us an accurate or useful map for navigating things. We can treat those old programs as fossils of bygone days and situations. We can program ourselves with our current languaging for living and loving fully. We can use our neuro-semantic powers as we meta-state and set higher frames of mind that will move beyond the old maps where we had sketched, *"Beyond there be Dragons."*

The Next Step in Dragon Taming and Transforming

We began with the NLP model about neuro-linguistic states. We then introduced the Meta-States model of neuro-semantic states. As we then described and illustrated how to use these models for state management in running our own brains, all of this has put into our hands a new way to think and talk about *our internal psychic forces* of thought, emotion, belief, value, perception, speech, and behavior. This new paradigm that models the structure of subjective experiences has also highlighted the two royal roads to "state" (i.e., the cognitive psychology of our internal representations of "thinking-emoting" and the behavioral psychology of our physiology).

What can we do with this?

It first gives us a new way to understand *what* causes us to get into Dragon States that we do and *how* we do so. It articulates a specific model for understanding our neuro-linguistic states which determine and govern the very *quality* of our lives, the quality of our thinking, remembering, perceiving, communicating, behaving, etc. No longer do our states have to "have" or dominate us. We can recognize them, acknowledge them, and shift them.

Secondly, we now have a pathway to true empowerment. The mechanisms and components of state (i.e., internal representations, sensory modalities, linguistics, submodalities, physiology, etc.) give us a multitude of ways for *taking charge of our states.* As we recognize our mental-emotional states, we can now *own* them as expressions of our basic powers. This changes our map. We no longer view them as alien forces that come upon us at unawares. We no longer think about them as "making" us think or feel or say or do anything. Operating from a sense of our own Power Zone, we feel and operate with an ever increasing sense of choice.

Thirdly, if we know *the mechanisms* within that model which cause or contribute to such, then we also have *a pathway for transforming things*. We no longer have to access Dragon States in response to the events of life. We can take charge of our mind at all of its higher levels so that we can set the kind of frames of mind and generate the kind of gestalt meta-states that will richly enhance our lives.

Fourthly, it gives us a way to constructively use our self-reflexive consciousness. Since we cannot avoid having thoughts-and-feelings about our thoughts-feelings, we will always and inescapably create meta-states, and meta-levels within meta-levels. What we expereince as our "personality" itself arises from the nested states *within* states (See *Personality Ordering and Disordering Using NLP and Neuro-Semantics*, 2000). Knowing this enables us to use our "going meta" power in a constructive and positive way so that we choose and experience meta-states that enhance our lives.

What Now?

1) *Use the model and the skills that it makes possible.*

In this work I have mentioned several Dragons common to most of us, yet this brief introduction by no means covers all of the possible Dragon States that afflict and torment human lives.

Over the years I have presented numerous workshops on Dragon Slaying and/or devoted a day to Dragon Slaying when presenting some specific training. All of this keeps revealing and flushing out new and additional Dragons. I got a lot of ideas from one of the questions I used to include in a Pre- and Post- questionnaire that I once used.

> "The unproductive, unuseful, Dragon States that I would like to conquer in my life include..."
>
> "What Dragons in others brings out Dragons in you?"

When I began trainings in selling excellence, wealth building, defusing hotheads, accelerated learning, and the like, I discovered such Dragons as the Cold-Calling Dragon, Fear of being Imperfect Dragon, Don't Deserve to Accumulate Wealth Dragon, Feel Like I'm Intruding Dragon, etc. And that doesn't even tough the hem of the garment about the wide range of Dragon States:

Addiction to Being Loved Dragon
Self-Blaming: Let's Beat Upon Me Dragon
Procrastination   Shame
Chronic Sadness   Negative Thinking

Fear of Failure
Raging Out-of-Control
Revengeful: I've Got to Get Even Dragon
Self-righteousness: I've Got to Always Be Right Dragon
Cowardice
Control Freak Dragon: I've Got to Monitor Everything!
Closed off to People: Emotionally Disconnected Dragon

Blaming	Worrisomeness
Paranoid	Painfully Self-Conscious
Gloomy & pessimistic	Sullen
Jealousy	Regretfulness

Over-Seriousness: "But it's Serious!" Dragon

Panic	Lying
Negativity	Mind-reading motives

Emptiness
Fretting about what I've missed
Failure to be emotional when I should be

2) *Take charge of your states.*
Knowing *how* to take charge of our states differs from actually *taking charge* of our states. The latter requires action, practice, decision, commitment, ongoing learning, etc. If you have any hesitation about taking a risk and practicing what you know, then meta-state yourself with a sense of adventure, courage, boldness, excitement, or whatever resource you need to set as your frame of mind so that *implementation* and *installation* just become part of your natural way of moving through the world. Taking charge of our states and our higher states involves an ongoing process. It involves taking charge in how we actually *use* our powers of thinking, representing, choosing, moving, etc.

3) *Keep designing and building powerful meta-states.*
While I have focused here on using the model to identify, tame, slay, and transform Dragons, the model offers much more than just getting rid of problematic states. With Meta-States, you can texture and qualify all of your mind-body states so that they enhance the very quality of your life. With this model, you can explore the very structure of excellence in any given field. Excellence, expertise, and even "genius" has a structure, a structure that brings out one's best and enables one to actualize the highest of potentials. This facet of Meta-States

describes the transcendence of the model and allows us to move up to the highest reach of human potential.

Since the introduction of the *Meta-States* model in 1994, *applications* of this model about the higher levels or frames of mind has opened up a vast range of domains. It has led to applications (and trainings) in such areas as:

Defusing Hotheads: Effectively handling someone who is hot, angry, and stressed-out.

Selling Excellence: the structure of expertise in selling.

Mind-Lines: Lines for Changing Minds: the structure of conversational reframing.

Advanced Flexibility using General Semantics: Mining the riches of Korzybski for new and additional processes.

Wealth Building Excellence: the structure of the states of mind for seeing and seizing opportunities, living passionately, and accumulating wealth in a healthy and balanced way.

Accelerated Learning: the structure of learning and the higher frames of mind that accelerates learning and wisdom.

Secrets of Personal Mastery: the structure of excellence that brings out one's best.

Summary

- All Dragons should beware of the power of the man or woman who knows how to run his or her own brain and to set the higher frames of mind that allows one to access the best states.
- Beyond Dragon States, we move on to casting spells for bringing out the Magician in ourselves and others. This speaks about the discovery of how magic lies in the language that we use, and that as a symbolic class of life who construct our realities, we can call forth the kind of worlds that are wonderful places to live.
- May you find yourself become a *Dragon Master* so that with just a word, just a leap to a meta-level, you can tame and transform and/or slay the Dragons that arise in your mind and in the minds of others. Use your Dragon Master powers wisely and with compassion. Avoid harm and aim for contributing to make the world a more wonderful place.

Appendix A:

E-PRIME / E-CHOICE

When I first wrote *Dragon Slaying,* I had just learned from David Bourland, Jr. how to handle the problem with *"is"* (e.g., the "is" of identity and the "is" of predication) by *E-Priming.*

If you don't know, *the "is" of identity* sets up identities between different things and generates a false-to-fact map. It confuses things that exist on different logical levels. "He is stupid!" and "She is lazy..." confuse a multi-dimensional person with a mental evaluation. It defines and limits the person to "being" whatever evaluation we declare about that person. That's what the person "is."

The "is" of predication, on the other hand, asserts or declares (hence, "predicates") that things which exist in the human nervous system as ideas, feelings, etc. exist "out there" beyond the nervous system. With this "is," we project. We take our hallucinations and project them out onto others. Hence, "It is good..." "That rose is red." As a language structure, this "is" implies that something "out there" contains those qualities of "goodness" or "redness." The "is" implies that such things exist independent of the speaker's experience and speaking. Yet that falsely maps the person's evaluations onto the world.

Actually, with both of these uses of "is" we have descriptions which speak about the speaker's *internal experience* (thinking, feeling, judgments, valuing, etc.) and which attempts to directly map that onto the structure of the world. We would speak more accurately if we said,

"I evaluate it as good..." "I believe she behaves in a lazy way..." "That statement strikes me as stupid..."

David Bourland, Jr. invented the extensional device of **E-Prime**. This means writing and producing **E**nglish primed of (or minus) the *"to be" verb family* (is, am, are, was, were, be, being, been).

Doing this leads to certain values. It obviously reduces the "is" of identity and the "is" of predication in our talking and thinking. And as one has to give up using this passive verb of "is," It forces one to use active verbs and to more precisely state what one means. For that reason I wrote the original text of *Dragon Slaying* in E-Prime.

Another value. Using the previous "is" statements actually distracts us from the true structure of things, since it confuses logical levels, and subtly leads to the unsanity that assumes that our value judgments and other terms of evaluation exist in the world of "objective" reality. When we talk that way, it's easy to forget that "it's just a way of talking," and isn't real. The evaluations (i.e., good, red, lazy, stupid) function only as definitions and interpretations. They only occur *in the "mind"* of some speaker. They are not real. And to say "The rose is red" falsely allocates the "redness" to a position outside of the person experiencing the redness via their interacting nervous system.

The "to be" verbs pose another danger. They presuppose that "things" (actually, events, processes) stay the same. This isn't true. Using the "to be" verbs can subtly create the impression of fixedness. They tend to set the world in concrete and to create "a frozen universe." In using them, the dynamic nature of processes become coded statically:

"Life is tough."
"I am no good at math."
"She always talks that way."

A long time ago, Ernest Fenollosa (1908) said, "'Is' suffers from "the tyranny of medieval logic." Such statements sound so definitive, so godlike. They sound like a pronouncement of the last word about reality. Bourland and Kellog have called this way of talking, *"the deity mode!"* No wonder some people so over-use "is" "am" and "are," etc.! It conveys a sense of power.

"That's the way it is!"

"To be" also carries with it a sense of completeness, finality, and time-independence. Yet if we can discern the difference between the map and the territory, then we know these phenomena exist on different logical levels. Using E-Prime helps to reduce slipping in groundless authoritarian statements.

Yet if we confuse the language we use in describing reality with reality, then we begin *"identifying"* unequal things. We begin to treat them as "the same." Korzybski said that this lies at the heart of *unsanity*. Actually, there "is" no absolute, final, non-changing "is" to which we can point. *"Is"* functions as a non-referencing word. To use it leads us into semantic mis-evaluations. Conversely, writing, thinking and speaking in E-Prime helps us to become more "conscious of abstracting," that is, mindful. Korzybski posited such conscious awareness as crucial for remaining sane.

Though I enjoyed using E-Prime because it facilitated speaking and thinking with more clarity and precision, it also makes for a certain awkwardness. My lack of experience with it created many stilted expressions. So even thought it invites a speaker or writer back to the level of first-person experience and reduces the passive verb tense ("It was done," "Mistakes were made"), it also can make for an unnecessary self-consciousness.

A close cousin to E-Prime is E-Choice, this seeks to reduce the "is" words as much as possible but using them when one so chooses, especially the other "is" words (the "is" of existence, the auxiliary "is," etc.). And so that's what I've used in this second edition of *Dragon Slaying.*

META-STATES GLOSSARY

Dragon State: A meta-level state wherein we have brought negative thoughts and feelings, especially judgments against ourselves. A meta-level structure that creates a distorted meaning that we cannot live in a healthy and/or productive way.

Dragon Slaying Sword: Using the Meta-Model to de-construct a negative morbid meta-state. Meta-modeling the linguistic structures of an induction de-frames and so *unglues* the state.

Floater Meta-states: States-about-other-states that we can install in the higher parts of our mind so that they continuously "float" above other states. This can provide a powerful and enhancing frame of mind.

Frames, Reframing, Outframing: Since all thought and perception occurs within some frame-of-reference, in reframing we put an idea inside of a new frame or context, in deframing we pull an old frame apart, in outframing we move up and set an entirely new frame over all of the concepts and perceptions.

Higher Meta-States: Any meta-state that *transcends* not only some primary state but also other meta-states so that we move up in our mind to some of our highest levels of awareness.

Languaging: Used as a verb, to "language" refers to using any symbol system (i.e., mathematics, music, iconic, linguistics, etc.) by which we represent information and concepts.

Meta-Awareness: The higher level awareness of a state about a state; an essential quality in human consciousness that enables us to not only think but experience at meta-levels.

Meta-Model: 12 linguistic distinctions that identify the structure of language, and how it can be ill-formed. Created by Bandler and Grinder in *"The Structure of Magic"* (1975). A model derived from Chomsky's Transformational Grammar. The Meta-Model provides a way to identify and challenge ill-formedness in our mental mapping. By it we can update limited and impoverished models and generate a fuller and more enriched model.

Meta-State: A state *about* another state, i.e. fear of fear, joy of anger, sadness about fear, etc., a higher state of mind and emotion about soem other state, typically coded by by linguistics or other symbols, a meta-level phenomenon, a higher logical level that operates as a class or category and so contains the members of the class at the lower level.

Meta-State Ecology: Stepping aside from an experience of thought or emotion and running a Quality Control on the values, usefulness, productivity, and other qualities.

Meta-State Elicitation: The specific way to elicit, access or create a meta-state.

Meta-States Linguistics: The language that enables us to *glue meta-state* structures together to give it a sense of stability, strength, and permanence. As a linguistically driven phenomenon, meta-states need linguistic structures, ideas, concepts, stories, narratives, etc. This enables us to anchor and hold a higher level state steady.

Meta-Level Linguistic Cues: About, beyond, of, concerning, regarding, transcend," etc., also, classifications, quotations, quotations within quotations, with this in mind, in terms of..., etc.

Meta-States Looping: Getting into a state that keeps looping back onto itself or onto a spiral of other states so that it keeps repeating the same thoughts-and-emotions and behaviors over and over. Getting caught in a non-ending loop.

Meta-State Permeation or Coalescing: When thoughts, ideas, understandings, beliefs, values, decisions, and all other higher neuro-semantic phenomena *permeates down through* to the primary states and so *coalesces* into them. This explains the power and pervasiveness of meta-states and the pervasive changes that can occur with meta-state transformations.

Meta-State Technologies: The tools, techniques, procedures, and processes for working with, eliciting, altering, and managing meta-states in contradistinction to those that only work with primary states.

Meta-State Strategy Analysis: Tracking the sequences of responses both linearly and non-linearly (e.g., vertically) as it moves up levels of mind and moves around in reflexive and recursive loops. The meta-level strategy gives explanation as to how we create meta-states and gestalt states.

Meta-State Questions: Questions that evoke one to access a state about a state. "How do you feel about feeling contempt toward yourself?" "What do you think about these reactive thoughts and feelings?" "What can you expect of yourself when you feel ...?"

Meta-Resources: Any resource that enable us to move to a meta-state, transform a meta-state, or enrich a meta-state.

Nominalizations: A Meta-Model distinction; the process of having turned a verb into a noun as in "relating" becomes "relationship." Nominalizing creates a "misplaced concreteness" or reification and so fails to map the movement and process and implies an untrue permanence and stability.

Primary State: A state of consciousness, a mind-body state driven by the basic modalities of sights, sounds, sensations, smells and tastes. Like the "primary emotions," examples of primary states include fear, anger, sadness, joy, attraction, aversion, relaxation, tension, pleasure, distress, etc.

Self-Expectancies: A meta-level of awareness, what we expect (about self, others, etc.), sets an expectational frame that works like an attractor in a self-organing system.

Strategy: The sequence of internal representations which describes the process where we put our neurology (body, physiology, emotions) into a certain state out of which we then produce behavior, actions, skills, etc.

Strategy Analysis: the NLP process for tracking down the sequence of where a brain goes as it creates its "programs." See *"NLP: The Structure of Subjectivity, Volume I."*

Unconscious Meta-States: Meta-states generally operate beyond our immediate awareness. The higher the meta-state and/or the more habitual, the more outside of consciousness. These set presuppositional frames, frames for epistemology, ontology, etc.

BIBLIOGRAPHY

Andreas, Connirae; Andreas, Tamara (1994). *Core transformation: Reaching the wellspring within.* Moab Utah: Real People Press.

Andreas, Steve (1991). *"Virginia Satir: The patterns of her magic,"* Palo Alto, CA: Science and Behavior Books.

Bandler, Richard and Grinder, John. (1975). *The structure of magic, Volume I: A book about language and therapy.* Palo Alto, CA: Science & Behavior Books.

Bandler, Richard and Grinder, John. (1976). *The structure of magic, Volume II.* Palo Alto, CA: Science & Behavior Books.

Bandler, Richard and Grinder, John. (1979). *Frogs into princes: Neuro-linguistic programming.* Moab, UT: Real people press.

Bandler, Richard and Grinder, John. (1982). *Reframing: Neuro-linguistic programming and the transformation of meaning.* UT: Real people press.

Bandler, Richard. (1985). *Magic in action.* Moab, UT: Real People Press.

Bandler, Richard. (1985). *Using your brain for a change: Neuro-linguistic programming.* UT: Real People Press.

Bateson, Gregory (1979). *Mind and nature: A necessary unity.* NY: Bantan.

Bateson, Gregory (1972). *Steps to an ecology of mind.* NY: Ballatine.

Bourland, D. David Jr. and Johnston, Paul Dennithorne (1991). *"To be or not: An E-prime anthology."*

Dilts, Robert; Grinder, John; Bandler, Richard; DeLozier, Judith. (1980). *Neuro-linguistic programming, Volume I: The study of the structure of subjective experience.* Cupertino. CA.: Meta Publications.

Dilts, Robert. (1983). *Applications of neuro-linguistic programming.* Cupertino CA: Meta Publications.

Dilts, Robert B. (1983). *Roots of neuro-linguistic programming.* Cupertino, CA: Meta Publications.

Ellis, Albert. (1973). *Humanistic psychotherapy: The rational-emotive approach.* NY: Julian Press.

Ellis, Albert and Harper, Robert A. (1976). *A new guide to rational living.* Englewood Cliffs, NJ: Prentice-Hall, Inc.

Frankl, V.E. (1957/1984). *Man's search for meaning: An introduction to logotherapy* (3rd.

ed.) NY: Simon & Schuster.

Frankl, Viktor (1953/1978). *The unheard cry for meaning.* NY: Washington Square Press.

Glasser, W. (1961). *Mental health or mental illness?* NY: Harper & Row.

Glasser, William (1965). *Reality therapy: A new approach to psychiatry.* NY: Harper & Row.

Hall, L. Michael (1995). *Meta-states: A new domain of logical levels, self-reflexiveness in human states of consciousness.* Grand Junction, CO: Empowerment Technologies.

Johnson, C.E. (1994). <u>The 7%, 38%, 55% Myth</u>. *Anchor Point Journal of NLP.* UT: Salt Lake City. (July 1994, pp. 32-36).

Kirsch, Irving (1990). *Changing expectations: A key to effective therapy.* Pacific Grove CA: Brooks/Cole.

Korzybski, Alfred (1941/1994 5th. ed.). *Science and sanity: An introduction to non-aristotelian systems and general semantics.* Lakeville, CT: Institute of General Semantics.

Maslow, Abraham H. (1954/1970). *Motivation and personality.* NY: Harper & Row.

Overstreet, Harry, Overstreet, Bonaro (1954). *"The mind alive,"* Norton Co.

Parry, Alan, and Doan, Robert E. (1994). *Story re-visions: Narrative therapy in the postmodern world.* NY: Guilford Press.

Seligman, Martin, E.P. (1975). *Helplessness: On depression, development, and death.* San Francisco: Freeman.

Seligman, Martin E.P. (1991). *Learned optimism.* NY: Alfred A. Knopf.

Smedes, Lewis (1983, Jan.). "The Power To Change The Past." *Christianity Today.*

Wolin, Sybil (1994). "Resilience: How Survivors of Troubled Families Keep the Past in its Place." *"Psychology Today"* (Jan/Feb. 1992, page 36ff).

Vaihinger, H. (1924). *The philosophy of 'as if.' A system of the theoretical, practical, and religious fictions of mankind.* (Translated by C.K. Ogden). NY: Harcourt, Brace.

White, Michael and Epston, David. (1990). *Narrative means to therapeutic ends.* NY: Norton.

TRAININGS AVAILABLE
The Institutes of Neuro-Semantics

Meta-State Trainings —
Accessing Personal Genius: Introduction to Meta-States as an advanced NLP model (3 days). This training introduces and teaches the *Meta-States Model* and is ideal for NLP Practitioners. It presupposes knowledge of the NLP Model and builds the training around accessing the kinds of states that will access and support "personal genius."

Advanced Modeling Using Meta-Levels: Advanced use of Meta-States by focusing on the domain of modeling excellence. This training typically occurs as the last 4 days of the 7 day Meta-States Certification. Based upon the modeling experiences of Dr. Hall and his book, *NLP: Going Meta— Advanced Modeling Using Meta-Levels,* this training looks at the formatting and structuring of the meta-levels in Resilience, Un-Insultability, and Seeing Opportunities. The training touches on modeling of Wealth Building, Fitness, Women in Leadership, Persuasion, etc.

Secrets of Personal Mastery: Awakening Your Inner Executive. This training presents the power of Meta-States *without* directly teaching the model as such. The focus instead shifts to *Personal Mastery* and the *Executive Powers* of the participants. Formatted so that it can take the form of 1, 2 or 3 days, this training presents a simpler form of Meta-States, especially good for those without NLP background or those who are more focused on Meta-States Applications than the model.

Frame Games: Persuasion Elegance. The first truly *User Friendly* version of Meta-States. Frame Games provides practice and use of Meta-States in terms of frame detecting, setting, and changing. As a model of frames, Frame Games focuses on the power of persuasion via frames and so presents how to influence or persuade yourself and others using the Levels of Thought or Mind that lies at the heart of Meta-States. Designed as a 3 day program, the first two days presents the model of Frame Games and lots of exercises. Day three is for becoming a true Frame Game Master and working with frames conversationally and covertly.

Wealth Building Excellence (Meta-Wealth). The focus of this training is on learning how to think like a millionaire, to develop the mind and meta-mind of someone who is structured and programmed to create wealth economically, personally, mentally, emotionally, relationally, etc. As a Meta-States Application Training, Wealth Building Excellence began as a modeling project and seeks to facilitate the replication of that excellence in participants.

Selling & Persuasion Excellence (Meta-Selling). Another Meta-States Application Training, modeled after experts in the fields of selling and persuasion and designed to replicate in participants. An excellent follow-up training to Wealth Building since most people who build wealth have to sell their ideas and dreams to others. This trainings goes way beyond mere Persuasion Engineering as it uses the Strategic Selling model of Heiman also known as Relational Selling, Facilitation Selling, etc.

Mind-Lines: Lines for Changing Minds. Based upon the book by Drs. Hall and Bodenhamer (1997), now in its third edition, Mind-Line Training is a training about Conversational Reframing and Persuasion. The Mind-Lines model began as a rigorous update of the old NLP "Sleight of Mouth" Patterns and has grown to become the persuasion language of the Meta-State moves. This advanced training is highly and mainly a linguistic model, excellent as a follow-up training for Wealth Building and Selling Excellence. Generally a two day format, although sometimes 3 and 4 days.

Accelerated Learning Using NLP & Meta-States (Meta-Learning). A Meta-State Application training based upon the NLP model for "running your own brain" and the Neuro-Semantic (Meta-States) model of managing your higher executive states of consciousness. Modeled after leading experts in the fields of education, cognitive psychologies, this training provides extensive insight into the Learning States and how to access your personal learning genius. It provides specific strategies for various learning tasks as well as processes for research and writing.

Defusing Hotheads: A Meta-States and NLP Application training for handling hot, stressed-out, and irrational people in Fight/Flight states. Designed to "talk someone down from a hot angry state," this training provides training in state management, first for the skilled negotiator or manager, and then for eliciting another into a more resourceful state.

Based upon the book by Dr. Hall, *Defusing Strategies (1987)*, this training has been presented to managers and supervisors for greater skill in conflict management, and to police departments for coping with domestic violence.

Advanced NLP Flexibility Training Using General Semantics. An advanced Neuro-Semantics training that explores the riches and treasures in Alfred Korzybski's work, *Science and Sanity.* Originally presented in London (1998, 1999) as "The Merging of the Models: NLP and General Semantics," this training now focuses almost exclusively on *developing Advanced Flexibility* using tools, patterns, and models in General Semantics. Recommend for the advanced student of NLP and Meta-States.

Meta-States Trainers Training. An advanced training for those who have been certified in Meta-States and Neuro-Semantics (the seven day program). This application training focuses the power and magic of Meta-States on the training experience itself—both public and individual training. It focuses first on the trainer, to access one's own Top Training States and then on how to meta-states or set the frames when working with others in coaching or facilitating greater resourcefulness.

Instant Relaxation. Another practical NLP and Meta-States Application Training designed to facilitate the advanced ability to quickly "fly into a calm." Based in part upon the book by Lederer and Hall (Instant Relaxation, 1999), this training does not teach NLP or Meta-States, but coaches the relaxation skills for greater "presence of mind," control over mind and neurology, and empowerment in handling stressful situations. An excellent training in conjunction with Defusing Hotheads.

About the Author

L. Michael Hall, Ph.D.   *Michael@neurosemantics.com*
P.O. Box 9231   *NLPMetaStates@OnLineCol.com*
Grand Jct. Co. 81501   www.neurosemantics.com
(970) 523-7877   www.learninstitute.com

Dr. L. Michael Hall is an entrepreneur who lives in the Rocky Mountains in Colorado. As a psychologist he had a private psychotherapeutic practice for many years, and then began teaching and training— first in Communication Training (Assertiveness, Negotiations, Relationships), then in NLP.

He studied NLP with co-founder, Richard Bandler in the late 1980s and became a Master Practitioner and Trainer. He wrote notes for the traingings at Bandler's request, edited *Time For a Change*. As a prolific author, he has written and published more than two dozen books including *The Spirit of NLP* (1996), *Dragon Slaying, Meta-States, Mind-Lines, Figuring Out People, The Structure of Excellence, Frame Games,* etc.

Michael earned his doctorate in Cognitive-Behavioral Psychology with an emphasis in psycho-linguistics. His doctoral dissertation dealt with the *languaging* of four psychotherapies (NLP, RET, Reality Therapy, Logotherapy) using the formulations of General Semantics. He addressed the Interdisciplinary International Conference (1995) presenting an integration of NLP and General Semantics.

In 1994, Michael developed *the Meta-States Model* while modeling *resilience* and presenting the findings at the International NLP Conference in Denver. He has hundreds of articles published in *NLP World, Anchor Point, Rapport, Connection, Meta-States Journal.*

Michael is the co-developer, along with Dr. Bob Bodenhamer, of Neuro-Semantics having co-authored a unified field model using the 3 Meta-Domains of NLP. They initiated *The Society of Neuro-Semantics,* and have begun to establish *Institute*s of Neuro-Semantics in the USA and around the world. Elvis Keith Lester joined the team in 1998, and then established the *LEARN Institute of Neuro-Semantics* in Tampa, Fl.

Today Michael spends his time researching and modeling, training internationally, and writing. Recent modeling projects have included modeling excellence in sales, persuasion, accelerated learning, state management, wealth building, women in leadership, fitness and health, etc. These are now Meta-State Gateway Trainings.

Books:
> Meta-States: Self-Reflexiveness in Human States of Consciousness (1995)
> Dragon Slaying: Dragons to Princes (1996)
> The Spirit of NLP: The Process, Meaning & Criteria for Mastering NLP (1996)
> Languaging: The Linguistics of Psychotherapy (1996)
> Patterns For "Renewing the Mind" (w. Dr. Bodenhamer) (1997)
> Time-Lining: Advance Time-Line Processes (w. Dr. Bodenhamer) (1997)
> NLP: Going Meta — Advanced Modeling Using Meta-Levels (1997)
> Figuring Out People: Design Engineering With Meta-Programs (w. Dr. Bodenhamer) (1997)
> A Sourcebook of Magic (formerly, How to Do What When (w. B. Belnap) (1999)
> Mind Lines: Lines For Changing Minds (w. Dr. Bodenharmer) (1997)
> The Secrets of Magic: Communicational Magic for the 21st. Century (1998)
> Meta-States Journal, Patterns, Volume I, II, III (97, 98, 99)
> The Structure of Excellence: Unmasking the Meta-Levels of Submodalities (Hall and Bodenhamer, 1999)
> Instant Relaxation (1999, Lederer & Hall)

Books in Development
> Personality Ordering & Disordering Using NLP and Neuro-Semantics (Hall , Bodenhamer, Bolstad, Harmblett, 2000, in press)
> Secrets of Personal Mastery (Fall, 2000, in press)
> Frame Games: Persuasion Elegance (2000, in press)
> Frame Games for Managers (2000, with Kearney)
> Frame Games for Fitness & Weight Control (2000, with Lester)
> Frame Games for Persuasion (2000)
> Accelerated Motivation: Human Propulsion Systems (2001)
> Neuro-Semantics (2001)